P9-DXH-628

FOR REFERENCE

Do Not Take From This Room

Decisions
of the
United States
Supreme Court

1999-00 TERM

---

by
The Editorial Staff
United States Supreme Court Reports,
Lawyers' Edition

LEXIS Publishing™

LEXIS-NEXIS® · MARTINDALE-HUBBELL®
MATTHEW BENDER® · MICHIE® · SHEPARD'S®

Riverside Community College
Library
4800 Magnolia Avenue
Riverside, CA 92506

DEC '00

REFERENCE

KF8741 .A5
Lawyers Co-operative
Publishing Company.
Decisions of the United
States Supreme Court.

LEXIS, NEXIS, *Shepard's* and Martindale-Hubbell are registered trademarks, LEXIS Publishing, and MICHIE are trademarks and *lexis.com* is a service mark of Reed Elsevier Properties Inc., used under license. Matthew Bender is a registered trademark of Matthew Bender Properties Inc.

Copyright © 2000
Matthew Bender & Company, Inc., one of the LEXIS Publishing™ companies.
All rights reserved

No copyright is claimed in the text of statutes, regulations, and excerpts from court opinions quoted within this work. Permission to copy material exceeding fair use, 17 U.S.C. § 107, may be licensed for a fee of $1 per page per copy from the Copyright Clearance Center, 222 Rosewood Drive, Danvers, MA, 01923, telephone (978) 750-8400.

ISBN 0-327-12376-1

7683512

Editorial Office

701 East Water Street, Charlottesville, VA 22902-7587
(800) 446-3410

www.lexis.com

Customer Service: 800/562-1197

CONTENTS

PAGE

Preface v

The Court's Personnel vii

Survey of the 1999-00 Term xxi

Summaries of Decisions 1

Glossary of Common Legal Terms 271

Table of Cases 281

Index Ind-1

PREFACE

This volume is designed to serve as a quick-reference guide to the work of the United States Supreme Court during its 1999–2000 Term. Its important features are described below.

The Court's Personnel. A list of the Justices of the Supreme Court is accompanied by photographs and biographical sketches of each Justice serving during the Term.

Survey of the Term. A succinct narrative statement outlines the high spots of the Term.

Summaries of Decisions. Every important decision of the Supreme Court is individually summarized. These summaries (reprinted from Vols. 145–147, Part 2 L Ed 2d) describe the manner in which the case came before the Court, the facts involved and issues presented, the holding of the Court and the reasons supporting that holding, the name of the Justice who wrote the opinion of the majority, and the names and views of those of the Justices who concurred or dissented.

The Summaries are printed in the order in which the cases were decided by the Court. Notations to Summaries indicate the volume and page at which the full opinion of the Court may be found in the official reports (US) published by the Federal Government, and the privately published United States Supreme Court Reports, Lawyers' Edition (L Ed 2d), and Supreme Court Reporter (S Ct).

Following each Summary is a listing of the attorneys who argued in behalf of the litigants.

Glossary. A glossary of common legal terms defines, in simple, nontechnical language, various legal words and phrases frequently used in the Supreme Court's decisions.

Table of Cases. A complete Table of Cases makes possible the location of the Summary of any case through the name of a party litigant.

Index. A detailed, alphabetical word index makes possible the location of the Summary of any case by consulting the index entries for appropriate factual and conceptual terms.

THE COURT'S PERSONNEL

JUSTICES

OF THE

SUPREME COURT OF THE UNITED STATES

1999–00Term

Chief Justice

HON. WILLIAM H. REHNQUIST

Associate Justices

HON. JOHN P. STEVENS

HON. SANDRA DAY O'CONNOR

HON. ANTONIN SCALIA

HON. ANTHONY M. KENNEDY

HON. DAVID H. SOUTER

HON. CLARENCE THOMAS

HON. RUTH BADER GINSBURG

HON. STEPHEN BREYER

BIOGRAPHIES OF THE
JUSTICES

Chief Justice Rehnquist was born in Milwaukee, Wisconsin, on October 1, 1924, the son of William B.

and Margery P. Rehnquist. He married Natalie Cornell in 1953. They have three children, James, Janet, and Nancy.

Chief Justice Rehnquist attended public schools in Shorewood, Wisconsin, and received his B.A. degree, with great distinction, and an M.A. degree from Stanford University in 1948. He also earned an M.A. degree from Harvard University in 1950, and then returned to Stanford University, where he received his LL.B. degree in 1952.

From 1952 to 1953, he served as law clerk for Justice Robert H. Jackson, Supreme Court of the United States. From 1953 to 1969, Chief Justice Rehnquist engaged in private practice in Phoenix, Arizona, and in 1969, he was appointed Assistant Attorney General, Office of Legal Counsel, by President Nixon.

Chief Justice Rehnquist served in the United States Army Air Corps in this country and overseas from 1943 to 1946, and was discharged with the rank of sergeant.

Chief Justice Rehnquist was nominated to the position of Associate Justice of the United States Supreme Court by President Nixon on October 21, 1971, and took office on January 7, 1972. On June 17, 1986, he was nominated Chief Justice by President Reagan, and on September 26, 1986, he was sworn in as Chief Justice.

Chief Justice Rehnquist's professional activities have included membership in the American Bar Association, the Arizona Bar Association, the Maricopa County (Arizona) Bar Association (President, 1963), the National Conference of Lawyers and Realtors, the National Conference of Commissioners of Uniform State Laws, and the Council of the Administrative Conference of the United States.

Justice Stevens was born in Chicago, Illinois, on April 20, 1920. He is married to Maryan Mulholland Stevens 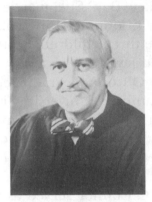 and has four children, John Joseph, Kathryn Stevens Tedlicka, Elizabeth Jane, and Susan Roberta.

Justice Stevens received an A.B. degree from the University of Chicago in 1941 and a J.D. degree, magna cum laude, from Northwestern University School of Law in 1947.

During the 1947–1948 Term of the United States Supreme Court, he was a law clerk to Justice Wiley Rutledge, and in 1949, he was admitted to practice law in Illinois. In 1951 and 1952, Justice Stevens was Associate Counsel to the Subcommittee on the Study of Monopoly Power of the Judiciary Committee of the United States House of Representatives, and from 1953 to 1955 he was a member of the Attorney General's National Committee to Study Anti-trust Law. From 1970 to 1975 he served as a Judge of the United States Court of Appeals for the Seventh Circuit.

Justice Stevens served in the United States Navy from 1942 to 1945.

Justice Stevens was appointed to the position of Associate Justice of the United States Supreme Court by President Ford on December 1, 1975, and took his seat on December 19, 1975.

Justice Stevens is a member of the Illinois Bar Association, Chicago Bar Association, Federal Bar Association, American Law Institute, and American Judicature Society.

Justice O'Connor was born in El Paso, Texas, on March 26, 1930, the daughter of Harold A. Day and Ada

Mae Wilkey Day. She married John Jay O'Connor III in 1952. They have three children, Scott, Brian, and Jay.

Justice O'Connor graduated from Stanford University in 1950 with a B.A. degree, magna cum laude. She earned her LL.B. degree at Stanford in 1952.

Justice O'Connor served as a deputy county attorney in San Mateo County, California, from 1952 to 1953, and as a civilian attorney for the Quartermaster Market Center in Frankfurt, Germany, from 1954 to 1957. She was in the private practice of law in Maryvale, Arizona, from 1958 to 1960, and served as an Assistant Attorney General in Arizona from 1965 to 1969.

Justice O'Connor was a member of the Arizona State Senate from 1969 to 1975. She was a judge of the Maricopa County Superior Court in Phoenix, Arizona, from 1975 to 1979, and served on the Arizona Court of Appeals from 1979 to 1981.

Justice O'Connor was appointed to the position of Associate Justice of the United States Supreme Court by President Reagan on July 7, 1981, and took office on September 25, 1981.

Justice Scalia was born on March 11, 1936 in Trenton, New Jersey. He married Maureen McCarthy, September 10, 1960. They have nine children: Ann Forrest, Eugene, John Francis, Catherine Elisabeth, Mary Clare, Paul David, Matthew, Christopher James, and Margaret Jane.

Justice Scalia attended Georgetown University and University of Fribourg (Switzerland), receiving his A.B. degree in 1957. He earned his LL.B. degree in 1960 from Harvard University.

Justice Scalia was admitted to the Ohio Bar, 1962, and the Virginia Bar, 1970. He was in private practice with Jones, Day, Cockley and Reavis, Cleveland, Ohio, from 1961 to 1967.

He served as general counsel, Office of Telecommunications Policy, Executive Office of the President, 1971 to 1972; chairman, Administrative Conference of the United States, 1972 to 1974; Assistant Attorney General, Office of Legal Counsel, U. S. Department of Justice, 1974 to 1977.

Justice Scalia was a professor of law at the University of Virginia from 1967 to 1974, a scholar in residence at the American Enterprise Institute in 1977, visiting professor of law at Georgetown University in 1977, professor of law at the University of Chicago from 1977 to 1982, and visiting professor of law at Stanford University from 1980 to 1981.

From 1982 to 1986, Justice Scalia served as a Judge of the United States Court of Appeals for the District of Columbia Circuit. He was nominated by President

Reagan as Associate Justice of the United States Supreme Court, and he took the oath of office on September 26, 1986.

Justice Kennedy was born in Sacramento, California, on July 23, 1936. He married Mary Davis on June 29,

1963, and they have three children, Justin Anthony, Gregory Davis, and Kristin Marie.

Justice Kennedy attended Stanford University and the London School of Economics, receiving a B.A. from Stanford in 1958. He then earned an LL.B. from Harvard Law School in 1961. From 1960 to 1961, he was on the board of student advisors, Harvard Law School.

Justice Kennedy was admitted to the California bar in 1962 and the United States Tax Court bar in 1971. From 1961 to 1963, he was an associate at Thelen, Marrin, Johnson & Bridges, San Francisco, then practiced as a sole practitioner in Sacramento from 1963 to 1967, and was a partner in Evans, Jackson & Kennedy, Sacramento, from 1967 to 1975. He was nominated to be a judge of the United States Court of Appeals for the Ninth Circuit by President Ford, and took the oath of office on May 30, 1975. In addition, Justice Kennedy has been a professor of constitutional law at McGeorge School of Law, University of the Pacific, from 1965 to 1988.

He has served in the California Army National Guard, 1961; the Judicial Conference of the United States Advisory Panel on Financial Disclosure Reports and Judicial Activities (subsequently renamed the Advisory Committee on Codes of Conduct), 1979 to 1987; and the board of the Federal Judicial Center, 1987 to 1988. He has been on the Committee on Pacific Territories, 1979 to 1988, and was named chairman 1982. He is a member of the American Bar Association,

Sacramento County Bar Association, State Bar of California, and Phi Beta Kappa.

Justice Kennedy was nominated by President Reagan as an Associate Justice of the Supreme Court, and took the oath of office on February 18, 1988.

Justice Souter was born in Melrose, Massachusetts on September 17, 1939, the son of Joseph Alexander and Helen Adams Hackett Souter.

He graduated from Harvard College in 1961 with an A.B. degree. After two years as a Rhodes Scholar, Justice Souter received an A.B. in Jurisprudence from Oxford University in 1963. He earned an LL.B. degree from Harvard Law School in 1966 and an M.A. degree from Oxford University in 1989.

Justice Souter was an associate at the law firm of Orr and Reno in Concord, New Hampshire from 1966 to 1968. He then became an Assistant Attorney General of New Hampshire. In 1971, he became Deputy Attorney General, and in 1976, Attorney General of New Hampshire. Justice Souter was named Associate Justice of the Superior Court of New Hampshire in 1978. In 1983, he was appointed as an Associate Justice of the Supreme Court of New Hampshire.

On May 25, 1990, Justice Souter became a Judge of the United States Court of Appeals for the First Circuit. He was nominated by President Bush as an Associate Justice of the United States Supreme Court, and he took his seat on October 9, 1990.

Justice Souter is a member of the National Association of Attorneys General, the New Hampshire Bar Association, and the American Bar Association.

Justice Thomas was born in Pinpoint, Georgia on June 23, 1948. He married Virginia Lamp on May 30,  1987, and has one child, Jamal Adeen.

Justice Thomas attended Conception Seminary and Holy Cross College, receiving an A.B. degree, cum laude, from Holy Cross in 1971. He earned a J.D. degree from Yale Law School in 1974.

He was admitted to the Missouri Bar in 1974, and after serving as Assistant Attorney General of Missouri from 1974 to 1977, he was an attorney for the Monsanto Company from 1977 to 1979.

Justice Thomas served as a legislative assistant to Senator John C. Danforth of Missouri from 1979 to 1981, before serving as Assistant Secretary for Civil Rights for the United States Department of Education from 1981 to 1982 and Chairman of the United States Equal Employment Opportunity Commission from 1982 to 1990.

On March 12, 1990, Justice Thomas became a Judge of the United States Court of Appeals for the District of Columbia Circuit. He was nominated by President Bush as Associate Justice of the United States Supreme Court, and he took the oath of office on October 23, 1991.

Justice Ginsburg was born in Brooklyn, New York, on March 15, 1933, the daughter of Nathan Bader and  Celia Amster Bader. She married Martin D. Ginsburg in 1954, and they have two children, Jane and James.

She received a B.A. degree, with high honors in Government and distinction in all subjects, from Cornell University in 1954. She attended Harvard Law School and Columbia Law School, receiving her L.L.B. degree from Columbia in 1959.

Justice Ginsburg was admitted to the New York Bar in 1959 and the District of Columbia Bar in 1975. She served as a law clerk for Judge Edmund L. Palmieri of the United States District Court for the Southern District of New York from 1959 to 1961.

Justice Ginsburg was a professor at the Rutgers University School of Law from 1963 to 1972 and at Columbia Law School from 1972 to 1980. In addition, she served the American Civil Liberties Union as general counsel from 1973 to 1980 and as a member of the national board of directors from 1974 to 1980.

On June 30, 1980, Justice Ginsburg became a Judge of the United States Court of Appeals for the District of Columbia Circuit. She was nominated by President Clinton as an Associate Justice of the United States Supreme Court, and she took the oath of office on August 10, 1993.

Justice Breyer was born in San Francisco, California, on August 15, 1938. He married Joanna Hare on  September 4, 1967, and they have three children, Chloe, Nell, and Michael.

Justice Breyer received an A.B. degree, with Great Distinction, from Stanford University in 1959. He attended Oxford University as a Marshall Scholar and received a B.A. degree, with 1st Class Honors, in 1961. He earned his LL.B. degree from Harvard Law School, magna cum laude, in 1964.

During the 1964-1965 Term of the United States Supreme Court, he served as clerk to Justice Arthur Goldberg. He served as Special Assistant to the Assistant Attorney General (Antitrust), Department of Justice, 1965 to 1967; Assistant Special Prosecutor, Watergate Special Prosecution Force, 1973; Special Counsel to the U.S. Senate Judiciary Committee, 1974 to 1975; and Chief Counsel to the U.S. Senate Judiciary Committee, 1979 to 1980.

At Harvard University, Justice Breyer was an assistant professor from 1967 to 1970, a professor of law from 1970 to 1980, a professor at the Kennedy School of Government from 1977 to 1980, and a lecturer since 1980. He was a visiting professor at the College of Law, Sydney, Australia, in 1975, and the University of Rome in 1993.

He was appointed to the United States Court of Appeals for the First Circuit in 1980, and served as Chief Judge of that Court from 1990 to 1994. He was nominated by President Clinton as Associate Justice of the United States Supreme Court and took office on August 4, 1994.

SURVEY OF THE 1999-2000 TERM

by

Karen Lussen Blair, J.D.

§ 1. Generally; statistics
§ 2. Landmark decisions
§ 3. Abortion
§ 4. Age discrimination
§ 5. Attorney fees
§ 6. Bankruptcy
§ 7. Boundry dispute
§ 8. Capital sentencing
§ 9. Certified question for interpretation of state law
§ 10. Child visitation
§ 11. Civil rights
§ 12. Clean Water Act
§ 13. Commerce clause
§ 14. Defendant's presence at trial
§ 15. Due process
§ 16. Elections
§ 17. Employee Retirement Income Security Act (ERISA)
§ 18. Equal protection
§ 19. Evidence of prior conviction
§ 20. Fair Labor Standards Act
§ 21. Federal Arbitration Act
§ 22. Federal court jurisdiction
§ 23. Federal habeas corpus
§ 24. Federal off-shore leases
§ 25. Federal pre-emption
§ 26. Federal Rules of Civil Procedure
§ 27. Federal taxation
§ 28. Firearms
§ 29. Food and Drug Administration (FDA)
§ 30. Freedom of association
§ 31. Freedom of speech and expression
§ 32. Indictment
§ 33. In forma pauperis proceedings

§ 34. Interstate Agreement on Detainers
§ 35. Jury selection
§ 36. Lanham Act
§ 37. Lesser included offense
§ 38. Medicare
§ 39. Miranda warnings
§ 40. Prisons and prisoners
§ 41. Racketeer Influenced and Corrupt Organizations Act (RICO)
§ 42. Retroactive application of state law
§ 43. Right to counsel
§ 44. —Search and seizure
§ 45. Secretary of the Interior - grazing lands
§ 46. Self-representation
§ 47. Separation of church and state
§ 48. Separation of powers
§ 49. Social Security
§ 50. Standing tosue
§ 51. State income taxation
§ 52. Voting rights

----

§ 1. Generally; statistics

The Supreme Court's 1999-2000 Term began on October 4, 1999. The court took a recess from June 29, 2000 until October 2, 2000, at which time the 1999-2000 Term adjourned.

Statistics released by the Office of the Clerk of the Supreme Court reveal that (1) 8,445 cases appeared on the Supreme Court's docket for the 1999-2000 Term, and (2) of these, 1,068 were carried over from the prior term, and 7,377 were docketed during the 1999-2000 Term.

Of the 8,445 cases on the docket during the 1999-2000 Term, 7,197 nonoriginal cases were disposed of by (1) the court's denial of review, (2) the court's dismissal, or (3) withdrawal. Another 50 nonoriginal cases were summarily decided. A total of 1,074 cases, including 8 original cases, were not acted upon, or remained undisposed of.

There were 124 cases available for argument during the 1999-00 Term, of which 83 cases were argued and 4 were dismissed or remanded without argument, leaving 37 cases still available for argument. Of the 83 cases that were argued, 79 were disposed of by signed opinion, 2 were disposed of by per curiam opinion, and 1 was set for reargument.

§ 2. Landmark decisions

During the 1999-2000 Term, the United States Supreme Court handed down a number of well-publicized landmark decisions. Among these decisions were cases that dealt with controversial issues such as the separation of church and state, child visitation rights, abortion, freedom of association and freedom of speech. The court continued to develop and refine the law concerning civil rights, search and seizure and Miranda Rights. Two cases were decided during the Term that involved the issue of the separation of church and state. The Supreme Court held that a school aid program, under which the Federal Government distributed funds to state and local government agencies, which in turn loaned educational materials and equipment to public and private schools—including religiously affiliated schools—was not prohibited by the Federal Constitution's First Amendment as a law respecting an establishment of religion (Mitchell v Helms (2000, US) 147 L Ed 2d 660, 120 S Ct 2530, infra § 47). Also, it was held that a Texas public school district's policy—which permitted a student-led and student-initiated "invocation and/or message" over a public address system before each high school varsity home football game—violated the prohibition, under the Federal Constitution's First Amendment, of an establishment of religion (Santa Fe Indep. Sch. Dist. v Doe (2000, US) 147 L Ed 2d 295, 120 S Ct 2266, infra § 47). The court held that application of a Wisconsin statute that allowed visitation rights to paternal grandparents—as well as other parties—violated the mother's due process right, under the Federal Constitution's Fourteenth Amendment, to raise her children (Troxel v Granville (2000, US) 147 L Ed 2d 49, 120 S Ct 2054, infra § 10). The Supreme Court held that a Nebraska statute that criminalized the performance of any "partial birth abortion" that was not necessary to save the life of the mother violated the Federal Constitution (Stenberg v Carhart (2000, US) 147 L Ed 2d 743, 120 S Ct 2597, infra § 3). In addition, the court held that the application of New Jersey's public accommodations law to require the Boy Scouts of America to admit an assistant scoutmaster violated the Boy Scouts' right of expressive association under the Federal Constitution's First Amendment, where the assistant scoutmaster's position had been revoked when the Boy Scouts learned that he was an avowed homosexual and gay activist (BSA v Dale (2000, US) 147 L Ed 2d 554, 120 S Ct 2446, infra § 30). Several cases were decided which addressed issues concerning freedom of speech. Among the most significant were: a case in which the Court held that a Colorado statute—which prohibited any person within 100 feet of a health care facility's entrance from knowingly approaching within 8 feet of another person, without that person's consent, for the purpose of passing a leaflet or handbill to, displaying a sign to, or engaging in oral protest, education, or counseling with such other person—did not violate the free speech provisions of the Federal Constitution's First Amendment (Hill v Colorado (2000, US) 147 L Ed 2d 597, 120 S Ct 2480, infra § 31), and a case in which it was held that the Telecommunications

Act of 1996 —which required cable television operators who provided channels primarily dedicated to sexually oriented programming either to fully scramble or block those channels or to "time channel," that is, limit transmission to hours when children were unlikely to be viewing—violated the free speech guarantee of the Federal Constitution's First Amendment, where it was not alleged that the programming in question was obscene (United States v Playboy Entertainment Group (2000, US) 146 L Ed 2d 865, 120 S Ct 1878, infra § 31). The court held in a civil rights action by a rejected applicant to a university's Ph. D. program—in which it was alleged that the university's race-conscious admissions process violated the equal protection clause of the Federal Constitution's Fourteenth Amendment and 42 USCS § 1983—that a Federal Court of Appeals had erred in holding that summary judgment for the university was inappropriate even if the university conclusively established that the applicant would have been rejected under a race-neutral policy. (Texas v Lesage (1999) 528 US 18, 145 L Ed 2d 347, 120 S Ct 467, infra § 11). The Supreme Court issued two decisions concerning search and seizure during the Term. The court held that a law enforcement officer's physical manipulation of a bus passenger's carry-on luggage—which consisted of squeezing the soft luggage which the passenger had placed in the overhead storage space—violated the proscription against unreasonable searches under the Federal Constitution's Fourth Amendment (Bond v United States (2000, US) 146 L Ed 2d 365, 120 S Ct 1462, infra § 44). On the other-hand, the court held that the actions of police officers in stopping an accused—who had fled upon seeing police officers patrolling an area known for heavy narcotics trafficking—did not violate the Federal Constitution's Fourth Amendment, as the police had a reasonable suspicion that the accused was involved in criminal activity (Illinois v Wardlow (2000) 528 US 119, 145 L Ed 2d 570, 120 S Ct 673, infra § 44). It was held that Miranda v Arizona (1966) 384 US 436, 16 L Ed 2d 694, 86 S Ct 1602, and its progeny in the Supreme Court would continue to govern the admissibility, in both state and federal courts, of statements made during custodial interrogation, as (1) the Miranda decision, being a federal constitutional ruling, could not be overruled by a subsequent statute, 18 USCS § 3501, which in essence made the admissibility of such statements turn on whether they were voluntary, and (2) the Supreme Court would decline to itself overrule Miranda (Dickerson v United States (2000, US) 147 L Ed 2d 405, 120 S Ct 2326, infra § 39). The Supreme Court decided two major cases in which the issues of Congressional authority and the delegation of that authority were addressed. In one case, the Supreme Court held that Congress had no authority—under the Federal Constitution's commerce clause (Art I, § 8, cl 3) or under § 5 of the Constitution's Fourteenth Amendment—to enact 42 USCS § 13981, which provided a federal civil remedy for victims of gender-motivated violence (United States v Morrison (2000, US) 146 L Ed 2d 658, 120 S Ct 1740, infra § 13), while in the other case, the court held that Congress had not given the Food and Drug Administration (FDA) the authority to assert jurisdiction to regulate tobacco products as customarily marketed (FDA v Brown & Williamson Tobacco Corp. (2000, US) 146 L Ed 2d 121, 120 S Ct 1291, infra § 29).

§ 3. Abortion

The Supreme Court held that a Nebraska statute that criminalized the performance of any "partial birth abortion" that was not necessary to save the life of the mother violated the Federal Constitution. [Stenberg v Carhart (2000, US) 147 L Ed 2d 743, 120 S Ct 2597.]

§ 4 Age discrimination

The court held that (1) the Age Discrimination in Employment Act of 1967 (29 USCS §§ 621 et seq.) contained a clear statement of Congress' intent to abrogate states' sovereign immunity under the Federal Constitution's Eleventh Amendment, but (2) such abrogation exceeded Congress' authority, under § 5 of the Constitution's Fourteenth Amendment, to enforce the provisions of the Fourteenth Amendment. [Kimel v Florida Bd. of Regents (2000) 528 US 62, 145 L Ed 2d 522, 120 S Ct 631.]

It was held that a prima facie case under the Age Discrimination in Employment Act (29 USCS §§ 621 et seq.), together with sufficient evidence to disbelieve an employer's justification, was potentially sufficient to support a finding of discrimination. [Reeves v Sanderson Plumbing Prods. (2000, US) 147 L Ed 2d 105, 120 S Ct 2097.]

§ 5 Attorney fees

The amendment of an attorney fees judgment in favor of a corporation to join the president of another corporation as a party and to make the president liable for the fee award, without an opportunity to contest personal liability, was held to violate due process. [Nelson v Adams USA, Inc. (2000, US) 146 L Ed 2d 530, 120 S Ct 1587.]

§ 6 Bankruptcy

It was held that for purposes of bankruptcy proceedings, 11 USCS § 506(c)—which provides that the trustee may recover from property subject to an allowed secured claim the reasonable and necessary costs of preserving or disposing of such property—does not provide administrative claimants with an independent right to seek payment of their claims from property encumbered by a secured creditor's lien. [Hartford Underwriters Ins. Co. v Union Planters Bank, N.A. (2000, US) 147 L Ed 2d 1, 120 S Ct 1942.]

The Supreme Court held that when the substantive law creating a tax obligation put the burden of proof on a taxpayer, the burden of proof on the tax claim in bankruptcy court remained where the substantive law put it, because the tax law was not a candidate for an exception to the general rule that one who asserts a claim is entitled to the burden of proof that normally comes with the claim. [Raleigh v Illinois Dep't of Revenue (2000, US) 147 L Ed 2d 13, 120 S Ct 1951.]

§ 7 Boundry disputes

The Supreme Court issued a decree adjudging the respective rights of the United States and the state of Alaska with respect to lands, minerals, and other natural resources underlying the Beaufort and Chukchi Seas along the coast of Alaska. [United States v Alaska (2000, US) 147 L Ed 2d 815, 120 S Ct 2767.] The Supreme Court held that the claims of the Quechan Tribe related to disputed boundary lands of the Fort Yuma (Quechan) Indian Reservation, made to increased rights to water from the Colorado River, were not foreclosed by (1) the court's decision in Arizona v California (1963) 373 US 546, 10 L Ed 2d 542, 83 S Ct 1468, concerning water rights on five Indian reservations, including the Fort Yuma Reservation, or (2) a 1983 consent decree which was (a) issued by the United States Court of Claims, and (b) allegedly extinguished the Quechan Tribe's claim to title in the disputed lands. [Arizona v California (2000, US) 147 L Ed 2d 374, 120 S Ct 2304.]

§ 8 Capital sentencing

The Supreme Court held that the Federal Constitution is not violated when a trial judge directs a capital sentencing jury's attention to a specific paragraph of a constitutionally sufficient jury instruction in response to a question by the jury regarding the proper consideration of mitigating circumstances. [Weeks v Angelone (2000, US) 145 L Ed 2d 727, 120 S Ct 727.]

The Supreme Court affirmed a Federal Court of Appeals judgment that, because a prior conviction that would have made an accused ineligible for parole was not final at the time of the accused's Virginia capital sentencing trial, the accused was not entitled to a jury instruction at the capital sentencing trial to the effect that the accused was ineligible for parole. [Ramdass v Angelone (2000, US) 147 L Ed 2d 125, 120 S Ct 2113.]

§ 9 Certified question for interpretation of state law

The United States Supreme Court held that it was necessary to certify to the Supreme Court of Pennsylvania the question whether the latter court's 1993 interpretation of a Pennsylvania statute concerning the operation of a hazardous waste facility stated the correct interpretation of Pennsylvania law at the date, in 1990, when the conviction of a hazardous waste disposal facility's owner under the statute became final, where (1) the owner, seeking federal habeas corpus relief, argued that he had been convicted for conduct that was not criminal under the 1993 interpretation; and (2) the answer to the certified question would help the United States Supreme Court determine whether the Federal Constitution required that the owner's conviction be set aside. [Fiore v White (1999) 528 US 23, 145 L Ed 2d 353, 120 S Ct 469.]

§ 10 Child visitation

The court held that application of a Wisconsin statute—which (1) permitted any person to petition a state court for child visitation rights at any time, and (2) authorized the court to order visitation rights for any person when visitation might serve the best interest of the child—to allow visitation rights to paternal grandparents violated the mother's due process right, under the Federal Constitution's Fourteenth Amendment, to raise her children. [Troxel v Granville (2000, US) 147 L Ed 2d 49, 120 S Ct 2054.]

§ 11 Civil rights

The court held—with respect to a civil rights action by a rejected applicant to a university's Ph. D. program, in which action it was alleged that the university's race-conscious admissions process violated the equal protection clause of the Federal Constitution's Fourteenth Amendment and 42 USCS § 1983—that a Federal Court of Appeals erred in holding that summary judgment for the university was inappropriate even if the university conclusively established that the applicant would have been rejected under a race-neutral policy. [Texas v Lesage (1999) 528 US 18, 145 L Ed 2d 347, 120 S Ct 467.]

§ 12 Clean Water Act

The Supreme Court held that a Federal Court of Appeals erred in concluding that a citizen suitor's civil penalties claim, under a provision of the Clean Water Act (33 USCS § 1365(a)), had to be dismissed as moot where the defendant, after commencement of the suit, came into compliance by the receipt of a National Pollutant Discharge Elimination System permit issued by a state department of health and environmental control. [Friends of the Earth, Inc. v Laidlaw Envtl.

Servs. (TOC) (2000) 528 US 167, 145 L Ed 2d 610, 120 S Ct 693, 163 ALR Fed 749.]

§ 13 Commerce clause

It was held that Congress had no authority—under the Federal Constitution's commerce clause (Art I, § 8, cl 3) or under § 5 of the Constitution's Fourteenth Amendment—to enact 42 USCS § 13981, which provided a federal civil remedy for victims of gender-motivated violence. [United States v Morrison (2000, US) 146 L Ed 2d 658, 120 S Ct 1740.]

The Supreme Court held that arson of an owner-occupied residence that was not currently used for any commercial purpose was not subject to prosecution under 18 USCS § 844(i)—which made it a federal crime to maliciously damage, by means of fire, any building used in interstate or foreign commerce or in any activity affecting interstate or foreign commerce—because such a residence was not "used" in commerce or commerce-affecting activity. [Jones v United States (2000, US) 146 L Ed 2d 902, 120 S Ct 1904.]

§ 14 Defendant's presence at trial

The Supreme Court held that a prosecutor's comments that a criminal defendant had the opportunity to hear all of the other witnesses before testifying, and to tailor his testimony accordingly, did not violate the defendant's (1) rights to be present at trial and confront his accusers under the Federal Constitution's Fifth and Sixth Amendments, or (2) right to due process under the Constitution's Fourteenth Amendment. [Portuondo v Agard (2000, US) 146 L Ed 2d 47, 120 S Ct 1119.]

§ 15 Due process

The court held that the due process clause of the Federal Constitution's Fourteenth Amendment required that any fact, other than the fact of a prior conviction, that increased the penalty for a state crime beyond the prescribed statutory maximum had to be (1) submitted to a jury, and (2) proved beyond a reasonable doubt. [Apprendi v New Jersey (2000, US) 147 L Ed 2d 435, 120 S Ct 2348.]

§ 16 Elections

It was held that the Organic Act of Guam (48 USCS §§ 1421 et seq.)—which provided that if no candidates for Governor and Lieutenant Governor of the Territory of Guam received a "majority of the votes cast in any election," a runoff election had to be held between the candidates receiving the highest and second highest number of votes cast (48 USCS § 1422)—did not compel a runoff election, where a candidate slate received a majority of the votes cast for Governor and Lieutenant Governor but did not receive a majority of the number of ballots cast in the simultaneous general election. [Gutierrez v Ada (2000, US) 145 L Ed 2d 747, 120 S Ct 740.]

The Supreme Court held that the federal limits on campaign contributions that were approved in Buckley v Valeo (1976) 424 US 1, 46 L Ed 2d 659, 96 S Ct 612, (1) were authority for state limits on contributions to state political candidates, but (2) did not define the scope of permissible state limits, either with or without adjustment of such federal limits for inflation. [Nixon v Shrink Mo. Gov't PAC (2000, US) 145 L Ed 2d 886, 120 S Ct 897.]

§ 17 Employee Retirement Income Security Act (ERISA)

It was held that mixed treatment-and-eligibility decisions made by a health maintenance organization (HMO), acting through its physician employees, are not fiduciary acts within the meaning of the Employee Retirement Income Security Act of 1974 (ERISA) (29 USC §§ 1001 et seq.). [Pegram v Herdrich (2000, US) 147 L Ed 2d 164, 120 S Ct 2143.]

The Supreme Court held that the authorization, under § 502(a)(3) of the Employee Retirement Income Security Act of 1974 (ERISA) (29 USCS § 1132(a)(3)), of a plan participant, beneficiary, or fiduciary to bring a civil action for "appropriate equitable relief" to address ERISA violations extends to a nonfiduciary party in interest to a transaction that is barred by § 406(a) of ERISA (29 USCS § 1106(a)). [Harris Trust & Sav. Bank v Salomon Smith Barney Inc. (2000, US) 147 L Ed 2d 187, 120 S Ct 2180.]

§ 18 Equal protection

It was held that a Federal Court of Appeals erred in concluding that an individual's suit—challenging, as violative of the equal protection component of the Federal Constitution's Fifth Amendment, the United States Department of Transportation's procedure for certifying contractors as disadvantaged business enterprises—should have been dismissed as moot after the individual was certified as a disadvantaged business enterprise by a state department of transportation. [Adarand Constructors, Inc. v Slater (2000) 528 US 216, 145 L Ed 2d 650, 120 S Ct 722.]

The court held (1) the number of individuals in a class was immaterial to establish a cause of action under the equal protection clause of the Federal Constitution's Fourteenth Amendment, and (2) thus, the equal protection clause could properly give rise to a cause of action on behalf of a "class of one," even though the plaintiff did not allege membership in a class or group. [Village of Willowbrook v Olech (2000, US) 145 L Ed 2d 1060, 120 S Ct 1073.]

§ 19 Evidence of prior conviction

The Supreme Court held that a federal criminal defendant who pre-emptively introduced evidence of a prior conviction on direct examination—after a Federal District Court, in ruling on a motion in limine, had granted the prosecution permission to introduce the prior conviction as impeachment evidence over the defendant's objection—was not entitled to challenge the District Court's in limine ruling on appeal. [Ohler v United States (2000, US) 146 L Ed 2d 826, 120 S Ct 1851.]

§ 20 Fair Labor Standards Act

It was held that nothing in the Fair Labor Standards Act of 1938 (FLSA) (29 USCS §§ 201 et seq.)—which permitted states and the political subdivisions of states to compensate employees for overtime work by granting them compensatory time in lieu of cash payment—or the FLSA's implementing regulations prohibited a public employer from compelling the use of compensatory time. [Christensen v Harris County (2000, US) 146 L Ed 2d 621, 120 S Ct 1655.]

§ 21 Federal Abitration Act

The Supreme Court held that the venue provisions of the Federal Arbitration Act (9 USCS §§ 9-11) were permissive, allowing a motion to confirm, vacate, or modify an arbitration award to be brought either in the district where the award was made or in any district proper under the general federal venue statute (28 USCS § 1391(a)(2)). [Cortez Byrd Chips, Inc. v Bill Harbert Constr. Co. (2000, US) 146 L Ed 2d 171, 120 S Ct 1331.

§ 22 Federal court jurisdiction

The Supreme Court affirmed by an equally divided court a United States Court of Appeals for the Fifth Circuit decision (176 F3d 298) with respect to a case in which a panel of the Court of Appeals had previously held (51 F3d 524) that—with respect to a class-action suit brought by purchasers of infant formula against formula manufacturers, which action alleged violations of state law—the federal supplemental jurisdiction statute (28 USCS § 1367) authorized a federal court to exercise jurisdiction over the claims of unnamed class members. [Free v Abbott Lab., Inc. (2000, US) 146 L Ed 2d 306, 120 S Ct 1578.]

§ 23 Federal habeas corpus

A federal habeas corpus petition filed by a state prisoner, after an initial petition was dismissed without adjudication on the merits, was held not to constitute a "second or successive" petition subject to dismissal for abuse of writ. [Slack v McDaniel (2000, US) 146 L Ed 2d 542, 120 S Ct 1595.]

A federal habeas corpus petitioner was held not to have "failed to develop" a factual basis for a claim in state court, so as to bar an evidentiary hearing under 28 USCS § 2254 (e) (2), absent a lack of diligence or some greater fault. [Williams v Taylor (2000, US) 146 L Ed 2d 435, 120 S Ct 1479.]

§ 24 Federal off-shore leases

The Supreme Court held that two oil companies were entitled to restitution of $158 million that they had paid the Federal Government in return for lease contracts that gave the companies conditional rights to explore for and develop oil off the North Carolina coast, where a change in federal law required the government to impose a delay that violated the contracts. [Mobil Oil Exploration & Producing Southeast, Inc. v United States (2000, US) 147 L Ed 2d 528, 120 S Ct 2423.]

§ 25 Federal pre-emption

The Supreme Court held that the National Traffic and Motor Safety Act of 1966 (15 USCS §§ 1381 et seq., later recodified at 49 USCS §§ 30101 et seq.)—read in conjunction with Federal Motor Vehicle Safety Standard (FMVSS) 208 (49 CFR § 571.208), which required auto manufacturers to equip some but not all 1987 vehicles with passive restraints—pre-empted a common-law tort action claiming that an auto manufacturer, who was in compliance with the standard, ought to have equipped a 1987 automobile with airbags. [Geier v American Honda Motor Co. (2000, US) 146 L Ed 2d 914, 120 S Ct 1913.]

It was held that the Federal Railroad Safety Act of 1970 (49 USCS §§ 20101 et seq.), in conjunction with 23 CFR §§ 646.214(b)(3) and (4), pre-empted state tort claims concerning a railroad's alleged failure to maintain adequate warning devices at crossings, where federal funds had been utilized in the devices' installation. [Norfolk Southern Ry. v Shanklin (2000, US) 146 L Ed 2d 374, 120 S Ct 1467.]

The court held (1) a Massachusetts statute, which generally barred state entities from buying goods and services from companies that were doing business with Burma (Myanmar), was pre-empted by a federal statute which imposed sanctions on Burma; and (2) thus, application of the state statute violated the Federal Constitution's supremacy clause (Art VI, cl 2). [Crosby v National Foreign Trade Council (2000, US) 147 L Ed 2d 352, 120 S Ct 2288.]

The Supreme Court held (1) the state of Washington's oil tanker regulations regarding general navigation watch procedures, crew English language skills and training, and maritime casualty reporting were pre-empted by a comprehensive federal regulatory scheme, and (2) the case would be remanded so that the validity of other Washington tanker regulations could be assessed in light of the considerable federal interest at stake. [United States v Locke (2000, US) 146 L Ed 2d 69, 120 S Ct 1135.]

§ 26 Federal Rules of Civil Procedure

The Supreme Court held that Rule 50 of the Federal Rules of Civil Procedure permitted an appellate court to direct the entry of a judgment as a matter of law when the appellate court determined that evidence was erroneously admitted at trial and that the remaining, properly admitted, evidence was insufficient to constitute a submissible case. [Weisgram v Marley Co. (2000, US) 145 L Ed 2d 958, 120 S Ct 1011.]

§ 27 Federal taxation

The court held that, despite an individual's exercise of his prerogative under Arkansas law to retroactively disclaim his interest as heir to his mother's estate, the interest constituted a "property" or "right to property" to which federal tax liens attached under 26 USCS § 6321. [Drye v United States (1999) 528 US 49, 145 L Ed 2d 466, 120 S Ct 474.]

Both remittance by a taxpayer of estimated federal income tax and remittance by the taxpayer's employer of federal withholding tax were held to be "paid" on the due date of the taxpayer's income tax return. [Baral v United States (2000, US) 145 L Ed 2d 949, 120 S Ct 1006.]

§ 28 Firearms

It was held that the word "machinegun" and similar terms used in 18 USCS § 924(c)—which provides that

(1) anyone who uses or carries a "firearm" during or in relation to a crime of violence shall, in addition to the sentence for that crime, be sentenced to 5 years imprisonment, and (2) if the firearm is of certain particular types, including a "machinegun," the additional sentence shall be 30 years—do not merely create sentencing factors, the existence of which may be determined by a judge, but state elements of an offense separate from that of using or carrying a "firearm," so that an indictment must identify the firearm type involved and the existence of those elements must be determined by a jury. [Castillo v United States (2000, US) 147 L Ed 2d 94, 120 S Ct 2090.]

§ 29 Food and Drug Administration (FDA)

The Supreme Court held that Congress had not given the Food and Drug Administration (FDA) the authority to assert jurisdiction to regulate tobacco products as customarily marketed. [FDA v Brown & Williamson Tobacco Corp. (2000, US) 146 L Ed 2d 121, 120 S Ct 1291.]

§ 30 Freedom of association

The court held that California's use of a "blanket" political primary election—in which (1) each voter's ballot listed every candidate regardless of political party affiliation and allowed the voter to choose freely among the candidates, and (2) the candidate of each party who won the most votes was that party's nominee for the general election—violated political parties' rights of association under the Federal Constitution's First Amendment. [California Democratic Party v Jones (2000, US) 147 L Ed 2d 502, 120 S Ct 2402.] The Supreme Court held that the application of New Jersey's public accommodations law to require the Boy Scouts of America to readmit an adult member to a

New Jersey Boy Scout troop violated the Boy Scouts' right of expressive association under the Federal Constitution's First Amendment, where the member's position as assistant scoutmaster had been revoked when the Boy Scouts learned that the member was an avowed homosexual and gay rights activist. [BSA v Dale (2000, US) 147 L Ed 2d 554, 120 S Ct 2446.]

§ 31 Freedom of speech and expression

It was held that Section 505 of the Telecommunications Act of 1996 (47 USCS § 561)—which required cable television operators who provided channels primarily dedicated to sexually oriented programming either to fully scramble or otherwise fully block those channels or to "time channel," that is, limit transmission to hours when children were unlikely to be viewing—violated the free speech guarantee of the Federal Constitution's First Amendment, where it was not alleged that the programming in question was obscene. [United States v Playboy Entertainment Group (2000, US) 146 L Ed 2d 865, 120 S Ct 1878.]

The First Amendment was held to permit a public university to use students' mandatory fees to fund extracurricular student speech, where there was viewpoint neutrality in allocation of funding to student organizations engaging in such speech. [Board of Regents v Southworth (2000, US) 146 L Ed 2d 193, 120 S Ct 1346.]

The court held that a Pennsylvania city's public indecency ordinance—which prohibited knowingly or intentionally appearing in public in a "state of nudity"—did not, as applied to nude dancing, violate freedom of expression under the Federal Constitution's First Amendment. [City of Erie v Pap's A.M. (2000, US) 146 L Ed 2d 265, 120 S Ct 1382.]

It was held that a Colorado statute—which prohibited any person within 100 feet of a health care facility's entrance from knowingly approaching within 8 feet of another person, without that person's consent, for the purpose of passing a leaflet or handbill to, displaying a sign to, or engaging in oral protest, education, or counseling with such other person—did not violate the free speech provisions of the Federal Constitution's First Amendment. [Hill v Colorado (2000, US) 147 L Ed 2d 597, 120 S Ct 2480.]

The Supreme Court held that a publisher was not entitled to prevail on a claim that a California statute—which restricted public access to the addresses of arrestees—was facially overbroad under the free speech clause of the Federal Constitution's First Amendment. [Los Angeles Police Dep't v United Reporting Publ'g Corp. (1999) 528 US 32, 145 L Ed 2d 451, 120 S Ct 483.]

§ 32 Indictment

The Supreme Court held that a former federal government official's federal indictment had to be dismissed, where the Federal Government could not prove that the evidence that it used to obtain the indictment—and proposed to use at trial—was derived from legitimate sources that were entirely independent of the documents produced by the official under a grant of prosecutorial immunity. [United States v Hubbell (2000, US) 147 L Ed 2d 24, 120 S Ct 2037.]

§ 33 In forma pauperis proceedings

A person who had filed eight frivolous certiorari petitions in the Supreme Court was denied leave to proceed in forma pauperis as to a petition for certiorari, and an order was entered barring the person's future in forma pauperis filings of petitions for certiorari in noncriminal matters. [Brancato v Gunn (1999) 528 US 1, 145 L Ed 2d 1, 120 S Ct 5.]

Similarly, a person who had filed 57 frivolous petitions in the Supreme Court was denied leave to proceed in forma pauperis as to 2 petitions for certiorari, and an order was entered barring the person's future in forma pauperis filings of petitions for certiorari or extraordinary writs in noncriminal matters. [Antonelli v Caridine (1999) 528 US 3, 145 L Ed 2d 4, 120 S Ct 4.]

The Supreme Court denied a person who had filed in the Supreme Court 12 frivolous petitions leave to proceed in forma pauperis as to a petition for certiorari, and the court entered an order barring the person's future in forma pauperis filings of petitions for certiorari or extraordinary writs in noncriminal matters. [Judd v United States Dist. Court (1999) 528 US 5, 145 L Ed 2d 7, 120 S Ct 1.]

Additionally, the court held that a person who had filed 19 frivolous certiorari petitions in the Supreme Court would be denied leave to proceed in forma pauperis as to a petition for certiorari, and an order was entered barring the person's future in forma pauperis filings of petitions for certiorari or extraordinary writs in noncriminal matters. [Dempsey v Martin (1999) 528 US 7, 145 L Ed 2d 10, 120 S Ct 2.]

Likewise, a person who had filed 10 frivolous certiorari petitions in the Supreme Court was denied leave to proceed in forma pauperis as to a petition for certiorari, and an order was entered barring the person's future in forma pauperis filings of petitions for certiorari in noncriminal matters. [Prunty v Brooks (1999) 528 US 9, 145 L Ed 2d 13, 120 S Ct 3.]

A person who had filed 12 frivolous petitions in the Supreme Court was denied leave to proceed in forma pauperis as to a petition for mandamus, and an order was entered barring the person's future in forma pauperis filings of petitions for certiorari or extraordinary writs in noncriminal matters. [In re Bauer (1999) 528 US 16, 145 L Ed 2d 21, 120 S Ct 6.]

§ 34 Interstate Agreement on Detainers

The Supreme Court held that an accused—who was returned from Ohio to New York, under the Interstate Agreement on Detainers (IAD) (18 USCS Appx), to face murder and robbery charges—was barred from seeking dismissal of the New York indictment on the ground that the trial did not occur within a 180-day period set by the IAD, where the accused's defense counsel had agreed to a trial date outside the 180-day period, as such agreement waived the accused's speedy trial rights under the IAD. [New York v Hill (2000) 528 US 110, 145 L Ed 2d 560, 120 S Ct 659.]

§ 35 Jury selection

It was held that a federal criminal defendant—who, after a trial judge erroneously refuses to dismiss a potential juror for cause, chooses to exercise a peremptory challenge to remove that juror—is not deprived of any constitutional or rule-based right, under the increased penalty clause of the Federal Constitution's Fifth Amendment or under Rule 24(b) of the Federal Rules of Criminal Procedure, where the defendant is subsequently convicted by a jury on which no biased juror sits. [United States v Martinez-Salazar (2000, US) 145 L Ed 2d 792, 120 S Ct 774.]

§ 36 Lanham Act

It was held that in an action for infringement of an unregistered trade dress under § 43(a) of the Lanham Act (15 USCS § 1125(a)), a product's design was distinctive, and therefore protectible, only upon a showing of secondary meaning. [Wal-Mart Stores, Inc. v Samara Bros. (2000, US) 146 L Ed 2d 182, 120 S Ct 1339.]

§ 37 Lesser included offense

The Supreme Court held that (1) the offense described in 18 USCS § 2113(b)—which punishes whoever takes and carries away, with intent to steal or purloin, any thing of value exceeding $1,000 belonging to, or in the possession of, any bank—is not a lesser included offense of the offense described in 18 USCS § 2113(a), which punishes whoever, by force and violence, or by intimidation, takes from the person or presence of another any thing of value belonging to, or in the possession of, any bank; and (2) an accused who had been charged with violating § 2113(a) was prohibited as a matter of law from obtaining a lesser-included-offense instruction on § 2113(b). [Carter v United States (2000, US) 147 L Ed 2d 203, 120 S Ct 2159.]

§ 38 Medicare

The Supreme Court held that 42 USCS § 405(h), as incorporated by 42 USCS § 1395ii—part of a special system of administrative and judicial review for denials of Medicare claims—barred a nursing home association from invoking federal-question jurisdiction (28 USCS § 1331) to challenge the validity of Medicare enforcement regulations. [Shalala v Illinois Council on Long Term Care, Inc. (2000, US) 146 L Ed 2d 1, 120 S Ct 1084.]

It was held that payments received by a health care provider—such as the one allegedly defrauded in the case at hand—from the Federal Government under the Medicare program were "benefits" within the meaning of a federal bribery statute (18 USCS § 666), prohibiting fraud and other offenses against organizations receiving federal benefits. [Fischer v United States (2000, US) 146 L Ed 2d 707, 120 S Ct 1780.]

§ 39 Miranda warnings

It was held that Miranda v Arizona (1966) 384 US 436, 16 L Ed 2d 694, 86 S Ct 1602, and its progeny in the Supreme Court would continue to govern the admissibility, in both state and federal courts, of statements made during custodial interrogation, as (1) the Miranda decision, being a federal constitutional ruling, could not be overruled by a subsequent statute, 18 USCS § 3501, which in essence made the admissibility of such statements turn on whether they were voluntary, and (2) the Supreme Court would decline to itself overrule Miranda. [Dickerson v United States (2000, US) 147 L Ed 2d 405, 120 S Ct 2326.]

§ 40 Prisons and prisoners

The Supreme Court held—with respect to a federal prisoner who was ordered by a Federal District Court to serve a new supervised release term following reimprisonment—that (1) at the time of the prisoner's conviction, 18 USCS § 3583(e)(3) gave the District Court the authority to reimpose supervised release; (2) 18 USCS § 3583(h), which was added in 1994 and explicitly gave the District Court such authority, did not apply retroactively; and (3) thus, no issue arose in the case at hand with respect to the Federal Constitution's Art I, § 9, cl 3 prohibition against ex post facto laws. Johnson v United States (No. 99-5153). (2000, US)146 L Ed 2d 727, 120 S Ct 1795. (see, § 19 below)

It was held that (1) under 18 USCS § 3624(e), a supervised release term was not reduced by reason of excess time served in prison, and (2) thus, a supervised release term did not commence until an individual was released from imprisonment. [United States v Johnson (2000, US) 146 L Ed 2d 39, 120 S Ct 1114.]

It was held that (1) Congress intended a Prison Litigation Reform Act of 1995 provision (18 USCS

§ 3626(e)(2))—which under certain circumstances, imposed an automatic stay of prospective relief in civil actions challenging prison conditions—to preclude courts from exercising their equitable powers to enjoin such a stay; and (2) the provision did not violate the Federal Constitution's separation-of-powers principles. [Miller v French (2000, US) 147 L Ed 2d 326, 120 S Ct 2246.]

§ 41 Racketeer Influenced and Corrupt Organizations Act (RICO)

It was held that the "injury and pattern discovery rule"—in which the statute of limitations period did not begin to run until a plaintiff discovered, or should have discovered, both the plaintiff's injury and a pattern of racketeering activity—did not govern the start of the 4-year limitations period for a civil Racketeer Influenced and Corrupt Organizations Act (RICO) claim under 18 USCS § 1964(c). [Rotella v Wood (2000, US) 145 L Ed 2d 1047, 120 S Ct 1075.]

The Supreme Court held that an injury caused by an overt act that was not an act of racketeering or otherwise wrongful under the Racketeer Influenced and Corrupt Organizations Act (RICO) (18 USCS §§ 1961 et seq.) did not give rise to a cause of action under 18 USCS § 1964(c) for a violation of 18 USCS § 1962(d). [Beck v Prupis (2000, US) 146 L Ed 2d 561, 120 S Ct 1608.]

§ 42 Retroactive application of state law

The Supreme Court held that the retroactive application of a state provision which permitted the extension of intervals between parole considerations did not necessarily violate the prohibition on ex post facto laws contained in Art I, § 10, cl 1 of the Federal Constitution. [Garner v Jones (2000, US) 146 L Ed 2d 236, 120 S Ct 1362.]

The court held that the retrospective application of a Texas statute modifying a corroboration requirement for conviction of a defendant charged with certain sexual offenses violated the ex post facto prohibition in Art I, § 10 of the Federal Constitution. [Carmell v Texas (2000, US) 146 L Ed 2d 577, 120 S Ct 1620.]

The Supreme Court held—with respect to a federal prisoner who was ordered by a Federal District Court to serve a new supervised release term following reimprisonment—that (1) at the time of the prisoner's conviction, 18 USCS § 3583(e)(3) gave the District Court the authority to reimpose supervised release; (2) 18 USCS § 3583(h), which was added in 1994 and explicitly gave the District Court such authority, did not apply retroactively; and (3) thus, no issue arose in the case at hand with respect to the Federal Constitution's Art I, § 9, cl 3 prohibition against ex post facto laws. [Johnson v United States (2000, US) 146 L Ed 2d 727, 120 S Ct 1795.]

§ 43 Right to counsel

The Supreme Court held that states are free to adopt procedures for determining whether an indigent's direct appeal is frivolous, other than the procedures set forth in Anders v California (1967) 386 US 738, 18 L Ed 2d 493, 87 S Ct 1396, so long as the adopted procedures adequately safeguard a defendant's right to appellate counsel under the Federal Constitution's Fourteenth Amendment. [Smith v Robbins (2000, US) 145 L Ed 2d 756, 120 S Ct 746.]

The court held that Strickland v Washington (1984) 466 US 668, 80 L Ed 2d 674, 104 S Ct 2052—which determined that under the Federal Constitution's Sixth Amendment, a convicted defendant alleging ineffective assistance of counsel had to show that (1) counsel's representation fell below an objective standard of rea-

sonableness, and (2) the deficient performance prejudiced the defendant—provided the proper framework
for evaluating a claim that counsel was constitutionally
ineffective for failing to file a notice of appeal. [Roe v
Flores-Ortega (2000, US) 145 L Ed 2d 985, 120 S Ct
1029.]

The Supreme Court held that (1) a Federal Court of
Appeals decision concluding that a federal habeas
corpus petitioner was not denied effective assistance of
counsel—as defined by Strickland v Washington (1984)
466 US 668, 80 L Ed 2d 674, 104 S Ct 2052—when the
petitioner's trial lawyers failed to investigate and to
present substantial mitigating evidence would be reversed, and (2) the case would be remanded for further
proceedings. [Williams v Taylor (2000, US) 146 L Ed 2d
389, 120 S Ct 1495.]

It was held that a procedurally defaulted ineffective-
assistance-of-counsel claim provided cause excusing a
procedural default of another claim in a federal habeas
corpus proceeding only if the petitioner showed cause
and prejudice with regard to the counsel claim. [Ed-
wards v Carpenter (2000, US) 146 L Ed 2d 518, 120 S Ct
1587.]

§ 44 Search and seizure

The Supreme Court held that a state trial court's
denial of an accused's motion to suppress evidence
seized in a warrantless search—on the grounds that
police were entitled to make such a search of a homicide crime scene and the objects found there—directly
conflicted with the rule of Mincey v Arizona (1977) 434
US 1343, 54 L Ed 2d 56, 98 S Ct 23, that there was no
"murder scene exception". [Flippo v West Virginia
(1999) 528 US 11, 145 L Ed 2d 16, 120 S Ct 7.]

The Supreme Court held that a law enforcement
officer's physical manipulation of a bus passenger's
carry-on luggage—which consisted of squeezing the

soft luggage which the passenger had placed in the overhead storage space—violated the proscription against unreasonable searches under the Federal Constitution's Fourth Amendment. [Bond v United States (2000, US) 146 L Ed 2d 365, 120 S Ct 1462.]

The court held that the actions of police officers in stopping an accused—who had fled upon seeing police officers patrolling an area known for heavy narcotics trafficking—did not violate the Federal Constitution's Fourth Amendment, as the police had a reasonable suspicion that the accused was involved in criminal activity. [Illinois v Wardlow (2000) 528 US 119, 145 L Ed 2d 570, 120 S Ct 673.]

It was held that under the Federal Constitution's Fourth Amendment, an anonymous tip that a person was carrying a gun was, without more, insufficient to justify a police officer's stop and frisk of that person. [Florida v J.L. (2000, US) 146 L Ed 2d 254, 120 S Ct 1375.]

§ 45 Secretary of the Interior

The Supreme Court held that certain federal grazing regulations (43 CFR §§ 4100.0-5, 4110.1(a), and 4120.3-2(b)) did not exceed the authority granted to the Secretary of the Interior by the Taylor Grazing Act (43 USCS §§ 315 et seq.). [Public Lands Council v Babbitt (2000, US) 146 L Ed 2d 753, 120 S Ct 1815.]

§ 46 Self-representation

The court held that neither the holding nor the reasoning of the court's decision in Faretta v California (1975) 422 US 806, 45 L Ed 2d 562, 95 S Ct 2525—which recognized an accused's right, under the Federal Constitution, to self-representation at trial—required a state to recognize a constitutional right to self-representation on direct appeal from a criminal conviction. [Martinez v Court of Appeal (2000) 528 US 152, 145 L Ed 2d 597, 120 S Ct 684.]

§ 47 Separation of church and state

The Supreme Court held that a school aid program, codified at 20 USCS §§ 7301 et seq., under which the Federal Government distributed funds to state and local government agencies, which in turn loaned educational materials and equipment to public and private schools—including religiously affiliated schools—was not, as applied in a particular Louisiana parish, prohibited by the Federal Constitution's First Amendment as a law respecting an establishment of religion. [Mitchell v Helms (2000, US) 147 L Ed 2d 660, 120 S Ct 2530.]

It was held that a Texas public school district's policy—which permitted a student-led and student-initiated "invocation and/or message" over a public address system before each high school varsity home football game—violated the prohibition, under the Federal Constitution's First Amendment, of an establishment of religion. [Santa Fe Indep. Sch. Dist. v Doe (2000, US) 147 L Ed 2d 295, 120 S Ct 2266.]

§ 48 Separation of powers

The court held that the enactment of the Drivers' Privacy Protection Act of 1994 (18 USCS §§ 2721-2725)—which regulates the disclosure of personal information contained in the records of state motor vehicle departments—by Congress (1) was a proper exercise of Congress' authority to regulate interstate commerce under the Federal Constitution's commerce clause (Art I, § 8, cl 3), and (2) did not run afoul of the federalism principles contained in the Federal Constitution. [Reno v Condon (2000) 528 US 141, 145 L Ed 2d 587, 120 S Ct 666.]

§ 49 Social Security

It was held that a Social Security benefits claimant—who had (1) exhausted the claimant's administrative remedies, and (2) obtained judicial review pursuant to 42 USCS § 405(g)—had not waived any issues that the claimant did not include in the claimant's request for review by the Social Security Appeals Council. [Sims v Apfel (2000, US) 147 L Ed 2d 80, 120 S Ct 2080.]

§ 50 Standing to sue

The Supreme Court held that (1) a private individual had standing, under Article III of the Federal Constitution, to bring an action on behalf of the United States under the False Claims Act (FCA) (31 USCS §§ 3729-3733), but (2) the FCA did not subject a state or a state agency to liability in a federal court suit by a private individual on behalf of the United States. [Vermont Agency of Natural Resources v United States ex rel. Stevens (2000, US) 146 L Ed 2d 836, 120 S Ct 1858.]

§ 51 State income tax

The Supreme Court held that California's interest-deduction-offset provision—which authorized a deduction for interest expense of the "unitary" income of a nondomiciliary corporation that carried out a particular business both inside and outside the state, but generally permitted use of the deduction only to the extent that the amount exceeded certain out-of-state income arising from the unrelated business activity of a discrete business enterprise—constituted impermissible taxation of income outside the state's jurisdictional reach, in violation of the due process clause of the Federal Constitution's Fourteenth Amendment and the Constitution's commerce clause (Art I, § 8, cl 3).

[Hunt-Wesson, Inc. v Franchise Tax Bd. (2000, US) 145 L Ed 2d 974, 120 S Ct 1022.]

§ 52 Voting rights

It was held that § 5 of the Voting Rights Act of 1965 (42 USCS § 1973c), as amended—which authorizes federal preclearance of a proposed voting change, by a covered state or its political subdivision, that does not have the purpose and will not have the effect of denying or abridging the right to vote on account of race or color—does not prohibit preclearance of a redistricting plan enacted with a discriminatory but nonretrogressive purpose. [Reno v Bossier Parish Sch. Bd. (2000, US) 145 L Ed 2d 845, 120 S Ct 866.]

It was held that the Federal Constitution's Fifteenth Amendment invalidated a Hawaii electoral qualification that permitted only "Hawaiians"—descendants of persons inhabiting Hawaii in 1778—to vote for trustees of a state agency that administered programs designed for the benefit of "native Hawaiians" and "Hawaiians". [Rice v Cayetano (2000, US) 145 L Ed 2d 1007, 120 S Ct 1044.]

SUMMARIES OF DECISIONS

DONALD H. BRANCATO, Petitioner

v

PRISCILLA F. GUNN et al.

528 US 1, 145 L Ed 2d 1, 120 S Ct 5

[No. 98-9913]

Decided October 12, 1999.

Decision: Person who filed eight frivolous certiorari petitions in Supreme Court denied leave to proceed in forma pauperis as to petition for certiorari; order entered barring person's future in forma pauperis filings of petitions for certiorari in non-criminal matters.

SUMMARY

An individual sought leave to proceed in forma pauperis in the United States Supreme Court under Supreme Court Rule 39 with respect to a petition for certiorari. The individual had filed, in the Supreme Court, seven previous petitions for certiorari, including a petition with respect to which the court, in the prior Term, had denied the person leave to proceed in forma pauperis by invoking Supreme Court Rule 39.8, which authorizes the court to deny such leave with respect to frivolous petitions. All of the previous petitions had been deemed frivolous by the court and had been denied without recorded dissent.

1

In a per curiam opinion expressing the view of REHNQUIST, Ch. J., and O'CONNOR, SCALIA, KENNEDY, SOUTER, THOMAS, GINSBURG, and BREYER, JJ., the Supreme Court (1) indicating that the instant petition was frivolous, invoked Rule 39.8 to deny the individual's request for leave to proceed in forma pauperis on the instant petition, and (2) directed the Clerk of the Supreme Court not to accept any further petitions for certiorari in noncriminal matters from the individual unless he complied with Supreme Court Rules 33.1 and 38.

STEVENS, J., dissented for reasons expressed in a previous Supreme Court case involving some similar issues.

———

MICHAEL C. ANTONELLI, Petitioner

v

DALE CARIDINE et al. (No. 98-9933)

———

MICHAEL C. ANTONELLI, Petitioner

v

UNITED STATES (No. 99-5445)

528 US 3, 145 L Ed 2d 4, 120 S Ct 4

[Nos. 98-9933 and 99-5445]

Decided October 12, 1999.

Decision: Person who filed 57 frivolous petitions in Supreme Court denied leave to proceed in forma pauperis as to 2 petitions for certiorari; order entered barring person's future in forma pauperis filings of petitions for certiorari or extraordinary writs in noncriminal matters.

SUMMARY

An individual sought leave to proceed in forma pauperis in the United States Supreme Court under Supreme Court Rule 39 with respect to two petitions for certiorari. The individual had filed, in the Supreme Court, 55 previous petitions for either certiorari or extraordinary writs, including 2 petitions with respect to which the court, in a previous Term, had denied the person leave to proceed in forma pauperis by invoking Supreme Court Rule 39.8, which authorizes the court to deny such leave with respect to frivolous petitions.

All of the previous petitions had been deemed frivolous by the court and had been denied without recorded dissent.

In a per curiam opinion expressing the view of REHNQUIST, Ch. J., and O'CONNOR, SCALIA, KENNEDY, SOUTER, THOMAS, GINSBURG, and BREYER, JJ., the Supreme Court (1) indicating that the instant petitions were frivolous, invoked Rule 39.8 to deny the individual's request for leave to proceed in forma pauperis on the instant petitions, and (2) directed the Clerk of the Supreme Court not to accept any further petitions for certiorari or for extraordinary writs in noncriminal matters from the individual unless he complied with Supreme Court Rules 33.1 and 38.

STEVENS, J., dissented for reasons expressed in a previous Supreme Court case involving some similar issues.

_____

KEITH RUSSELL JUDD, Petitioner

v

UNITED STATES DISTRICT COURT FOR THE
WESTERN DISTRICT OF TEXAS et al.

528 US 5, 145 L Ed 2d 7, 120 S Ct 1

[No. 99-5260]

Decided October 12, 1999.

Decision: Person who filed 12 frivolous petitions in
Supreme Court denied leave to proceed in forma
pauperis as to petition for certiorari; order entered
barring person's future in forma pauperis filings of
petitions for certiorari or extraordinary writs in
noncriminal matters.

SUMMARY

An individual sought leave to proceed in forma
pauperis in the United States Supreme Court under
Supreme Court Rule 39 with respect to a petition for
certiorari. The individual had filed, in the Supreme
Court, 11 previous petitions for either certiorari or
extraordinary writs, including a petition for an extraordinary writ, with respect to which the court, in a
previous Term, had denied the person leave to proceed
in forma pauperis by invoking Supreme Court Rule
39.8, which authorizes the court to deny such leave with
respect to frivolous petitions. All of the previous petitions had been deemed frivolous by the court and had
been denied without recorded dissent.

In a per curiam opinion expressing the view of
REHNQUIST, Ch. J., and O'CONNOR, SCALIA, KENNEDY,
SOUTER, THOMAS, GINSBURG, and BREYER, JJ., the Su-

preme Court (1) indicating that the instant petition was frivolous, invoked Rule 39.8 to deny the individual's request for leave to proceed in forma pauperis on the instant petition, and (2) directed the Clerk of the Supreme Court not to accept any further petitions for certiorari or for extraordinary writs in noncriminal matters from the individual unless he complied with Supreme Court Rules 33.1 and 38.

STEVENS, J., dissented for reasons expressed in a previous Supreme Court case involving some similar issues.

JOHN B DEMPSEY, Petitioner

v

RALPH MARTIN, District Attorney for Suffolk
County

528 US 7, 145 L Ed 2d 10, 120 S Ct 2

[No. 99-5283]

Decided October 12, 1999.

Decision: Person who filed 19 frivolous certiorari petitions in Supreme Court denied leave to proceed in
forma pauperis as to petition for certiorari; order
entered barring person's future in forma pauperis
filings of petitions for certiorari or extraordinary
writs in noncriminal matters.

SUMMARY

An individual sought leave to proceed in forma
pauperis in the United States Supreme Court under
Supreme Court Rule 39 with respect to a petition for
certiorari. The individual had filed, in the Supreme
Court, 18 previous petitions for either certiorari or
extraordinary writs, including a petition for certiorari,
with respect to which the court, in a previous Term, had
denied the person leave to proceed in forma pauperis
by invoking Supreme Court Rule 39.8, which authorizes
the court to deny such leave with respect to frivolous
petitions. All of the previous petitions had been
deemed frivolous by the court and had been denied
without recorded dissent.

In a per curiam opinion expressing the view of
REHNQUIST, Ch. J., and O'CONNOR, SCALIA, KENNEDY,
SOUTER, THOMAS, GINSBURG, and BREYER, JJ., the Su-

preme Court (1) indicating that the instant petition was frivolous, invoked Rule 39.8 to deny the individual's request for leave to proceed in forma pauperis on the instant petition, and (2) directed the Clerk of the Supreme Court not to accept any further petitions for certiorari or for extraordinary writs in noncriminal matters from the individual unless he complied with Supreme Court Rules 33.1 and 38.

STEVENS, J., dissented for reasons expressed in a previous Supreme Court case involving some similar issues.

ROBERT E. PRUNTY, Petitioner

v

W. BROOKS et al.

528 US 9, 145 L Ed 2d 13, 120 S Ct 3

[No. 99-5316]

Decided October 12, 1999.

Decision: Person who filed 10 frivolous certiorari petitions in Supreme Court denied leave to proceed in forma pauperis as to petition for certiorari; order entered barring person's future in forma pauperis filings of petitions for certiorari in noncriminal matters.

SUMMARY

An individual sought leave to proceed in forma pauperis in the United States Supreme Court under Supreme Court Rule 39 with respect to a petition for certiorari. The individual had filed, in the Supreme Court, nine previous petitions for certiorari, including a petition with respect to which the court, in the prior Term, had denied the person leave to proceed in forma pauperis by invoking Supreme Court Rule 39.8, which authorizes the court to deny such leave with respect to frivolous petitions. All of the previous petitions had been deemed frivolous by the court and had been denied without recorded dissent.

In a per curiam opinion expressing the view of REHNQUIST, Ch. J., and O'CONNOR, SCALIA, KENNEDY, SOUTER, THOMAS, GINSBURG, and BREYER, JJ., the Supreme Court (1) indicating that the instant petition was frivolous, invoked Rule 39.8 to deny the individual's request for leave to proceed in forma pauperis on the instant petition, and (2) directed the Clerk of the Supreme Court not to accept any further petitions for certiorari in noncriminal matters from the individual unless he complied with Supreme Court Rules 33.1 and 38.

STEVENS, J., dissented for reasons expressed in a previous Supreme Court case involving some similar issues.

_____

JAMES MICHAEL FLIPPO, Petitioner

v

WEST VIRGINIA

528 US 11, 145 L Ed 2d 16, 120 S Ct 7

[No. 98-8770]

Decided October 18, 1999. §§ * Petitioner sought a writ directed to the West Virginia Supreme Court of Appeals. That court, however, merely declined to exercise discretionary review. The last State court to rule on the merits of this case was the Circuit Court of West Virginia, Fayette County, to which the writ is therefore addressed. .

Decision: Police held not entitled to make warrantless search of anything and everything found within homicide crime scene area, where no exceptions to warrant requirement of Federal Constitution's Fourth Amendment are invoked.

SUMMARY

In response to a 911 telephone call, police officers arrived at a cabin in a West Virginia state park and found the body of a woman with fatal head wounds. The officers closed off the area and searched the exterior and environs of the cabin. For over 16 hours inside the cabin, the officers took photographs, collected evidence, and searched through the contents of the cabin. In the course of the search, the officers found and opened a closed briefcase, in which were discovered various photographs and negatives that allegedly incriminated the woman's husband. The husband, having been indicted for murder, moved in the

11

Circuit Court of West Virginia, Fayette County, to suppress the photographs and negatives on the grounds that (1) the police had obtained no warrant, and (2) no exception to the warrant requirement of the Federal Constitution's Fourth Amendment had justified the search and seizure. The Circuit Court denied the motion to suppress on the ground that the officers, having secured the homicide crime scene for investigative purposes, had been within the law to conduct a thorough investigation and examination of anything and everything found within the crime scene area. On appeal of this ruling, the Supreme Court of Appeals of West Virginia denied discretionary review.

The United States Supreme Court (1) granted the husband's motion for leave to proceed in forma pauperis and petition for certiorari, (2) reversed the Circuit Court's judgment, and (3) remanded the case for further proceedings. In a per curiam opinion expressing the unanimous view of the court, it was held that (1) after a homicide crime scene is secured for police investigation, the police are not entitled to make a warrantless search of anything and everything found within the crime scene area, where none of the exceptions to the Fourth Amendment's warrant requirement are invoked; and (2) in the case at hand, such matters as the applicability of any exception to the warrant requirement or the alleged harmlessness of any error in receiving the evidence in question could properly be resolved on remand, if such matters were to be properly raised.

————

IN RE FREDERICK W. BAUER, Petitioner

528 US 16, 145 L Ed 2d 21, 120 S Ct 6

[No. 99-5440]

Decided October 18, 1999.

Decision: Person who filed 12 frivolous petitions in Supreme Court denied leave to proceed in forma pauperis as to petition for mandamus; order entered barring person's future in forma pauperis filings of petitions for certiorari or extraordinary writs in noncriminal matters.

SUMMARY

An individual sought leave to proceed in forma pauperis in the United States Supreme Court under Supreme Court Rule 39 with respect to a petition for mandamus. The individual had filed, in the Supreme Court, 11 previous petitions for either certiorari or extraordinary writs, including a petition for an extraordinary writ, with respect to which the court, in a previous Term, had denied the person leave to proceed in forma pauperis by invoking Supreme Court Rule 39.8, which authorizes the court to deny such leave with respect to frivolous petitions. All of the previous petitions had been deemed frivolous by the court and had been denied without recorded dissent.

In a per curiam opinion expressing the view of REHNQUIST, Ch. J., and O'CONNOR, SCALIA, KENNEDY, SOUTER, THOMAS, GINSBURG, and BREYER, JJ., the Supreme Court (1) indicating that the instant petition was frivolous, invoked Rule 39.8 to deny the individual's request for leave to proceed in forma pauperis on the

13

instant petition, and (2) directed the Clerk of the Supreme Court not to accept any further petitions for certiorari or for extraordinary writs in noncriminal matters from the individual unless he complied with Supreme Court Rules 33.1 and 38.

STEVENS, J., dissented for reasons expressed in a previous Supreme Court case involving some similar issues.

_____

TEXAS et al., Petitioners

v

FRANÇOIS DANIEL LESAGE and UNITED STATES

528 US 18, 145 L Ed 2d 347, 120 S Ct 467

[No. 98-1111]

Decided November 29, 1999.

Decision: Federal Court of Appeals held to have erred—with respect to rejected applicant's damages claim against university that allegedly had race-conscious admissions process—in holding that university was not entitled to summary judgment even if applicant would have been rejected under race-neutral policy.

SUMMARY

An African immigrant of Caucasian descent applied for admission to a Ph. D. program at the University of Texas. The university, which undisputedly considered the race of the applicants at some stage during the review process, rejected this applicant and offered admission to at least one member of a minority group. The rejected applicant filed suit for monetary, declaratory, and injunctive relief in the United States District Court for the Western District of Texas against the state of Texas, the university and several of its subdivisions, and various university officials in their official capacities. The suit alleged that the university had established and was maintaining a race-conscious admissions process in violation of the equal protection clause of the Federal Constitution's Fourteenth Amendment and various federal civil rights statutes (42 USCS §§ 1981,

15

1983, and 2000d). The defendants, in seeking summary judgment, offered evidence that even if the university's admissions process had been completely colorblind, the applicant would not have been admitted. The District Court, concluding that considerations of race had no effect on the applicant's rejection, granted summary judgment for the defendants with respect to all of the applicant's claims. The United States Court of Appeals for the Fifth Circuit, in reversing and remanding, reasoned that (1) the District Court's determination that there was no genuine issue as to whether the applicant would have been rejected under a colorblind admissions process was irrelevant to the pertinent issue on the motion for summary judgment; (2) the pertinent issue was whether the state had violated the applicant's constitutional rights by rejecting his application in the course of operating a racially discriminatory admissions program and thus indirectly injuring the applicant by rendering him unable to compete on an equal footing; and (3) because there remained a factual dispute as to whether the stage of review during which the applicant was eliminated was in some way race conscious, summary judgment for the defendants was inappropriate (158 F3d 213).

The United States Supreme Court (1) granted the defendants' petition for certiorari, (2) reversed the Court of Appeals' judgment, and (3) remanded the case for further proceedings. In a per curiam opinion expressing the unanimous view of the court, it was held that (1) insofar as the Court of Appeals had held that summary judgment for the defendants on the § 1983 damages claim was inappropriate even if it was conclusively established that the applicant would have been rejected under a race-neutral policy, that decision was inconsistent with the Supreme Court's framework for analyzing such claims; and (2) the questions whether the applicant's claims under §§ 1981 and 2000d remained and whether the applicant had abandoned his claim for injunctive relief on the ground that the defendants were continuing to operate a discriminatory admissions process were matters open on remand.

WILLIAM FIORE, Petitioner

v

GREGORY WHITE, Warden, et al.

528 US 23, 145 L Ed 2d 353, 120 S Ct 469

[No. 98-942]

Argued October 12, 1999.
Decided November 30, 1999.

Decision: Question as to interpretation of Pennsylvania hazardous-waste-facility statute certified to Pennsylvania Supreme Court to help determine proper state-law predicate for determination of federal constitutional questions raised in case.

SUMMARY

Pennsylvania authorities alleged that (1) the owner of a hazardous waste disposal facility in Pennsylvania, together with the facility's general manager, had deliberately altered a monitoring pipe to hide a leakage problem; and (2) such conduct had gone so far beyond the terms of the facility's operating permit that the operation effectively had taken place without a permit at all, in violation of a Pennsylvania statute. In the Court of Common Pleas of Allegheny County, Pennsylvania, the owner and the general manager were convicted of operating the facility without a permit. The owner appealed his conviction to the Superior Court of Pennsylvania, which affirmed the conviction (391 Pa Super 634, 563 A2d 189). In 1990, the Supreme Court of Pennsylvania denied the owner leave to appeal (525 Pa 577, 575 A2d 109); shortly thereafter, his conviction became final. However, the general manager appealed
18

his own conviction to the Commonwealth Court of Pennsylvania, which—noting the existence of a "valid permit" and setting aside the general manager's conviction in pertinent part—reversed the Court of Common Pleas' judgment in pertinent part and ordered a remand (141 Pa Cmwlth 560, 596 A2d 892). On appeal in 1993, the Pennsylvania Supreme Court—authoritatively interpreting the relevant statute for the first time and agreeing that the general manager's conduct did not constitute the operation of the facility without a permit—affirmed the Commonwealth Court's judgment (535 Pa 273, 634 A2d 1109). The owner, having been denied review by the Pennsylvania Supreme Court, was refused collateral relief by the Court of Common Pleas, and this refusal was affirmed by the Superior Court (445 Pa Super 401, 665 A2d 1185). The owner then sought federal habeas corpus relief in the United States District Court for the Western District of Pennsylvania on the ground that he had been imprisoned for conduct which was not criminal under the statutory section charged. The District Court granted a writ of habeas corpus, but the United States Court of Appeals for the Third Circuit reversed, on the ground that state courts were under no federal constitutional obligation to apply their own decisions retroactively (149 F3d 221). The United States Supreme Court granted the owner's petition for certiorari to consider whether the due process clause of the Federal Constitution's Fourteenth Amendment required the owner's conviction to be set aside (526 US ——, 143 L Ed 2d 497, 119 S Ct 1332).

On certiorari, the United States Supreme Court (1) certified to the Pennsylvania Supreme Court the question whether the latter court's 1993 interpretation of the statute stated the correct interpretation of Pennsylvania law at the date when the owner's conviction became final, and (2) reserved judgment and further proceedings in the case at hand pending receipt of a response from the Pennsylvania Supreme Court. In an opinion by BREYER, J., expressing the unanimous view of the court, it was held that certification was necessary because the answer to the certified question would help the United States Supreme Court determine the proper state-law predicate for a determination of the federal constitutional questions raised in the case at hand.

COUNSEL

James B. Lieber argued the cause for petitioner.
Robert A. Graci argued the cause for respondents.

———————

LOS ANGELES POLICE DEPARTMENT, Petitioner

v

UNITED REPORTING PUBLISHING CORPORA-
TION

528 US 32, 145 L Ed 2d 451, 120 S Ct 483

[No. 98-678]

Argued October 13, 1999.
Decided December 7, 1999.

Decision: Publisher held not entitled to prevail on
claim that California statute—under which arrestee's address disclosed by government agency could
not be used to sell product or service—was facially
overbroad under First Amendment.

SUMMARY

A former version of a California public records
statute generally required a state or local law enforcement agency to make public the name, address, and
occupation of every individual arrested by the agency.
In 1996, the statute was amended to require that a
person requesting an arrestee's address declare, under
penalty of perjury, that (1) the request was being made
for journalistic, scholarly, political, governmental, or
investigative purposes, and (2) the address would not
be used directly or indirectly to sell a product or
service. A private publishing service had obtained
names and addresses of recently arrested individuals
from law enforcement agencies under the statute's
former version and had provided such information to
customers such as attorneys, insurance companies,
drug and alcohol counselors, and driving schools.

21

However, on the effective date of the statutory amendment, various law enforcement agencies denied the publishing service access to the address information, allegedly because the service's employees did not sign declarations pursuant to the amended statute. The publishing service, which had previously filed suit in the United States District Court for the Southern District of California against various state officials and local agencies for declaratory and injunctive relief pursuant to 42 USCS § 1983—on the theory that the amended statute violated the Federal Constitution's First and Fourteenth Amendments—amended the complaint and sought a temporary restraining order. The District Court issued such an order and subsequently issued a preliminary injunction. Ultimately, the District Court—stating that the case at hand presented a facial challenge to the amended statute—granted the service's motion for summary judgment, on the ground that the amended statute was an impermissible restriction on commercial speech and thus violated the First Amendment (946 F Supp 822). The United States Court of Appeals for the Ninth Circuit, in affirming, expressed the view that (1) the amended statute restricted commercial speech, which was entitled to a limited measure of First Amendment protection; and (2) although an asserted governmental interest in protecting arrestees' privacy was substantial, the amended statute's numerous exceptions precluded the statute from directly and materially advancing such an interest (146 F3d 1133).

On certiorari, the United States Supreme Court reversed. In an opinion by REHNQUIST, Ch. J., joined by O'CONNOR, SCALIA, SOUTER, THOMAS, GINSBURG, and BREYER, JJ., it was held that the publishing service was not entitled to prevail on a claim that the amended statute was invalid as facially overbroad under the First

Amendment, for (1) at least for purposes of assessing the propriety of a facial invalidation, the amended statute was not an abridgment of anyone's right to engage in speech, commercial or otherwise, but simply a law regulating access to information in the hands of law enforcement agencies; (2) the case was not one in which the government was prohibiting a speaker from conveying information that the speaker already possessed; (3) to the extent that the facial challenge sought to rely on the effect of the amended statute on parties not before the Supreme Court—for example, the publishing service's potential customers—the claim did not fit within the case law allowing courts to entertain facial challenges; and (4) resort to a facial challenge was thus not warranted, as there was no possibility that protected speech would be muted.

SCALIA, J., joined by THOMAS, J., concurring, expressed the view that (1) insofar as the case presented a facial challenge to the amended statute, the fact that the amended statute was formally nothing but a restriction upon access to government information was determinative; (2) the Supreme Court's opinion was to be understood as (a) not addressing a challenge to the amended statute as applied, and (b) leaving that question open upon remand; and (3) such a course was permissible under the circumstances.

GINSBURG, J., joined by O'CONNOR, SOUTER, and BREYER, JJ., concurring, expressed the view that (1) the amended statute was properly analyzed as a restriction on access to government information, not as a restriction on protected speech, and (2) that consideration was sufficient reason to reverse the Court of Appeals' judgment.

STEVENS, J., joined by KENNEDY, J., dissenting, expressed the view that (1) the publishing service had

23

advanced both a facial and an "as applied" challenge to the amended statute's constitutionality; (2) the service's allegations of direct injury justified the decision of the District Court and the Court of Appeals to pass on the validity of the amended statute; and (3) the amended statute was invalid as applied to the service, because (a) California was making information available to some while denying access to a narrow category of persons solely because such persons intended to use the information for a constitutionally protected purpose, and (b) such discrimination was not justified by a state interest in protecting arrestees' privacy or preventing lawyers from soliciting business.

COUNSEL

Thomas C. Goldstein argued the cause for petitioner.

Edward C. DuMont argued the cause for the United States, as amicus curiae, by special leave of court.

Bruce J. Ennis argued the cause for respondent.

ROHN F. DRYE, Jr., et al., Petitioners

v

UNITED STATES

528 US 49, 145 L Ed 2d 466, 120 S Ct 474

[No. 98-1101]

Argued November 8, 1999.
Decided December 7, 1999.

Decision: Taxpayer's interest as heir to estate held to
constitute "property" or "righ[t] to property" to
which federal tax liens attached under 26 USCS
§ 6321, despite taxpayer's exercise of prerogative
Arkansas law accorded to disclaim interest retroactively.

SUMMARY

A taxpayer inherited an approximately $233,000 es-
tate in Arkansas from his mother, who died intestate.
Under Arkansas law, the taxpayer was the sole heir to
the estate. At the time of the mother's death, (1) the
taxpayer was insolvent, (2) the taxpayer owed the
Federal Government approximately $325,000 on un-
paid tax assessments, and (3) the Internal Revenue
Service (IRS) had valid tax liens against all of the
taxpayer's "property and rights to property" pursuant
to 26 USCS § 6321. After petitioning for the position,
the taxpayer was appointed as administrator of the
decedent's estate by the Pulaski County Probate Court
in August 1994. The taxpayer resigned as administrator
in February 1995, after filing in the Probate Court and
county land records a written disclaimer of all interests
in the estate. Under Arkansas law, (1) such a disclaimer

created the legal fiction that the disclaimant prede-
ceased the decedent, (2) the disclaimant's share of the
estate passed to the person next in line to receive that
share, and (3) the disavowing heir's creditors could not
reach property thus disclaimed. The Probate Court
declared valid the taxpayer's disclaimer in March 1995.
The estate then passed to the taxpayer's daughter, who
succeeded the taxpayer as administrator and established a trust with the funds from the estate, of which
trust she and, during their lifetimes, her parents were
the beneficiaries. The trust was spendthrift, and under
state law, its assets were shielded from creditors seeking
to satisfy the debts of the trust's beneficiaries. When the
taxpayer revealed to the IRS his beneficial interest in
the trust, the IRS in April 1996 (1) filed a notice of
federal tax lien against the trust as the taxpayer's
nominee, (2) served a notice of levy on accounts held
in the trust's name by an investment bank, and (3)
notified the trust of the levy. The trust then filed a
wrongful levy action against the United States in the
United States District Court for the Eastern District of
Arkansas. The Federal Government counterclaimed
against the trust, the trustee, and the trust beneficiaries, seeking to (1) reduce to judgment the tax assessments against the taxpayer, (2) confirm the government's rights to seize the trust's assets in collection of
those debts, (3) foreclose on the tax liens, and (4) sell
the trust property. On cross-motions for summary
judgment, the District Court ruled in the government's
favor (1997 US Dist LEXIS 6755). The United States
Court of Appeals for the Eighth Circuit affirmed,
reading the United States Supreme Court's precedents
to convey that state law determines whether a given set
of circumstances creates a right or interest, but federal
law dictates whether that right or interest constitutes

26

"property" or the "righ[t] to property" under § 6321
(152 F3d 892, 1998 US App LEXIS 20084).

On certiorari, the Supreme Court affirmed. In an
opinion by GINSBURG, J., expressing the unanimous
view of the court, it was held that, in the case at hand,
the taxpayer's interest as heir to the estate constituted
"property" or a "righ[t] to property" to which the
federal tax liens attached under § 6321, despite the
taxpayer's exercise of the prerogative state law accorded him to disclaim the interest retroactively, as,
among other matters, (1) the Internal Revenue Code's
prescriptions are most sensibly read to look to state law
for delineation of a taxpayer's rights or interests, but to
leave to federal law the determination whether those
rights or interests constitute "property" or "rights to
property" within the meaning of § 6321; (2) once it has
been determined that state law creates sufficient interests in a taxpayer to satisfy the requirements of the
federal tax lien provision, state law is inoperative to
prevent the attachment of liens created by federal
statutes in favor of the United States; and (3) Congress'
broad use of the term "property" in § 6321 and 26
USCS § 6331(a) revealed that the legislature aimed to
reach every species of right or interest protected by law
and having an exchangeable value.

COUNSEL

Daniel M. Traylor argued the cause for petitioners.
Kent L. Jones argued the cause for respondent.

J. DANIEL KIMEL, Jr., et al., Petitioners

v

FLORIDA BOARD OF REGENTS et al. (No. 98-791)

UNITED STATES, Petitioners

v

FLORIDA BOARD of REGENTS et al. (No. 98-796)

528 US 62—, 145 L Ed 2d 522, 120 S Ct 631

[Nos. 98-791 and 98-796]

Argued October 13, 1999.
Decided January 11, 2000.

Decision: Age Discrimination in Employment Act held to contain clear statement of Congress' intent to abrogate states' Eleventh Amendment immunity from suit in federal court by private individuals, but purported abrogation held to exceed Congress' authority under § 5 of Fourteenth Amendment.

SUMMARY

Section 5 of the Federal Constitution's Fourteenth Amendment grants Congress the power to enforce, by appropriate legislation, the Fourteenth Amendment's provisions, which include the equal protection clause. The Age Discrimination in Employment Act of 1967, as amended (ADEA) (29 USCS §§ 621 et seq.), which prohibits employment discrimination on the basis of age against individuals age 40 and over, provides in 29 USCS § 626(b) that the ADEA shall be enforced in accordance with the powers, remedies, and procedures provided in certain Fair Labor Standards Act (FLSA) provisions that include (1) 29 USCS § 216(b), which authorizes employees to maintain suits against a public agency in any federal or state court of competent jurisdiction, and (2) 29 USCS § 203(x), which defines "public agency" to include the government of a state or its political subdivision and any agency of a state or its political subdivision. Three suits—one by two associate professors at an Alabama state university, one by a group of current and former faculty and librarians of two Florida state universities, and one by an employee of the Florida department of corrections—were filed under the ADEA, which suits sought, among other remedies, money damages from state employers for alleged age discrimination. The United States District Court for the Northern District of Alabama dismissed the Alabama suit on the basis that—although the ADEA contained a clear statement of Congress' intent to abrogate the states' immunity, under the Constitution's Eleventh Amendment, from suit in federal court by private individuals—Congress did not enact or extend the ADEA under Congress' Fourteenth Amendment enforcement power. In the two Florida suits, the United States District Court for the Northern District of Florida, expressing the view that the ADEA had properly abrogated the states' Eleventh Amendment immunity under § 5, denied the state employers' motions to dismiss on the basis of the Eleventh Amendment. On appeal, the United States intervened in all three cases to defend the ADEA's abrogation of the states' Eleventh Amendment immunity, and the United States Court of Appeals for the Eleventh Circuit consolidated the three cases. The Court of Appeals, in affirming the judgment of the Alabama District Court and in reversing the judgments of the Florida District Court, expressed the view that the ADEA did not abrogate the states' Eleventh Amendment immunity (139 F3d 1426).

On certiorari, the United States Supreme Court affirmed. In an opinion by O'CONNOR, J., joined by REHNQUIST, Ch. J., and STEVENS, SCALIA, SOUTER, GINSBURG, and BREYER, JJ., as to holding 1 below, and by REHNQUIST, Ch. J., and SCALIA, KENNEDY, and THOMAS, JJ., as to holding 2 below, it was held that (1) the ADEA contained a clear statement of Congress' intent to abrogate the states' Eleventh Amendment immunity, where read as a whole, the plain language of §§ 203(x), 216(b), and 626(b) clearly demonstrated Congress' intent to subject the states to suit for money damages at the hands of individual employees; but (2) that purported abrogation exceeded Congress' enforcement authority under § 5, because the ADEA was not appropriate legislation under § 5, as the substantive requirements that the ADEA imposed on state and local governments could not be understood as responsive to, or designed to, prevent unconstitutional behavior.

STEVENS, J., joined by SOUTER, GINSBURG, and BREYER, JJ., concurring in part and dissenting in part, (1) agreed that Congress had clearly expressed its intention to subject states to suits by private parties under the ADEA, but (2) expressed the view that (a) Congress' power to authorize federal remedies against state agencies that violate federal statutory obligations is coextensive with Congress' power to impose those obligations on the states, and (b) neither the Eleventh Amendment nor the doctrine of sovereign immunity places any limit on that power.

THOMAS, J., joined by KENNEDY, J., concurring in part and dissenting in part, (1) agreed that the purported abrogation of the states' Eleventh Amendment immunity in the ADEA fell outside Congress' enforcement power under § 5, but (2) expressed the view that

Congress had not made its intention to abrogate unmistakably clear in the text of the ADEA, as (a) § 626(b) did not clearly incorporate the part of § 216(b) that established a private right of action against employers, and (b) even if it was assumed that § 626(b) incorporated § 216(b) in its entirety, § 216(b) itself fell short of an unmistakably clear expression of Congress' intent to abrogate the states' Eleventh Amendment immunity.

COUNSEL

Jeremiah A. Collins argued the cause for petitioners in No. 98-791.

Barbara D. Underwood argued the cause for petitioners in No. 98-796.

Jeffrey S. Sutton argued the cause for respondents.

NEW YORK, Petitioner

v

MICHAEL HILL

528 US 110, 145 L Ed 2d 560, 120 S Ct 659

[No. 98-1299]

Argued November 2, 1999.
Decided January 11, 2000.

Decision: Criminal defense counsel's agreement to trial
date outside time period set by Article III(a) of
Interstate Agreement on Detainers (18 USCS
Appx) held to bar defendant from seeking dismissal on ground that trial did not occur within
that period.

SUMMARY

New York lodged a detainer, under the Interstate
Agreement on Detainers (IAD) (18 USCS Appx),
against an individual who was an Ohio prisoner. The
individual (1) signed a request for disposition of the
detainer pursuant to Article III of the IAD, and (2) was
returned to New York to face murder and robbery
charges. Article III(a) of the IAD provides that upon
such a request, a prisoner must be brought to trial
within 180 days, "provided that for good cause shown
. . . , the prisoner or his counsel being present, the
court . . . may grant any necessary or reasonable
continuance." The individual's defense counsel filed
several motions, which, it was uncontested, tolled the
time limits during their pendency. On January 9, 1995,
the prosecutor and defense counsel appeared in court
to set a trial date. After an agreement was made

between the two attorneys, the court scheduled trial to begin on May 1, 1995. On April 17, 1995, the individual moved to dismiss the indictment and argued that the IAD's time limit had expired. The trial court found that as of January 9, when the trial date was set, 167 nonexcludable days had elapsed, so that if the subsequent time period were chargeable to the state, the 180-day time period had expired. However, the trial court concluded that defense counsel's explicit agreement to the trial date set beyond the 180-day period constituted a waiver or abandonment of the individual's IAD rights. Accordingly, the court denied the individual's motion to dismiss (164 Misc 2d 1032, 627 NYS2d 234, 1995 NY Misc LEXIS 221). Following a jury trial, the individual was convicted of murder in the second degree and robbery in the first degree. On appeal, the individual argued that the trial court erred in declining to dismiss the indictment for lack of a timely trial under the IAD. The New York Supreme Court, Appellate Division, affirmed the decision of the trial court (244 AD2d 927, 668 NYS2d 126, 1997 NY App Div LEXIS 12288). The New York Court of Appeals, however, reversed and ordered that the indictment against the individual be dismissed, as the Court of Appeals expressed the view that defense counsel's agreement to a later trial date did not waive the individual's speedy trial rights under the IAD (92 NY2d 406, 681 NYS2d 775, 704 NE2d 542, 1998 NY LEXIS 4028).

On certiorari, the United States Supreme Court reversed. In an opinion by SCALIA J., expressing the unanimous view of the court, it was held that in the case at hand, the defense counsel's agreement to a trial date outside the time period set by Article III(a) of the IAD barred the defendant from seeking a dismissal on the ground that the trial did not occur within that period, as among other matters, (1) in the context of a broad array of constitutional and statutory provisions, a general rule presumes the availability of waiver; and (2) while a defendant must personally make an informed waiver for certain fundamental rights, the text of Article III(a) contemplated that scheduling questions could properly be left to counsel.

COUNSEL

Robert Mastrocola argued the cause for petitioner.

Lisa S. Blatt argued the cause for the United States, as amicus curiae, by special leave of court.

Brian Shiffrin argued the cause for respondent.

ILLINOIS, Petitioner

v

WILLIAM WARDLOW, aka SAM WARDLOW

528 US 119, 145 L Ed 2d 570, 120 S Ct 673

[No. 98-1036]

Argued November 2, 1999.
Decided January 12, 2000.

Decision: Police officer held not to have violated Federal Constitution's Fourth Amendment when officer stopped individual after individual fled upon seeing police caravan patrolling area known for heavy narcotics trafficking.

SUMMARY

An accused, who was holding an opaque bag, fled upon seeing a caravan of four police cars converge on an area known for heavy narcotics trafficking. When the two uniformed officers who were in the last car cornered the accused on the street, one of the officers exited the car, stopped the accused, and immediately conducted a pat-down search for weapons because, in the officer's experience, it was common for there to be weapons in the near vicinity of narcotics transactions. During the frisk, the officer discovered in the bag a handgun and live ammunition, whereupon the officer arrested the accused. After an Illinois trial court, expressing the view that the gun had been recovered during a lawful stop and frisk, denied the accused's motion to suppress, the accused was convicted of unlawful use of a weapon by a felon. The Illinois Appellate Court, expressing the view that the gun

35

should have been suppressed, reversed the accused's conviction (287 Ill App 3d 367, 678 NE2d 65). The Illinois Supreme Court, in affirming, expressed the view that because sudden flight in a high crime area does not create a reasonable suspicion under Terry v Ohio (1968) 392 US 1, 20 L Ed 2d 889, 88 S Ct 1868—which authorizes a brief investigatory stop of an individual when a police officer has a reasonable and articulable suspicion that criminal activity is afoot—the stop and subsequent arrest of the accused violated the prohibition under the Federal Constitution's Fourth Amendment against unreasonable searches and seizures (183 Ill 2d 306, 701 NE2d 484).

On certiorari, the United States Supreme Court reversed and remanded. In an opinion by REHNQUIST, Ch. J., joined by O'CONNOR, SCALIA, KENNEDY, and THOMAS, JJ., it was held that the police officer did not violate the Fourth Amendment when he stopped the accused, because the officer was justified in suspecting that the accused was involved in criminal activity and, therefore, in investigating further, as (1) officers are not required to ignore the relevant characteristics of a location in determining whether the circumstances are sufficiently suspicious to warrant further investigation, (2) headlong flight, which is the consummate act of evasion, is suggestive of wrongdoing, and (3) the determination of reasonable suspicion must be based on commonsense judgments and inferences about human behavior.

STEVENS, J., joined by SOUTER, GINSBURG, and BREYER, JJ., concurring in part and dissenting in part, (1) agreed with the court's rejection of both the rule requested by Illinois, which rule would authorize the detention of anyone who flees at the mere sight of a police car, and the rule requested by the accused—that such flight would never, by itself, justify a stop authorized by Terry v Ohio—but (2) expressed the view that even in a high crime neighborhood, unprovoked flight does not invariably lead to reasonable suspicion justifying a stop and frisk.

COUNSEL

Richard A. Devine argued the cause for petitioner.

Malcolm L. Stewart argued the cause for the United States, as amicus curiae, by special leave of court.

James B. Koch argued the cause for respondent.

JANET RENO, Attorney General, et al., Petitioners

v

CHARLIE CONDON, Attorney General of South Carolina, et al.

528 US 141, 145 L Ed 2d 587, 120 S Ct 666

[No. 98-1464]

Argued November 10, 1999.
Decided January 12, 2000.

Decision: Driver's Privacy Protection Act (18 USCS §§ 2721-2725) held not violative of principles of federalism contained in Federal Constitution.

SUMMARY

State departments of motor vehicles (DMVs) required drivers and automobile owners to provide personal information—which may have included a person's name, address, telephone number, vehicle description, Social Security number, medical information, and photograph—as a condition of obtaining a driver's license or registering an automobile. Congress, finding that many states, in turn, sold this personal information to individuals and businesses, enacted the Driver's Privacy Protection Act (DPPA) (18 USCS §§ 2721-2725), which (1) generally prohibited any state DMV, or officer, employee, or contractor thereof, from knowingly disclosing or otherwise making available to any person or entity personal information about any individual obtained by the department in connection with a motor vehicle record; (2) provided that (a) the ban on disclosure of personal information did not apply if drivers had consented to the release of their
38

data, and (b) the prohibition of nonconsensual disclo-
sures was subject to a number of statutory exceptions;
(3) regulated the resale and redisclosure of drivers'
personal information by private persons who obtained
that information from a state DMV; and (4) established
several penalties to be imposed on states and private
actors that failed to comply with the DPPA's requirements. South Carolina law—under which the information contained in the state's DMV records was available
to any person or entity that filled out a form listing the
requester's name and address and stating that the
information would not be used for telephone
solicitation—conflicted with the DPPA. South Carolina
and its attorney general filed suit in the United States
District Court for the District of South Carolina, and
alleged that the DPPA violated the Federal Constitution's Tenth and Eleventh Amendments. The District
Court (1) concluded that the DPPA was incompatible
with the principles of federalism inherent in the Constitution's division of power between the states and the
Federal Government, (2) granted summary judgment
for South Carolina, and (3) permanently enjoined the
DPPA's enforcement against South Carolina and its
officers (972 F Supp 977). The United States Court of
Appeals for the Fourth Circuit affirmed the decision of
the District Court (155 F3d 453).

On certiorari, the United States Supreme Court
reversed. In an opinion by REHNQUIST, Ch. J., expressing the unanimous view of the court, it was held that
(1) the personal, identifying information that the DPPA
regulated was a thing in interstate commerce; (2) the
sale or release of that information in interstate commerce was therefore a proper subject of congressional
regulation; and (3) Congress, in enacting the DPPA,
did not run afoul of the federalism principles, contained in the Constitution, which were enunciated by

the Supreme Court in New York v United States (1992) 505 US 144, 120 L Ed 2d 120, 112 S Ct 2408, and Printz v United States (1997) 521 US 898, 138 L Ed 2d 914, 117 S Ct 2365, as the DPPA did not require (a) the states in their sovereign capacity to regulate their own citizens, (b) the South Carolina legislature to enact any laws or regulations, or (c) state officials to assist in the enforcement of federal statutes regulating private individuals.

COUNSEL

Seth P. Waxman argued the cause for petitioners.
Charles Condon argued the cause for respondents.

SALVADOR MARTINEZ, Petitioner

v

COURT OF APPEAL OF CALIFORNIA, FOURTH
APPELLATE DISTRICT

528 US 152, 145 L Ed 2d 597, 120 S Ct 684

[No. 98-7809]

Argued November 9, 1999.
Decided January 12, 2000.

Decision: Lay appellant who wished to represent himself held not to have been deprived of federal
constitutional right, where California courts required him to accept state-appointed attorney on
direct appeal from state criminal conviction.

SUMMARY

The United States Supreme Court held in Faretta v
California (1975) 422 US 806, 45 L Ed 2d 562, 95 S Ct
2525, that a criminal defendant has a federal constitutional right to proceed without counsel at trial, where
the defendant voluntarily and intelligently elects to do
so. An office assistant at a law firm was accused of
converting $6,000 of a client's money to his own use.
The accused chose to represent himself at a jury trial, as
he claimed that no attorney would believe him because
of his past criminal record. The jury convicted the
accused of embezzlement, and a California trial court
imposed a prison sentence of 25 years to life. The
accused filed a notice of appeal as well as a motion to
represent himself and a waiver of counsel. The Court of
Appeal of California—which had expressed the view, in
a prior case, that notwithstanding Faretta v California,

there was no federal constitutional right to self-representation on an initial appeal as of right—denied the accused's motion. The Supreme Court of California denied the accused's application for a writ of mandate (1998 Cal LEXIS 7438).

On certiorari, the United States Supreme Court affirmed. In an opinion by STEVENS, J., joined by REHNQUIST, Ch. J., and O'CONNOR, KENNEDY, SOUTER, THOMAS, GINSBURG, and BREYER, JJ., it was held that on direct appeal from a state criminal conviction, a state is not required to recognize a federal constitutional right to self-representation—and thus, the California courts did not deprive the accused of a federal constitutional right in requiring him to accept a state-appointed attorney against his will—for (1) although historical evidence arguably demonstrated that early lawmakers had intended to preserve the right of self-representation at trial, the historical evidence did not provide any support for an affirmative federal constitutional right to appellate self-representation; (2) neither the structure of the Federal Constitution's Sixth Amendment nor inquiries into historical English practices provided any basis for finding a right to self-representation on appeal; (3) although there was a risk that the appellant would be skeptical as to whether a government-appointed lawyer would serve the appellant's cause with undivided loyalty, the risk of either disloyalty or suspicion of disloyalty was not a sufficient concern—under currently prevailing practices—to conclude that a right of self-representation was a necessary component of a fair appellate proceeding under the Constitution's due process guarantee; and (4) the states were within their discretion to conclude that in the appellate context, the government's interests in the

fair and efficient administration of justice outweighed an invasion of the appellant's interest in self-representation.

KENNEDY, J., concurring, expressed the view that in resolving the case at hand, it was unnecessary to cast doubt on the rationale of Faretta v California as to an accused's right of self-representation at trial, for different considerations applied in the appellate system.

BREYER, J., concurring, expressed the view that without some strong factual basis for believing that the holding of Faretta v California had proved counterproductive in practice, the Supreme Court was not in a position to reconsider the federal constitutional assumptions underlying that case.

SCALIA, J., concurring in the judgment, expressed the view that (1) the decision in Faretta v California was correct, and (2) the question whether the Faretta holding applied to self-representation on appeal was readily answered by the fact that there is no federal constitutional right to appeal.

COUNSEL

Ronald D. Maines argued the cause for petitioner.
Robert M. Foster argued the cause for respondent.

FRIENDS of the EARTH, INCORPORATED, et al.,
Petitioners

v

LAIDLAW ENVIRONMENTAL SERVICES (TOC),
Inc.

528 US 167, 145 L Ed 2d 610, 120 S Ct 693

[No. 98-822]

Argued October 12, 1999.
Decided January 12, 2000.

Decision: Environmental groups' claim for civil penalties against owner of hazardous waste facility under § 505(a) of Clean Water Act (33 USCS § 1365(a)) held not necessarily mooted by owner's compliance with permit or closing of facility.

SUMMARY

The owner of a South Carolina hazardous waste incinerator facility that included a wastewater treatment plant was granted a National Pollutant Discharge Elimination System (NPDES) permit by a South Carolina state agency acting under § 402(a)(1) of the Clean Water Act (CWA) (33 USCS § 1342(a)(1)). The permit authorized the company to discharge treated water into a nearby river, but placed limits on the discharge of several pollutants. In June 1992, two environmental organizations (subsequently joined by a third), alleging that the owner's discharges of pollutants had exceeded the limits set by the permit, notified the owner of an intention to file a citizen suit under § 505(a) of the CWA (33 USCS § 1365(a)) after the expiration of a 60-day notice period. Meanwhile, at the owner's own request, the state agency agreed to file a separate lawsuit against the owner. On the last day before the 60-day notice period expired, the owner and the state agency reached a settlement with respect to the separate lawsuit, which settlement required the owner to pay civil penalties and to make every effort to comply with the permit obligations. Nevertheless, the environmental organizations filed a citizen suit against the owner in the United States District Court for the District of South Carolina shortly afterward, in which suit the organizations alleged noncompliance with the NPDES permit and sought declaratory and injunctive relief and an award of civil penalties. The owner moved for summary judgment on the ground that the organizations had failed to present evidence demonstrating injury in fact and therefore lacked standing under the Federal Constitution's Article III to bring the suit. In opposition to this motion, the organizations submitted affidavits and deposition testimony from some members of the organizations who lived near the river and who alleged that the owner's discharges (1) had curtailed those members' recreational use of the river, and (2) would subject those members to other economic and aesthetic harms. In 1993, the District Court denied the summary judgment motion upon finding that the organizations had standing. In 1997, the District Court issued a judgment—consisting of findings of fact, conclusions of law, and an order—in which it was concluded that (1) although there was no demonstrated proof of harm to the environment from the discharge violations, the owner had gained an economic benefit as a result of noncompliance with the permit; (2) a civil penalty of $405,800 was appropriate; and (3) injunctive relief was inappropriate, because the owner had been in substantial compliance with the permit since at least August 1992 (956 F Supp 588). The organizations appealed the District Court's civil penalty judgment on the ground that the penalty was inadequate, but they did not appeal the denial of declaratory or injunctive relief. In a cross-appeal, the owner argued, among other matters, that the organizations lacked standing to bring the suit. On appeal, the United States Court of Appeals for the Fourth Circuit (1) assumed, without deciding, that the organization had initially had standing; (2) concluded that the case had become moot, because the only remedy currently available to the organizations—civil penalties payable to the government—would not have redressed any injury that the organizations had suffered; (3) vacated the District Court's order; and (4) remanded the case with instructions to dismiss (149 F3d 303). The owner subsequently asserted that after the Court of Appeals issued its decision, but before the United States Supreme Court granted certiorari in 1999, the entire facility was closed, dismantled, and put up for sale, and that all discharges from the facility permanently ceased.

On certiorari, the Supreme Court reversed the Court of Appeals' judgment and remanded the case for further proceedings. In an opinion by GINSBURG, J., joined by REHNQUIST, Ch. J., and STEVENS, O'CONNOR, KENNEDY, SOUTER, and BREYER, JJ., it was held that (1) the organizations had demonstrated sufficient alleged injury in fact, by means of the members' affidavits and testimony, to establish the organizations' standing to bring the suit, even if there was no proof of harm to the environment from the facility owner's alleged violations; (2) the organizations had standing to seek civil penalties, as such penalties (a) were for alleged violations that were ongoing at the time of the complaint and that could continue into the future if undeterred, and (b) carried with them a deterrent effect that made it likely that the penalties would redress the organiza-

46

tions' injuries by abating current violations and preventing future ones; (3) the organizations' failure to appeal the District Court's denial of injunctive relief did not moot the civil penalties claim on appeal; (4) the civil penalties claim had possibly become moot when the owner came into compliance with the permit or closed the facility, but only if one or the other of these events made it absolutely clear that the permit violations could not reasonably be expected to recur; and (5) the effect of the owner's compliance and the facility's closure on the prospect of future violations was a disputed factual matter that remained open for consideration on remand.

STEVENS, J., concurring, expressed the view that the claim for civil penalties would not have been moot even if it had been absolutely clear that (1) the facility's owner had gone out of business and posed no threat of future permit violations, or (2) the owner's violations could not reasonably have been expected to recur because of the owner's achievement of substantial compliance with the permit requirements after the organizations filed their complaint but before the District Court entered judgment.

KENNEDY, J., concurring, expressed the view that questions concerning the permissibility—in view of the responsibilities committed to the executive by Article II of the Constitution—of exactions of public fines by private litigants and the delegation of executive power which might be inferable from such authorization were best reserved for a later case.

SCALIA, J., joined by THOMAS, J., dissenting, expressed the view that (1) injury in fact ought not to have been found on the basis of the affidavits presented by the organizations, as those affidavits were vague and were undermined by the District Court's express finding that the facility owner's discharges caused no demonstrable harm to the environment; (2) it was a violation of traditional principles of federal standing to hold that a civil penalty, payable to the public, remedied a threatened private harm and sufficed to sustain a private suit; and (3) while the Supreme Court might have been correct in stating that the parallel between standing and mootness was imperfect, this did not change the underlying principle that the requisite personal interest that must exist at the commencement of the litigation must continue throughout the litigation's existence.

COUNSEL

Bruce J. Terris argued the cause for petitioners.

Jeffrey P. Minear argued the cause for the United States, as amicus curiae, by special leave of court.

Donald A. Cockrill argued the cause for respondent.

ADARAND CONSTRUCTORS, INC., Petitioner

v

RODNEY SLATER, Secretary of Transportation, et al.

528 US 216, 145 L Ed 2d 650, 120 S Ct 722

[No. 99-295]

Decided January 12, 2000.

Decision: Federal Court of Appeals held to have erred
in deciding subcontractor's suit challenging
United States Department of Transportation's procedure for certifying contractors as disadvantaged
business enterprises ought to be dismissed as
moot.

SUMMARY

A subcontractor, whose principal was a white man,
(1) brought suit against various federal officials and (2)
alleged that a United States Department of Transportation (DOT) contract's subcontractor compensation
clause, inserted pursuant to a Small Business Act provision (15 USCS § 637(d)), and in particular the race-
based presumption that formed the clause's founda-
tion, violated the subcontractor's Fifth Amendment
right to equal protection under the Federal Constitution. The subcontractor compensation clause was required to be included by all federal agencies in their
prime contracts and rewarded the prime contractor for
subcontracting with disadvantaged business enterprises. Eventually, the United States Court of Appeals
for the Tenth Circuit, applying intermediate scrutiny,
upheld the use of the clause and the presumption (16
F3d 1537). However, the United States Supreme Court

reversed and remanded on the ground that the use of race-based measures by the DOT ought to have been subjected to strict scrutiny (515 US 200, 132 L Ed 2d 158, 115 S Ct 2097). On remand, the United States District Court for the District of Colorado held that (1) the clause and the presumption failed strict scrutiny because they were not narrowly tailored; (2) the presumption that members of the enumerated racial groups were socially disadvantaged was both overinclusive and underinclusive, since it (a) included members of those groups who were not disadvantaged, and (b) excluded members of other groups who were; and (3) the DOT was enjoined from using the clause and its presumption (965 F Supp 1556). Filing a second suit against certain Colorado officials in the District Court, the subcontractor then challenged the state's use of the federal guidelines in certifying disadvantaged-business enterprises for federally assisted projects on the same grounds. Shortly after this suit was filed, and in response to the District Court's decision on remand, Colorado amended its certification procedure by (1) removing the presumption of social disadvantage for certain minorities and women, (2) substituting a requirement that all applicants certify on their own account that each of the firm's majority owners had experienced social disadvantage based upon the effects of racial, ethnic, or gender discrimination, and (3) requiring no further showing of social disadvantage by an applicant. The District Court (1) took judicial notice of its previous holding that the Federal Government had discriminated against the subcontractor's owner by the application of unconstitutional rules and regulations, (2) denied the subcontractor's request for a preliminary injunction, and (3) reasoned that the subcontractor was likely eligible for disadvantaged-business status under Colorado's system for certifying businesses for federally assisted projects. Meanwhile, the federal officials' appeal from the District Court's earlier decision was pending before the Court of Appeals. After learning that the subcontractor received disadvantaged-business status from the Colorado department of transportation, the Court of Appeals ruled that the cause of action was moot and vacated the District Court's judgment favorable to the subcontractor (169 F3d 1292).

The Supreme Court (1) granted the subcontractor's petition for certiorari, (2) reversed the Court of Appeals' judgment, and (3) remanded the case for further proceedings. In a per curiam opinion expressing the unanimous view of the court, it was held that the Court of Appeals erred in holding that the subcontractor's suit challenging the DOT's procedure for certifying contractors as disadvantaged business enterprises ought to be dismissed as moot after subcontractor was so certified by Colorado's department of transportation, as among other matters, (1) federal officials did not satisfy the heavy burden of persuading a court that the challenged conduct—or the utilization of the subcontractor compensation clause—could not reasonably be expected to recur; (2) the DOT had not approved, as was required under 49 CFR § 26.21(b)(1), the state agency's procedure for certifying disadvantaged business enterprises; and (3) the state agency's procedure under which subcontractor was certified applied no presumption in favor of minority groups, as was required under 49 CFR § 26.67(a)(1), and accepted without investigation the firm's self-certification of entitlement to disadvantaged-business status.

LONNIE WEEKS, Jr., Petitioner

v

RONALD J. ANGELONE, Director, Virginia Department of Corrections

528 US 225, 145 L Ed 2d 727, 120 S Ct 727

[No. 99-5746]

Argued December 6, 1999.
Decided January 19, 2000.

Decision: Federal Constitution held not violated by Virginia trial judge who, during capital trial's penalty phase, directed jury's attention to allegedly ambiguous paragraph of jury instruction in response to jury's question as to mitigating evidence.

SUMMARY

In the Circuit Court for Prince William County, Virginia, a trial jury found a defendant guilty of capital murder. A 2-day penalty phase followed, during which the prosecution sought to prove two aggravating circumstances and the defense presented witnesses in mitigation. The trial judge gave the jury a three-paragraph instruction on fixing the penalty, which instruction was a state pattern instruction that was subsequently upheld by the United States Supreme Court in another case, Buchanan v Angelone (1998) 522 US 269, 139 L Ed 2d 702, 118 S Ct 757, as constitutionally sufficient to allow a capital jury to consider mitigating evidence. The first paragraph provided that before the penalty could be fixed at death, the prosecution had to prove beyond a reasonable doubt at least one of two alternative aggravating cir-
52

cumstances. The second paragraph provided that if the jury were to find from the evidence that the prosecution had proved beyond a reasonable doubt either of the two alternatives, then the jury would be permitted to fix the punishment of the defendant at death, "or if you believe from all the evidence that the death penalty is not justified, then you shall fix the punishment of the defendant at life imprisonment" or imprisonment for life and a fine. The third paragraph provided that if the prosecution failed to prove beyond a reasonable doubt at least one of the alternatives, then the jury had to fix the punishment at life imprisonment or imprisonment for life and a fine. In addition, (1) the judge gave a specific instruction that the jury would have to consider a mitigating circumstance if the jury found that there was evidence to support that circumstance, and (2) defense counsel specifically explained to the jury during closing argument that the jury could find both aggravating factors proven and still not sentence the defendant to death. During deliberations, the jury sent the trial judge a note asking whether, if the jury believed the accused guilty of at least one of the aggravating circumstances, it was the jury's duty to (1) issue the death penalty, or (2) decide whether to issue the death penalty or a life sentence. The judge responded by directing the jury to the instruction's second paragraph. After 2 more hours of deliberation, the jury returned a verdict stating that the jury, having unanimously found that the defendant's conduct had satisfied one of the aggravating circumstances— and having considered the evidence in mitigation—unanimously fixed the punishment at death. The jurors were polled and all responded affirmatively that the foregoing was their verdict. In a direct appeal to the Supreme Court of Virginia, the defendant presented 47 assignments of error, including as number 44 an assignment of error respecting the judge's answer to the jury's question about mitigating circumstances. However, the Virginia Supreme Court affirmed the defendant's conviction and sentence on direct appeal (248 Va 460, 450 SE2d 379, cert den 516 US 829, 133 L Ed 2d 55, 116 S Ct 100) and subsequently dismissed the defendant's state habeas corpus petition. The United States District Court for the Eastern District of Virginia, in denying the defendant federal habeas corpus relief, (1) noted that the defendant had alleged, among other matters, that his federal constitutional rights were violated when the trial court refused to give a proposed alternative jury instruction; and (2) concluded that although the proposed instruction was a clearer statement of the law than the instruction actually given, the latter instruction was constitutionally sufficient (4 F Supp 2d 497). The United States Court of Appeals for the Fourth Circuit denied a certificate of appealability and dismissed the defendant's habeas corpus petition (176 F3d 249).

On certiorari, the United States Supreme Court affirmed. In an opinion by REHNQUIST, Ch. J., joined by O'CONNOR, SCALIA, KENNEDY, and THOMAS, JJ., it was held that under the circumstances presented, the Constitution was not violated, for the defendant had demonstrated at best only that there existed a slight possibility that the jury had considered itself precluded from considering mitigating evidence.

STEVENS, J., joined by GINSBURG and BREYER, JJ., and joined in part (except for point 2(a) below) by SOUTER, J., dissenting, expressed the view that (1) it was virtually certain that the jury did not understand that the law authorized the jury not to issue the death penalty even though the jury found the defendant guilty of at least one aggravating circumstance; and (2) this conclusion was cumulatively supported by (a) the text of the instructions, (b) the judge's responses to the jury's inquiries, (c) the verdict forms given to the jury, and (d) the court reporter's transcription of the polling of the jury, which transcription indicated that a majority of the jurors were in tears when affirming the verdict.

COUNSEL

Mark E. Olive argued the cause for petitioner.

Robert H. Anderson, III argued the cause for respondent.

CARL T. C. GUTIERREZ and MADELINE Z. BOR-
DALLO, Petitioners

v

JOSEPH F. ADA and FELIX P. CAMACHO

528 US 250, 145 L Ed 2d 747, 120 S Ct 740

[No. 99-51]

Argued December 6, 1999.
Decided January 19, 2000.

Decision: Runoff election in Guam held not required
where candidate slate received majority of votes
cast for Governor and Lieutenant Governor, but
not majority of total number of ballots cast.

SUMMARY

The Organic Act of Guam (48 USCS §§ 1421 et seq.)
provided that if no candidates for Governor and Lieutenant Governor of the Territory of Guam received a
"majority of the votes cast in any election," a runoff
election would be held between the candidates who
received the highest and second highest number of
votes cast (48 USCS § 1422). In the November 1998
Guam general election, a slate of candidates for Governor and Lieutenant Governor, headed by Carl T. C.
Gutierrez, received 24,250 votes, which represented
49.83 percent of the total number of ballots cast in the
general election. An opposing slate, headed by Joseph
F. Ada, received 21,200 votes. A number of persons cast
ballots that were blank as to the gubernatorial election.
The Guam Election Commission (1) found that, after
deducting the blank ballots, the Gutierrez slate received 51.21 percent of the vote in the gubernatorial

election, and (2) certified the Gutierrez slate as the winner. Ada and his running mate brought suit in the United States District Court for the District of Guam and alleged that the Gutierrez slate had not received a majority of the votes cast as required by the Organic Act. The District Court (1) read the statute to require a majority of the total number of voters casting ballots in the general election, and (2) issued a writ of mandamus for a runoff election to be held in December 1998. The United States Court of Appeals for the Ninth Circuit affirmed the District Court's issuance of the writ (179 F3d 672).

On certiorari, the United States Supreme Court reversed the judgment of the Court of Appeals and remanded the case for further proceedings. In an opinion by SOUTER, J., expressing the unanimous view of the court, it was held that the Guam Organic Act did not compel a runoff election, as (1) the phrase "any election" in § 1422 could not have referred to anything except an election for Governor and Lieutenant Governor, since (a) the section contained six express references to an election for Governor and Lieutenant Governor, (b) the reference to "any election" was preceded by two references to gubernatorial election and was followed by four such references, and (c) words are known by their companions; (2) such a reading was confirmed by the other clues in § 1422 and other provisions; and (3) a reading of "any election" as referring to an election for Governor and Lieutenant Governor was not undermined by (a) the drafting difference between 48 USCS § 1422 and 48 USCS § 1712, which included a specific statement that "a majority of the votes cast for the office of Delegate" to Congress was necessary to elect a Guam Delegate, or (b) the rule against attributing redundancy to Congress.

COUNSEL

Seth M. Hufstedler argued the cause for petitioners.
Dennis P. Riordan argued the cause for respondents.

GEORGE SMITH, Warden, Petitioner

v

LEE ROBBINS

528 US 259, 145 L Ed 2d 756, 120 S Ct 746

[No. 98-1037]

Argued October 5, 1999.
Decided January 19, 2000.

Decision: States held free to adopt procedures for determining whether indigent's direct appeal is frivolous, other than procedures set forth in Anders v California (1967) 386 US 738, 18 L Ed 2d 493, 87 S Ct 1396, so long as procedures adequately safeguard defendant's Fourteenth Amendment right to appellate counsel.

SUMMARY

In Anders v California (1967) 386 US 738, 18 L Ed 2d 493, 87 S Ct 1396, the United States Supreme Court, in holding that California's then existing procedure for handling potentially frivolous criminal appeals by convicted indigents violated the Federal Constitution's Fourteenth Amendment, set out what would be an acceptable procedure for treating such appeals, under which procedure (1) counsel who finds an appeal to be frivolous should so advise the appellate court and request permission to withdraw, (2) counsel's request must be accompanied by a brief referring to anything in the record that might arguably support the appeal, and (3) the court then decided whether the case is frivolous. Subsequently, the California Supreme Court adopted a new procedure, under which (1) counsel (a)

59

upon concluding that an appeal would be frivolous, filed a brief with the appellate court that summarized the procedural and factual history of the case, (b) attests that counsel has reviewed the record, explained counsel's evaluation of the case to the client, provided the client with a copy of the brief, and informed the client of the client's right to file a pro se supplemental brief, (c) requests that the court independently examine the record for arguable issues, (d) neither explicitly states a conclusion that an appeal would be frivolous nor requests leave to withdraw, (e) is silent on the merits of the case, and (f) expresses counsel's availability to brief any issues on which the court might desire briefing; and (2) the appellate court must conduct a review of the entire record. An accused who, after representing himself at a California state court trial, had been convicted of murder and grand theft, received appointed counsel on appeal. Counsel, concluding that an appeal would be frivolous, filed a brief that complied with the new California procedure, and the accused filed a pro se supplemental brief. After the California Court of Appeal affirmed the accused's conviction, the California Supreme Court denied the accused's petition for review. The accused filed, in the United States District Court for the Central District of California pursuant to 28 USCS § 2254, a writ of habeas corpus alleging, among other things, that the accused had been denied effective assistance of appellate counsel because counsel's brief filed in accordance with the new California procedure failed to comply with the procedure set forth in Anders v California. The District Court, in agreeing with the accused's allegation, ordered California to either grant the accused a new trial within 30 days or release him from custody. The United States Court of Appeals for the Ninth Circuit agreed with the District Court on the Anders issue, but remanded for the District Court to consider the accused's 11 claims of trial error, reasoning that if the accused prevailed on any of these claims, then it would be unnecessary to order the California Court of Appeal to grant a new direct appeal (152 F3d 1062).

On certiorari, the United States Supreme Court reversed and remanded. In an opinion by THOMAS, J., joined by REHNQUIST, Ch. J., and O'CONNOR, SCALIA, and KENNEDY, JJ., it was held that (1) states are free to adopt procedures for determining whether an indigent accused's direct criminal appeal is frivolous, other than the procedure set forth in Anders v California (1967) 386 US 738, 18 L Ed 2d 493, 87 S Ct 1396, so long as the adopted procedures adequately safeguard an accused's right, under the Federal Constitution's Fourteenth Amendment, to appellate counsel, and (2) the new California procedure did not violate the Fourteenth Amendment, as the procedure provided a criminal appellant pursuing a first appeal as of right the minimum safeguards necessary to make that appeal adequate and effective.

STEVENS, J., joined by GINSBURG, J., dissenting, expressed the view that the new California procedure violated the principle of substantial equality that had been part of the law for decades, because the procedure did not provide an indigent appellant with anything approaching representation by a paid attorney.

SOUTER, J., joined by STEVENS, GINSBURG, and BREYER, JJ., dissenting, expressed the view that the new California procedure failed to assure representation by counsel with the adversarial character demanded by the Constitution, as the procedure failed to provide an advocate's analysis of issues as a predicate of court review.

61

COUNSEL

Carol F. Jorstad argued the cause for petitioner.
Ronald J. Nessim argued the cause for respondent.

———————

UNITED STATES, Petitioner

v

ABEL MARTINEZ-SALAZAR

528 US 304, 145 L Ed 2d 792, 120 S Ct 774

[No. 98-1255]

Argued November 29, 1999.
Decided January 19, 2000.

Decision: Accused's exercise of peremptory challenges pursuant to Rule 24 of Federal Rules of Criminal Procedure held not to be denied or impaired when accused chose to use such challenge to remove juror who ought to have been excused for cause.

SUMMARY

An accused and his codefendant were tried by a jury in the United States District Court for the District of Arizona for narcotics and weapons offenses. As instructed by Rule 24(b) of the Federal Rules of Criminal Procedure, the District Court allotted 10 peremptory challenges to the codefendants that could be used jointly in the selection of 12 jurors. When a prospective juror indicated on his questionnaire and in his discussion with the trial judge that he would favor the prosecution, the codefendants challenged the juror for cause, but the District Court declined to excuse the juror. After two unsuccessful objections to the for-cause ruling, the accused used a peremptory challenge to remove the juror. Subsequently, the codefendants exhausted all of their peremptory challenges. When jury selection was completed, the District Court read the names of the jurors to be seated and asked if the prosecutor or defense counsel had any objections to any of those jurors. Counsel for the accused responded: "None from us." At the conclusion of the trial, the accused was convicted on all counts. On appeal, the accused contended that (1) the District Court abused its discretion in refusing to strike the juror for cause, and (2) this error forced the accused to use a peremptory challenge on the juror. The United States Court of Appeals for the Ninth Circuit expressed the view that (1) the District Court's refusal to strike the juror for cause was an abuse of discretion; (2) the error did not violate the Federal Constitution's Sixth Amendment, because the juror was removed and the impartiality of the jury ultimately seated was not challenged; (3) the District Court's mistake resulted in a violation of the accused's due process rights under the Constitution's Fifth Amendment, since the District Court's error in denying the for-cause challenge forced the accused to use a peremptory challenge curatively, thereby impairing his right to the full complement of peremptory challenges to which he was entitled under federal law; and (4) such an error required automatic reversal (146 F3d 653, 1998 US App LEXIS 10899).

On certiorari, the United States Supreme Court reversed. In an opinion by GINSBURG, J., joined by REHNQUIST, Ch. J., and STEVENS, O'CONNOR, SOUTER, THOMAS, and BREYER, JJ., it was held that an accused's exercise of peremptory challenges pursuant to Rule 24 of the Federal Rules of Criminal Procedure was not denied or impaired when, as in the case at hand, the accused chose to use such challenge to remove a juror who, it was uncontested, ought to have been excused for cause, as among other matters, (1) peremptory challenges were auxiliary and not of federal constitutional dimension, and (2) the loss of a peremptory challenge did not constitute a violation of the Sixth Amendment right to an impartial jury.

SOUTER, J., concurring, expressed the opinion that this case did not present the issue whether the refusal to afford a defendant a peremptory challenge beyond the maximum otherwise allowed was reversible error, when the defendant has (1) used a peremptory challenge to cure an erroneous denial of a challenge for cause, and (2) showed that the defendant would otherwise have used the full complement of peremptory challenges for the noncurative purposes that are the focus of the peremptory right.

SCALIA, J., joined by KENNEDY, J., concurring in the judgment, expressed the view that (1) the accused was accorded the full number of peremptory challenges to which he was entitled, (2) the court unnecessarily pronounced upon the accused's ability to complain about the seating of the biased juror if he had not expended his peremptory challenge, and (3) uncertainty exists as to whether normal principles of waiver disable a defendant from objecting on appeal to the seating of a juror that he was able to prevent.

COUNSEL

Michael R. Dreeben argued the cause for petitioner. Michael Gordon argued the cause for respondent.

JANET RENO, Attorney General, Appellant

v

BOSSIER PARISH SCHOOL BOARD (No. 98-405)

GEORGE PRICE, et al., Appellants

v

BOSSIER PARISH SCHOOL BOARD (No. 98-406)

528 US 320, 145 L Ed 2d 845, 120 S Ct 866

Argued April 26, 1999.
Reargued October 6, 1999.
Decided January 24, 2000.

Decision: Section 5 of Voting Rights Act of 1965 (42 USCS § 1973c) held not to prohibit preclearance of covered jurisdiction's redistricting plan that was enacted with discriminatory but nonretrogressive purpose.

SUMMARY

Under § 5 of the Voting Rights Act of 1965 (42 USCS § 1973c), some states and their political subdivisions may not implement any change in a voting qualification, prerequisite, standard, practice, or procedure unless the state or subdivision first obtains either (1) administrative preclearance of that change from the United States Attorney General, or (2) judicial preclearance from the United States District Court for the District of Columbia. Bossier Parish, Louisiana, was a jurisdiction subject to the § 5 preclearance requirements. In order to equalize the population distribution among the 12 electoral districts for the parish's school board, the board, in 1992, adopted a redistricting plan

which had been recently adopted by the Bossier Parish
police jury—the parish's primary governing body—to
govern the jury's own elections. This plan, for which
the jury had obtained the Attorney General's preclearance, likewise contained 12 districts. None of the
districts in the board's existing plan or in the jury plan
contained a majority of black residents. In adopting the
jury plan, the board rejected an alternative 12-district
plan that would have included two districts each containing a majority of voting-age black residents. The
Attorney General (1) objected to the board's use of the
jury plan on the basis of new information not previously available, that is, the alternative plan; (2) asserted
that the board's redistricting plan violated § 2 of the
Voting Rights Act (42 USCS § 1973) by unnecessarily
limiting the opportunity for minority voters to elect
their candidates of choice; and (3) concluded that the
board's plan warranted a denial of preclearance. The
board filed a preclearance action in the District Court
against the Attorney General. The District Court, in
granting preclearance, said that the District Court
would not (1) deny preclearance of a proposed voting
change under § 5 simply because the change violated
§ 2, or (2) permit § 2 evidence to prove discriminatory
purpose under § 5 (907 F Supp 434). The United States
Supreme Court, in vacating the District Court's judgment and in remanding the case for further proceedings, held that (1) a proposed voting change could not
be denied preclearance simply because the change
violated § 2; and (2) evidence of a dilutive but nonretrogressive effect forbidden by § 2 could, in some circumstances, be relevant to whether a plan was enacted
with a retrogressive purpose forbidden by § 5 (520 US
471, 137 L Ed 2d 730, 117 S Ct 1491). On remand, the
District Court, in again granting preclearance, (1)
expressed the view that retrogressive intent had not

been established, but (2) left open the question, which the Supreme Court had left open on remand, as to whether the § 5 purpose inquiry extended beyond the search for retrogressive intent (7 F Supp 2d 29).

On certiorari, the Supreme Court affirmed. In an opinion by SCALIA, J., expressing the unanimous view of the court as to holding 1 below, and joined by REHNQUIST, Ch. J., and O'CONNOR, KENNEDY, and THOMAS, JJ., as to holding 2 below, it was held that (1) the instant case and its companion case concerning the 1992 plan were not mooted on the theory that they no longer presented a live case or controversy for purposes of the Federal Constitution's Article III, as the 1992 plan probably would serve as the baseline against which the next plan would be evaluated for preclearance purposes; and (2) § 5 did not prohibit preclearance of a redistricting plan that was enacted with a discriminatory but nonretrogressive purpose, as, when considered in light of the court's longstanding interpretation of the "effect" prong of § 5 as covering only retrogressive dilution, the language of § 5 led to the conclusion that the "purpose" prong of § 5 covered only retrogressive dilution.

THOMAS, J., concurring, expressed the view that the election, while the instant litigation was pending, of three blacks from majority-white districts to serve on the school board illustrated that the federal intervention that spawned the litigation was unnecessary.

SOUTER, J., joined by STEVENS, GINSBURG, and BREYER, JJ., concurring in part and dissenting in part, (1) agreed that the cases were not moot, but (2) expressed the view that (a) the behavior of the parish was a plain effort to deny the voting equality that the Constitution just as plainly guaranteed, (b) the point of § 5 was to thwart the ingenuity of the school board's efforts to stay ahead of challenges under § 2, and (c) under the Supreme Court's decision, executive and judicial officers of the United States would be forced to preclear illegal and unconstitutional voting schemes patently intended to perpetuate discrimination.

STEVENS, J., joined by GINSBURG, J., dissenting, expressed the view that even if retrogression were assumed to be an acceptable standard for identifying prohibited effects, that assumption did not justify an interpretation of the § 5 word "purpose" that was at war with controlling precedent and the plain meaning of the statutory text.

BREYER, J., dissenting, expressed the view that § 5 prohibited preclearance of a voting change that had the purpose of unconstitutionally depriving minorities of the right to vote.

COUNSEL

Paul R. Q. Wolfson argued and reargued the cause for appellant in No. 98-405.

Patricia A. Brannan argued and reargued the cause for appellants in No. 98-406.

Michael A. Carvin argued and reargued the cause for appellee.

_____

JEREMIAH W. NIXON, Attorney General of Missouri,
et al., Petitioners

v

SHRINK MISSOURI GOVERNMENT PAC et al.

528 US 377, 145 L Ed 2d 886, 120 S Ct 897

[No. 98-963]

Argued October 5, 1999.
Decided January 24, 2000.

Decision: Missouri statute limiting permissible amounts
of contributions to candidates for state
office—including $1,075 limit with respect to state-
wide offices—held not to violate Federal Constitution's First Amendment.

SUMMARY

In 1994, the Missouri legislature enacted a statute to
restrict the permissible amounts of monetary contributions to candidates for state office. The statute took
effect in 1995, after a ballot initiative with even stricter
contribution limits—although approved by 74 percent
of Missouri voters—had been invalidated as violative of
the Federal Constitution's First Amendment by the
United States Court of Appeals for the Eighth Circuit,
which had nevertheless noted alleged improprieties
with respect to contributions to Missouri political fig-
ures (72 F3d 633, cert den 518 US 1033, 135 L Ed 2d
1094, 116 S Ct 2579). The statute provided, among
other matters, that (1) with respect to elections for
statewide offices, including state auditor, the amount of
contributions made by or accepted from any person
other than the candidate was not to exceed $1,000; (2)

contributions to candidates for some other state offices were to be limited to as little as $250; and (3) the statutory dollar amounts were to be adjusted each even-numbered year by taking into account the consumer price index. Thus, as of 1998, the limit was adjusted to $1,075 for contributions to candidates for statewide office, while the limit on contributions to candidates for some other state offices was adjusted to $275. A political action committee (PAC) gave a candidate for state auditor $1,025 in 1997 and another $50 in 1998. The PAC, alleging that it would have contributed more to the candidate's campaign but for the limitation—and the candidate, alleging that he could campaign effectively only with more generous contributions than those allowed by the statute—brought suit in the United States District Court for the Eastern District of Missouri against various Missouri officials to enjoin enforcement of the statute as assertedly violating the Federal Constitution's First and Fourteenth Amendments. The District Court, in granting summary judgment in favor of the officials, (1) cited evidence including (a) an affidavit from a Missouri state senator—the co-chair of the legislature's campaign finance reform committee at the time that the contribution limits were enacted—who said that large contributions had the real potential to buy votes, and (b) newspaper reports supporting inferences of impropriety with respect to contributions to Missouri political figures; (2) found adequate support for the statute in the proposition that large contributions raised suspicions of influence peddling that tended to undermine citizens' confidence in the integrity of government; and (3) concluded that the case was controlled by Buckley v Valeo (1976) 424 US 1, 46 L Ed 2d 659, 96 S Ct 612, in which the United States Supreme Court had upheld the constitutionality of a federal statute establishing a

$1,000 limitation on contributions to any single candidate for federal office (5 F Supp 2d 734). However, the Court of Appeals (1) enjoined enforcement of the law pending appeal (151 F3d 763); and (2) ultimately reversed and ordered a remand, as the Court of Appeals reasoned in part that Missouri's claim of a compelling interest in avoiding the corruption or the perception of corruption with respect to large campaign contributions was insufficient by itself to satisfy the requisite strict scrutiny (161 F3d 519, reh, en banc, den 1999 US App LEXIS 5241).

On certiorari, the Supreme Court reversed the Court of Appeals' judgment and remanded the case for further proceedings. In an opinion by SOUTER, J., joined by REHNQUIST, Ch. J., and STEVENS, O'CONNOR, GINSBURG, and BREYER, JJ., it was held that (1) state limits may—consistent with the First Amendment—be placed on contributions to state political candidates, where such state regulation is comparable to the federal regulation of federal campaign contributions approved in Buckley v Valeo; (2) those federal limits do not (a) define the scope of permissible state limits on contributions to state political candidates, either with or without adjustment of such limits for inflation, or (b) set a minimum constitutional threshold for contribution limits; (2) the state statute in question was not void, under the First Amendment, for want of evidence to justify the statute's limits, as the evidence was enough to show that the substantiation of the congressional concerns reflected in Buckley v Valeo with respect to federal contribution limits had a counterpart that supported the state statute; (3) the state statute's contribution limits were not so different in kind from the federal limits upheld in Buckley v Valeo as to raise a First Amendment issue about the adequacy of the state statute's tailoring to serve the state statute's purposes, for there was no showing that the limitations had prevented candidates and political committees from amassing the resources necessary for effective advocacy; and (4) for First Amendment purposes, the state statute's limits did not differ in kind, owing to inflation since 1976, from the federal limits.

STEVENS, J., concurring, expressed the view that the First Amendment did not provide the same measure of protection to the use of money to accomplish campaign goals as the First Amendment provided to the use of ideas to achieve the same results.

BREYER, J., joined by GINSBURG, J., concurring, expressed the view that (1) in cases involving limits on campaign finances, where there were competing constitutional interests, there was no place for a strong presumption against constitutionality, nor would the mechanical application of "strict scrutiny" properly resolve the constitutional problem posed; (2) the state statute in question was valid under the appropriate balance-of-interests approach; and (3) if Buckley v Valeo denied the political branches sufficient leeway to enact comprehensive solutions to the problems posed by campaign finance, then the Constitution would require the Supreme Court to reconsider that decision.

KENNEDY, J., dissenting, expressed the view that (1) the state statute in question could not pass any serious standard of First Amendment review; (2) Buckley v Valeo, which had upheld contribution limits but had invalidated campaign expenditure limits, ought to be overruled as causing a distortion of political speech; and (3) Congress or state legislatures ought to be free to attempt some new reform in which there were some limits on both expenditures and contributions.

THOMAS, J., joined by SCALIA, J., dissenting, expressed the view that (1) campaign contribution limitations ought to be subject to strict First Amendment scrutiny; (2) under such scrutiny, the state statute in question was unconstitutional; and (3) Buckley v Valeo ought to be overruled as failing to provide an adequate justification for limiting individual contributions to political candidates.

COUNSEL

Jeremiah W. Nixon argued the cause for petitioners.

Seth P. Waxman argued the cause for the United States as amicus curiae, by special leave of court.

D. Bruce La Pierre argued the cause for respondents.

DAVID H. BARAL, Petitioner

v

UNITED STATES

528 US 431, 145 L Ed 2d 949, 120 S Ct 1006

[No. 98-1667]

Argued January 18, 2000.
Decided February 22, 2000.

Decision: Remittance by taxpayer of estimated federal income tax, as well as remittance by taxpayer's employer of federal withholding tax, held to be "paid" on due date of taxpayer's income tax return.

SUMMARY

Under § 6511(b)(2)(A) of the Internal Revenue Code (IRC) (26 USCS § 6511(b)(2)(A)), the amount of credit or refund to which a taxpayer is entitled as compensation for an overpayment of federal income tax shall not exceed the portion of the tax paid within the period, immediately preceding the filing of the taxpayer's claim, equal to 3 years plus the period of any extension of time for filing the tax return on which the credit or refund is claimed. Two remittances—a withholding of $4,104 from a calendar year taxpayer's wages throughout 1988 by the taxpayer's employer, and an estimated income tax of $1,100 remitted on January 15, 1999 by the taxpayer—were made to the Internal Revenue Service (IRS) toward the taxpayer's 1988 federal income tax liability. After receiving a filing extension from April 15, 1989 until August 15, 1989, the taxpayer failed to file his 1988 federal income tax

75

return until June 1, 1993. On the return, he claimed a $1,175 overpayment and asked the IRS to apply this amount as a credit toward his 1989 taxable year. The IRS denied the requested credit on the basis that the ceiling imposed by § 6511(b)(2)(A) for a refund or credit of the taxpayer's income tax payments for 1988 was zero, because the relevant look-back period supposedly extended 3 years and 4 months from June 1, 1993 to February 1, 1990, during which period, according to the IRS, the taxpayer had paid none of overpaid taxes. The taxpayer commenced a refund suit in a Federal District Court. After the District Court entered a summary judgment for the IRS, the United States Court of Appeals for the District of Columbia Circuit, in affirming, concluded that both the withholding and the estimated taxes had been paid on April 15, 1989 (172 F3d 918).

On certiorari, the United States Supreme Court affirmed. In an opinion by THOMAS, J., expressing the unanimous view of the court, it was held that the § 6511(b)(2)(A) ceiling on the requested $1,175 was zero, because, rather than being paid within the look-back period, both the withholding and the estimated taxes had been "paid" on April 15, 1989, as for purposes of § 6511, (1) § 6513(b)(1) of the IRC (26 USCS § 6513(b)(1)) provided that income tax withheld from a taxpayer was deemed to have been paid on the fifteenth day of the fourth month following the close of the taxpayer's taxable year, and (2) § 6513(b)(2) of the IRC (26 USCS § 6513(b)(2)) provided that estimated income tax for any taxable year was deemed to have been paid on the last day prescribed for filing a tax return under § 6012 of the IRC (26 USCS § 6012), which required calendar year taxpayers to file on the April 15 following the close of the calendar year.

COUNSEL

Walter J. Rockler argued the cause for petitioner.
Kent L. Jones argued the cause for respondent.

CHAD WEISGRAM, et al., Petitioners

v

MARLEY COMPANY et al.

528 US 440, 145 L Ed 2d 958, 120 S Ct 1011

[No. 99-161]

Argued January 18, 2000.
Decided February 22, 2000.

Decision: Federal Court of Appeals held to have appropriately directed entry of judgment as matter of law upon determination that (1) some evidence was erroneously admitted at trial, and (2) remaining evidence was insufficient to support verdict.

SUMMARY

A plaintiff, individually and on behalf of his mother's heirs, brought a diversity action in the United States District Court for the District of North Dakota against the manufacturer of an electric baseboard heater. The plaintiff, presenting a strict products liability claim under North Dakota law, sought wrongful death damages on the theory that a defect in the heater had caused a house fire and the death of the plaintiff's mother. At trial, the plaintiff introduced the testimony of three witnesses, proffered as experts, in an endeavor to prove the alleged defect and a causal connection between the defect and the fire. The District Court overruled the manufacturer's objections, lodged before and during the trial, that this testimony was unreliable and thus inadmissible under Rule 702 of the Federal Rules of Evidence. Also, the manufacturer unsuccessfully moved under Rule 50 of the Federal

Rules of Civil Procedure (FRCP) for judgment as a
matter of law on the ground that the plaintiff had
allegedly failed to meet the burden of proof on the
issues of defect and causation. The jury returned a
verdict for the plaintiff. The manufacturer, reasserting
that the expert testimony was unreliable and thus
inadmissible, again requested judgment as a matter of
law and also requested, in the alternative, a new trial
pursuant to Rules 50 and 59 of the FRCP. The District
Court denied the motions and entered judgment for
the plaintiff. On appeal, the United States Court of
Appeals for the Eighth Circuit—in vacating the District
Court's judgment and in ordering a remand of the case
with instructions to grant the manufacturer judgment
as a matter of law—(1) concluded that the expert
testimony was unreliable and therefore inadmissible
under Rule 702; (2) considered the remaining evidence in the light most favorable to the plaintiff; (3)
found such evidence insufficient to support the jury
verdict; and (4) rejected the contention that the Court
of Appeals was required to order a remand for a new
trial, as (a) the case was not a close one, (b) the plaintiff
had had a fair opportunity to prove the strict liability
claim, and (c) there was no reason to give the plaintiff
a second chance (169 F3d 514). In a petition for
rehearing, the plaintiff argued that the Court of Appeals (1) had misapplied North Dakota law, (2) did not
have the authority to direct judgment, and (3) had
failed to give adequate deference to the District Court's
evidentiary rulings. The Court of Appeals denied rehearing (1999 US App LEXIS 7977).

On certiorari, the United States Supreme Court
affirmed. In an opinion by GINSBURG, J., expressing the
unanimous view of the court, it was held that (1) under
Rule 50, a Court of Appeals may appropriately direct a
District Court to enter judgment for a jury-verdict loser

as a matter of law upon the Court of Appeals' determination that some of the verdict winner's evidence was erroneously admitted at trial and that the verdict winner's remaining and properly admitted evidence is insufficient to constitute a submissible case, where the Court of Appeals concludes that (a) the verdict winner has had a full and fair opportunity to present the case, including arguments for a new trial, and (b) further proceedings are thus unwarranted; (2) under such circumstances, the Court of Appeals need not remand the case to the District Court for a determination whether (a) final judgment should be entered for the verdict loser, or (b) a new trial should be ordered; and (3) under the circumstances in the case at hand, the Court of Appeals did not abuse its discretion by directing the District Court to enter judgment for the manufacturer as a matter of law.

APPEARANCES OF COUNSEL ARGUING CASE

Paul A. Strandness argued the cause for petitioners.

Christine A. Hogan argued the cause for respondents.

_____

HUNT-WESSON, INC., Petitioner

v

FRANCHISE TAX BOARD OF CALIFORNIA

528 US 458, 145 L Ed 2d 974, 120 S Ct 1022

[No. 98-2043]

Argued January 12, 2000.
Decided February 22, 2000.

Decision: California's interest-deduction-offset provision held to constitute impermissible taxation of income outside state's jurisdictional reach, in violation of due process clause of Federal Constitution's Fourteenth Amendment and Constitution's commerce clause (Art I, § 8, cl 3).

SUMMARY

Pursuant to the requirements of the Federal Constitution's commerce clause (Art I, § 8, cl 3) and the due process clause of the Constitution's Fourteenth Amendment, a state could tax a proportionate share of the "unitary" income of a nondomiciliary corporation that carried out a particular business both inside and outside of the state. However, the state could not tax "nonunitary" income received by a nondomiciliary corporation from an unrelated business activity which constituted a discrete business enterprise. California's unitary system for determining the state's taxable share of a multistate corporation's business income authorized a deduction for interest expense, but generally permitted use of that deduction only to the extent that the amount exceeded certain out-of-state income arising from the unrelated business activity of a discrete

81

business enterprise. A corporation was a successor in interest to a nondomiciliary business of California that incurred interest expense during the years at issue. California disallowed the deduction for that expense insofar as the nondomiciliary business had received relevant nonunitary dividend and interest income. The successor corporation challenged the constitutional validity of the disallowance. The California Court of Appeal found the disallowance constitutional, and the California Supreme Court denied review (1999 Cal LEXIS 1672).

On certiorari, the United States Supreme Court reversed the judgment of the California Court of Appeal and remanded the case for further proceedings. In an opinion by BREYER, J., expressing the unanimous view of the court, it was held that California's interest-deduction-offset provision constituted impermissible taxation of income outside the state's jurisdictional reach, in violation of the due process clause and the commerce clause, as, among other matters, the provision (1) denied a taxpayer use of a portion of a deduction from unitary income, (2) measured the amount of additional unitary income that became subject to taxation by precisely the amount of nonunitary income that a taxpayer had received, and (3) assumed that a corporation that borrowed any money at all had really borrowed that money to purchase or carry the corporation's nonunitary investments.

COUNSEL

Walter Hellerstein argued the cause for petitioner.
David Lew argued the cause for respondent.

ERNEST C. ROE, Warden, Petitioner

v

LUCIO FLORES-ORTEGA

528 US 470, 145 L Ed 2d 985, 120 S Ct 1029

[No. 98-1441]

Argued November 1, 1999.
Decided February 23, 2000.

Decision: Strickland v Washington (1984) 466 US 668,
80 L Ed 2d 674, 104 S Ct 2052, held to provide
proper framework for evaluating claim that criminal defense counsel was constitutionally ineffective
for failing to file notice of appeal.

SUMMARY

An accused pleaded guilty in a California court to
second-degree murder. At sentencing, the trial judge
advised the accused that there were 60 days for the
accused to file an appeal. While the accused's counsel
wrote "bring appeal papers" in a file, no notice of
appeal was filed within that time. The accused's following attempt to file such notice was rejected as untimely,
and efforts to secure state habeas corpus relief were
unsuccessful. Subsequently, the accused filed a federal
habeas corpus petition, alleging constitutionally ineffective assistance of counsel on the basis of the attorney's failure to file the notice of appeal after allegedly
promising to do so. The United States District Court for
the Eastern District of California denied relief. However, the United States Court of Appeals for the Ninth
Circuit reversed, finding that the accused was entitled
to relief because, under the Court of Appeals' prece-

dent, a habeas corpus petitioner needed only to show that counsel's failure to file a notice of appeal was without the petitioner's consent (160 F3d 534, 1998 US App LEXIS 27933).

On certiorari, the United States Supreme Court vacated and remanded the case for further proceedings. In an opinion by O'CONNOR, J., expressing the unanimous view of the court as to holding 2 below, and otherwise joined by REHNQUIST, Ch. J., and SCALIA, KENNEDY, THOMAS, and BREYER, JJ., it was held that Strickland v Washington (1984) 466 US 668, 80 L Ed 2d 674, 104 S Ct 2052, provided the proper framework for evaluating a claim that counsel was constitutionally ineffective for failing to file a notice of appeal, as, among other matters, (1) counsel had a constitutionally imposed duty to consult the criminal defendant only when there was reason to think either that (a) a rational defendant would have wanted to appeal, or (b) a particular defendant reasonably demonstrated to counsel that he was interested in appealing; and (2) the defendant was required to demonstrate that there was a reasonable probability that, but for counsel's deficient failure to consult with him about an appeal, the defendant would have timely appealed.

BREYER, J., concurring, expressed the view that counsel almost always had a constitutional duty to consult with a criminal defendant about an appeal after a trial.

SOUTER, J., joined by STEVENS and GINSBURG, JJ., concurring in part and dissenting in part, expressed the view that (1) a lawyer had a duty to consult with a client about the choice to appeal almost always in those criminal cases in which a plea of guilty had not obviously waived any claims of error, and (2) the failure to do that in the case at hand violated the objective reasonableness standard in Strickland v Washington.

GINSBURG, J., concurring in part and dissenting in part, expressed the view that the duty to consult was not satisfied in this case.

COUNSEL

Paul E. O'Connor argued the cause for petitioner.

Edward C. DuMont argued the cause for the United States, as amicus curiae, by special leave of court.

Quin Denvir argued the cause for respondent.

HAROLD F. RICE, Petitioner

v

BENJAMIN J. CAYETANO, Governor of Hawaii

528 US 495, 145 L Ed 2d 1007, 120 S Ct 1044

[No. 98-818]

Argued October 6, 1999.
Decided February 23, 2000.

Decision: Hawaii statute permitting only "Hawaiians"—that is, descendants of aboriginal peoples inhabiting Hawaiian Islands in 1778—to vote for trustees of state agency held to violate Federal Constitution's Fifteenth Amendment.

SUMMARY

In 1921, Congress enacted the Hawaiian Homes Commission Act (HHCA) with the purpose of rehabilitating the native Hawaiian population, which was defined to include "any descendant of not less than one-half part of the blood of the races inhabiting the Hawaiian Islands previous to 1778." Upon Hawaii's admission as a state in 1959, a federal statute granting Hawaii title to public lands provided that those lands—and the proceeds and income that the lands generated—were to be held as a public trust for various purposes, including the betterment of the conditions of native Hawaiians. In 1978, Hawaii established the Office of Hawaiian Affairs (OHA), a state agency that was to be (1) independent from other branches of state government; and (2) responsible for programs and activities relating to (a) "native Hawaiians," the statutory definition of which term incorporated the definition given by the HHCA, and (b) "Hawaiians," defined by state statute as descendants of the aboriginal peoples inhabiting the Hawaiian Islands in 1778. Among the OHA's responsibilities was the administration of a share of the revenue from some of the lands granted to Hawaii upon admission. The OHA was overseen by a board of trustees who were required by state statute to be elected by "Hawaiians." A citizen of Hawaii who was not a "Hawaiian" as statutorily defined applied to vote in an election for OHA trustees, but the state denied his application. The citizen, alleging that his exclusion from the election violated the Federal Constitution's Fourteenth and Fifteenth Amendments, brought suit in the United States District Court for the District of Hawaii against Hawaii's governor. The District Court granted summary judgment to the state on the grounds that (1) Congress and Hawaii had recognized a guardian-ward relationship with the native Hawaiians, (2) this relationship was analogous to the relationship between the United States and the Indian tribes, (3) the electoral scheme was rationally related to the state's responsibilities toward the native Hawaiians, and (4) the voting restriction did not violate the Constitution's ban on racial classifications (963 F Supp 1547). The United States Court of Appeals for the Ninth Circuit affirmed (146 F3d 1075).

On certiorari, the United States Supreme Court reversed. In an opinion by KENNEDY, J., joined by REHNQUIST, Ch. J., and O'CONNOR, SCALIA, and THOMAS, JJ., it was held that Hawaii's electoral qualification at issue violated the Fifteenth Amendment, because the qualification was a racial classification that was not sustainable under (1) Supreme Court cases (a) allowing the differential treatment of Indian tribes, or (b) holding that the Fourteenth Amendment's one-person, one-vote requirement did not pertain to some special-purpose election districts; or (2) an argument that the voting restriction did no more than insure an alignment of interests between fiduciaries and beneficiaries of a trust.

BREYER, J., joined by SOUTER, J., concurring in the result, expressed the view that Hawaii could not justify the electoral qualification through analogy to a trust for an Indian tribe, because (1) for purposes of the case at hand, there was no "trust" for native Hawaiians, and (2) the OHA's electorate, as defined in the state statute, did not sufficiently resemble an Indian tribe.

STEVENS, J., joined in part (as to point 1 below) by GINSBURG, J., dissenting, expressed the view that (1) the election provision was justified under the Fourteenth Amendment, because (a) legislation targeting native Hawaiians had to be evaluated according to the same understanding of equal protection that has been applied to Indians, that is, that special treatment must be tied rationally to the fulfillment of Congress' unique obligation toward native peoples, and (b) the election provision rationally furthered such a governmental purpose; and (2) the election provision did not violate the Fifteenth Amendment, because (a) ancestry was not a proxy for race under the circumstances presented, and (b) the ancestry classification was based on the permissible assumption that "Hawaiians" had a claim to compensation and self-determination that others did not have.

GINSBURG, J., dissenting, expressed the view that (1) Congress' prerogative to enter into special trust relationships with indigenous peoples was not confined to tribal Indians, but encompassed native Hawaiians; (2) this federal trust responsibility had been delegated by Congress to Hawaii; (3) the voting scheme at issue was tied rationally to the fulfillment of that obligation; and

(4) no more was needed to demonstrate the validity of the voting provision under the Fourteenth and Fifteenth Amendments.

COUNSEL

Theodore B. Olson argued the cause for petitioner.

Edwin S. Kneedler argued the cause for the United States, as amicus curiae, by special leave of court.

John G. Roberts, Jr. argued the cause for respondent.

MARK ROTELLA, Petitioner

v

ANGELA M. WOOD et al.

528 US 549, 145 L Ed 2d 1047, 120 S Ct 1075

[No. 98-896]

Argued November 3, 1999.
Decided February 23, 2000.

Decision: "Injury and pattern discovery" rule held not
to govern start of limitations period for civil treble
damages action under Racketeer Influenced and
Corrupt Organizations Act (RICO) (18 USCS §§
1961 et seq.).

SUMMARY

The Racketeer Influenced and Corrupt Organizations Act (RICO) (18 USCS §§ 1961 et seq.) provides
that (1) it is unlawful to conduct an enterprise's affairs
through a pattern of racketeering activity (18 USCS
§ 1962(c)), (2) a pattern requires at least two acts of
racketeering activity, the last of which occurs within 10
years after the commission of a prior act (18 USCS
§ 1962(c)), and (3) a person injured by a RICO violation can bring a civil RICO action (18 USCS § 1964(c)).
The United States Supreme Court, in Agency Holding
Corp. v Malley-Duff & Associates, Inc. (1987) 483 US
143, 97 L Ed 2d 121, 107 S Ct 2759, determined that the
limitations period applicable to a civil RICO action was
the 4-year period applicable to the Clayton Act (15
USCS § 15b). In 1997, a former patient of a psychiatric
facility brought an action in the United States District
Court for the Northern District of Texas, which action
90

alleged that a group of doctors and their related business entities had violated RICO by improperly conspiring to admit, treat, and retain the patient at the facility for reasons related to their own financial interests rather than the patient's psychiatric condition. The patient had been admitted to the facility in 1985 and discharged in 1986. In 1994, the facility's parent company and one of its directors had pleaded guilty to charges of criminal fraud perpetrated through improper relationships and illegal agreements between the company and its doctors, and the patient had learned of the plea agreement in the same year. The District Court (1) expressed the view that (a) the limitations period for civil RICO claims began to run when the plaintiff discovered his injury, and (b) under this "injury discovery" rule the limitations period expired in 1990; and (2) ordered summary judgment for the defendants. The patient appealed to the United States Court of Appeals for the Fifth Circuit and argued that the RICO limitations period did not begin to run until he had discovered, or should have discovered, both the injury and the pattern of racketeering activity. However, the Court of Appeals affirmed the decision of the District Court (147 F3d 438).

On certiorari, the Supreme Court affirmed. In an opinion by SOUTER, J., expressing the unanimous view of the court, it was held that the patient's action was not timely, because the start of the 4-year limitations period applicable to a civil RICO action was not governed by an "injury and pattern discovery" accrual rule—under which such a civil claim would accrue only when the claimant discovered, or should have discovered, both an injury and a pattern of racketeering activity—as (1) the injury-and-pattern-discovery rule would extend the potential limitations period for most civil RICO cases well beyond the time when a plaintiff's cause of action

91

was complete; (2) such a rule would have allowed proof more remote from time of trial and, hence, litigation more at odds with the basic policies of limitations provisions; (3) in the circumstance of medical malpractice, a person suffering from inadequate treatment was responsible for determining within the limitations period then running whether the inadequacy was malpractice; (4) there was no good reason for accepting a lesser degree of responsibility on a RICO plaintiff's part; (5) there was a clear legislative record of congressional reliance on the Clayton Act when RICO was under consideration; and (6) the Clayton Act's injury-focused accrual rule was well established by the time civil RICO was enacted.

COUNSEL

Richard P. Hogan, Jr. argued the cause for petitioner.

Charles T. Frazier, Jr. argued the cause for respondents.

VILLAGE OF WILLOWBROOK, et al., Petitioners

v

GRACE OLECH

528 US 562, 145 L Ed 2d 1060, 120 S Ct 1073

[No. 98-1288]

Argued January 10, 2000.
Decided February 23, 2000.

Decision: Fourteenth Amendment's equal protection clause held to give rise to cause of action on behalf of "class of one" where property owner's equal protection claim against village did not allege membership in class or group.

SUMMARY

A married couple asked a village to connect their property to the municipal water supply. After the couple objected to the village's conditioning of the connection on the couple's granting the village a 33-foot easement—where the couple asserted that the village required only a 15-foot easement from other property owners who sought access to the water supply—the village, following some delay, agreed to provide the couple water service with a 15-foot easement. The wife, whose husband had died, brought against the village in a Federal District Court a suit alleging that the village's demand of an additional 18-foot easement had violated the equal protection clause of the Federal Constitution's Fourteenth Amendment. The wife, who did not allege membership in a class or group, asserted that (1) the 33-foot easement demand was (a) "irrational and wholly arbi-

93

trary," (b) motivated by ill will resulting from the couple's previous filing of an unrelated unsuccessful lawsuit against the village; and (2) the village had acted either (a) with the intent to deprive the wife of her rights, or (b) in reckless disregard of her rights. The District Court dismissed the suit pursuant to Rule 12(b)(6) of the Federal Rules of Civil Procedure for failure to state a cognizable claim under the equal protection clause. The United States Court of Appeals for the Seventh Circuit, in reversing, expressed the view that the wife's complaint alleged an equal protection claim by asserting that the village's action was motivated solely by spite (160 F3d 386).

On certiorari, the United States Supreme Court affirmed. In a per curiam opinion expressing the view of REHNQUIST, Ch. J., and STEVENS, O'CONNOR, SCALIA, KENNEDY, SOUTER, THOMAS, and GINSBURG, JJ., it was held that (1) the wife's complaint could fairly be construed as alleging that the village intentionally had demanded a 33-foot easement as a condition of connecting her property to the municipal water supply, while requiring only a 15-foot easement from other similarly situated property owners; and (2) this allegation, combined with the allegations in the wife's complaint that the village's demand was "irrational and wholly arbitrary" and that the village ultimately connected her property after receiving a clearly adequate 15-foot easement, were sufficient to state a claim for relief as a "class of one" under traditional equal protection analysis.

BREYER, J., concurring in the result, expressed the view that this case did not directly raise the question whether the simple and common instance of a faulty zoning decision would violate the equal protection clause.

COUNSEL

James L. DeAno argued the cause for petitioners.

Irving L. Gornstein argued the cause for the United States, as amicus curiae, by special leave of court.

John R. Wimmer argued the cause for respondent.

DONNA E. SHALALA, Secretary of Health and Human Services, et al., Petitioners

v

ILLINOIS COUNCIL ON LONG TERM CARE, INC.

529 US —, 146 L Ed 2d 1, 120 S Ct 1084

[No. 98-1109]

Argued November 8, 1999.
Decided February 29, 2000.

Decision: 42 USCS § 405(h), as incorporated by 42 USCS § 1395ii, held to bar nursing home association from invoking federal-question jurisdiction (28 USCS § 1331) to challenge validity of Medicare enforcement regulations.

SUMMARY

Under the Medicare Act (42 USCS §§ 1395 et seq.), 42 USCS § 1395cc(b)(2) gives the United States Secretary of Health and Human Services power to terminate a provider agreement with a nursing home where, for example, the Secretary determines that a home has failed to comply substantially with the statute and the regulations. According to 42 USCS § 1395cc(h)(1), a nursing home that is dissatisfied with a determination described in § 1395cc(b)(2) is entitled to (1) an administrative hearing to the same extent as is provided in the Social Security Act (42 USCS § 405(b)), and (2) judicial review of the final decision of the Secretary after such hearing as is provided in 42 USCS § 405(g). An association of nursing homes did not rely on these provisions when it (1) filed suit in the United States District Court for the Northern District of Illinois against defendants including the Secretary, and (2) challenged the validity of Medicare regulations that imposed sanctions or remedies on nursing homes that violated certain substantive standards. Rather, the association of nursing homes invoked federal-question jurisdiction (28 USCS § 1331). The District Court (1) dismissed the case for lack of jurisdiction, and (2) found that 42 USCS § 405(h), as interpreted in Weinberger v Salfi (1975) 422 US 749, 45 L Ed 2d 522, 95 S Ct 2457, and Heckler v Ringer (1984) 466 US 602, 80 L Ed 2d 622, 104 S Ct 2013, barred a § 1331 suit. The United States Court of Appeals for the Seventh Circuit reversed, expressing the view that Bowen v Michigan Academy of Family Physicians (1986) 476 US 667, 90 L Ed 2d 623, 106 S Ct 2133, had significantly modified such earlier case law (143 F3d 1072, 1998 US App LEXIS 9313).

On certiorari, the United States Supreme Court reversed. In an opinion by BREYER J., joined by REHNQUIST, Ch. J., and O'CONNOR, SOUTER, and GINSBURG, JJ., it was held that the association of nursing homes was barred from invoking federal-question jurisdiction under § 1331 to challenge the validity of Medicare enforcement regulations, as, among other matters, § 405(h), as incorporated into the Medicare Act by 42 USCS § 1395ii, (1) provided that no action to recover on any claim arising under the Medicare laws would be brought under federal-question jurisdiction, and (2) channeled most, if not all, Medicare claims through a special administrative review system.

STEVENS, J., dissenting, expressed the view that the language in § 1395ii that made § 405(h) applicable to the Medicare Act to the same extent as that section applied to the Social Security Act encompassed claims made by patients, but did not necessarily encompass providers' challenges to the regulations of the Secretary.

SCALIA, J., dissenting, expressed the view that there was no basis for holding that (1) 1395ii had a different meaning with regard to Medicare Part A than with regard to Part B, or (2) the subsequent addition of a judicial-review provision related to § 1395ii altered the determination pronounced in Bowen v Michigan Academy of Family Physicians.

THOMAS, J., joined by STEVENS and KENNEDY, JJ., and joined in part (as to point 1 below) by SCALIA, J., dissenting, expressed the view that (1) § 1395ii, as interpreted by Bowen v Michigan Academy of Family Physicians, did not, in the case at hand, incorporate § 405(h)'s preclusion of federal-question jurisdiction; and (2) this conclusion was especially correct in light of the presumption in favor of pre-enforcement review.

COUNSEL

Jeffrey A. Lamken argued the cause for petitioner.

Kimball R. Anderson argued the cause for respondent.

UNITED STATES, Petitioner

v

ROY LEE JOHNSON

529 US —, 146 L Ed 2d 39, 120 S Ct 1114

[No. 98-1696]

Argued December 8, 1999.
Decided March 1, 2000.

Decision: 18 USCS § 3624(c) held not to reduce length
of supervised release term by reason of excess time
served in prison.

SUMMARY

An accused was convicted in a Federal District Court
for multiple violations of federal criminal provisions,
including two counts of possession with an intent to
distribute controlled substances. The accused was sentenced terms of imprisonment for the violations and, in
addition, a 3-year mandatory term of supervised release
for the drug possession offenses. While the accused was
serving time in a federal prison, two of his convictions,
not including the drug possession convictions, were
declared invalid. As a result, the accused had served too
much prison time. The District Court ordered his
immediate release. The accused filed a motion requesting that the District Court reduce his supervised release
term by 2.5 years, which was the amount of extra time
he had served on the vacated convictions. The District
Court denied relief, and explained that (1) pursuant to
18 USCS § 3624(e), the supervised release commenced
upon the accused's actual release from incarceration,
not before, and (2) granting the accused credit would

undermine Congress' aim of using supervised release to assist convicted felons in their transitions to community life. However, the United States Court of Appeals for the Sixth Circuit (1) accepted the accused's argument that his term of supervised release commenced when his lawful term of imprisonment expired, and (2) reversed the decision of the District Court (154 F3d 569).

On certiorari, the United States Supreme Court reversed the judgment of the Court of Appeals and remanded the case for further proceedings. In an opinion by KENNEDY, J., expressing the unanimous view of the court, it was held that the accused's excess prison time should not have been credited to his term of supervised release, because under § 3624(e), the accused's term of supervised release began on the date of his actual release from incarceration, as, among other matters, (1) the language of § 3624(e) directed that a supervised release term did not commence until an accused was "released from imprisonment"; (2) the ordinary and commonsense meaning of "release" was to be freed from confinement; and (3) § 3624(e) also provided that (a) a term of supervised release came after imprisonment, once the prisoner was released by the Bureau of Prisons to the supervision of a probation officer, and (b) supervised release did not run while an individual remained in the custody of the Bureau.

COUNSEL

Barbara B. McDowell argued the cause for petitioner. Kevin M. Schad argued the cause for respondent.

LEONARD PORTUONDO, Superintendent, Fishkill
Correctional Facility, Petitioner

v

RAY AGARD

529 US —, 146 L Ed 2d 47, 120 S Ct 1119

[No. 98-1170]

Argued November 1, 1999.
Decided March 6, 2000.

Decision: Prosecutor's comments that accused had
opportunity to hear all other witnesses before
testifying and tailor testimony accordingly held not
to violate accused's rights under Federal Constitution's Fifth, Sixth, or Fourteenth Amendments.

SUMMARY

At the trial of one accused of multiple criminal
charges in the state of New York, the accused gave
testimony that conflicted with the testimony of the
alleged victim and the alleged victim's friend. During
summation, the prosecutor challenged the accused's
credibility by calling the jury's attention to the fact that
the accused had the opportunity to (1) hear all other
witnesses testify, and (2) tailor testimony accordingly.
The trial court rejected the accused's objection that
these comments violated the accused's right to be
present at trial. The accused was convicted of one count
of sodomy and two counts of possession of a weapon.
On direct appeal, the New York Supreme Court reversed one of the accused's convictions for possession
of a weapon, but affirmed the remaining convictions
(199 App Div 2d 401, 606 NYS2d 239). The New York

Court of Appeals denied leave to appeal (83 NY2d 868, 613 NYS2d 129, 635 NE2d 298). The accused then filed a habeas corpus petition in a Federal District Court and included claims that the prosecutor's comments violated the accused's (1) rights under the Federal Constitution's Fifth and Sixth Amendments to be present at trial and confront his accusers, and (2) right to due process under the Constitution's Fourteenth Amendment. The District Court denied the habeas corpus petition, but the United States Court of Appeals for the Second Circuit reversed, expressing the view that the prosecutor's comments violated the accused's Fifth, Sixth, and Fourteenth Amendment rights (117 F3d 696, rehearing denied 159 F3d 98).

On certiorari, the United States Supreme Court reversed and remanded. In an opinion by SCALIA, J., joined by REHNQUIST, Ch. J., and O'CONNOR, KENNEDY, and THOMAS, JJ., it was held that the prosecutor's comments at issue did not violate the accused's rights, under the Fifth and Sixth Amendments, to be present at trial, to be confronted with the witnesses against him, or to testify on his own behalf—and also did not violate the accused's right to due process under the Fourteenth Amendment—as, among other matters, it was natural and irresistible for the jury, in evaluating the relative credibility of an accused who testified last, to have in mind and weigh in the balance the fact that the accused had heard the testimony of the preceding witnesses.

STEVENS, J., joined by BREYER, J., concurring in the judgment, expressed the view that while the prosecutor's argument in the case at hand survived constitutional scrutiny, states or trial courts were not deprived of the power to (1) prevent such prosecutor comment entirely, or (2) provide juries with instructions that explained the necessity, and the justification, for a defendant's attendance at trial.

GINSBURG, J., joined by SOUTER, J., dissenting, expressed the view that (1) when a defendant's exercise of a constitutional right is insolubly ambiguous as between innocence and guilt, a prosecutor may not unfairly encumber the right by urging the jury to construe the ambiguity against the defendant, and (2) that principle ought to decide the case at hand, in which the irrebuttable prosecutorial comment at issue, tied only to the accused's presence in the courtroom and not to his actual testimony, tarnished the innocent no less than the guilty.

COUNSEL

Andrew Zwerling argued the cause for petitioner.

Jonathan A. Nuechterlein argued the cause for the United States, as amicus curiae, by special leave of court.

Beverly Van Ness argued the cause for respondent.

UNITED STATES, Petitioner

v

GARY LOCKE, Governor of Washington, et al. (No.
98-1701)

INTERNATIONAL ASSOCIATION OF INDEPEN-
DENT TANKER OWNERS (INTERTANKO), Petitioner

v

GARY LOCKE, Governor of Washington, et al. (No.
98-1706)

529 US —, 146 L Ed 2d 69, 120 S Ct 1135

Argued December 7, 1999.
Decided March 6, 2000.

Decision: State of Washington's rules regarding oil
tanker ship crew training and English language
skills, navigation watch, and marine casualty reporting held pre-empted by federal law; case remanded so validity of other Washington tanker
rules could be assessed.

SUMMARY

A trade association that represented operators of oil
tanker ships brought, in the United States District
Court for the Western District of Washington, a suit
seeking declaratory and injunctive relief against state
and local officials who were responsible for enforcing
certain Washington rules that imposed tanker design,
equipment, reporting, and operating requirements.
Environmental groups intervened in defense of the
rules. The District Court, rejecting the trade associa-

tion's arguments that the rules invaded areas long occupied by the Federal Government and imposed unique requirements in an area where national uniformity was mandated, upheld the rules (947 F Supp 1484). After the United States intervened on the trade association's behalf at the appeal stage, the United States Court of Appeals for the Ninth Circuit determined that the state could enforce all of the rules except one that required tankers to install certain navigation and towing equipment (148 F3d 1053). The Court of Appeals denied petitions for rehearing en banc (159 F3d 1220).

On certiorari, the United States Supreme Court reversed and remanded. In an opinion by KENNEDY, J., expressing the unanimous view of the court, it was held that (1) three of the state rules—one that required a comprehensive training program for tanker crews, one that imposed English language proficiency requirements on tanker crews, and one that imposed certain navigation watch requirements—were pre-empted by 46 USCS § 3703(a), which required the United States Coast Guard to issue regulations for the design, construction, alteration, repair, maintenance, operation, equipping, personnel qualifications, and manning of tankers; (2) a fourth state rule, which required tankers to report certain marine casualties, was pre-empted by other sources of federal regulation of the same subject; and (3) the case would be remanded so that the Court of Appeals or the District Court could consider, after the development of a full record by all interested parties, whether the remaining state rules at issue were pre-empted by federal law.

COUNSEL

C. Jonathan Benner argued the cause for petitioner in No. 98-1706.

David C. Frederick argued the cause for petitioner in No. 98-1701.

William B. Collins argued the cause for respondents.

FOOD AND DRUG ADMINISTRATION, et al., Petitioners

v

BROWN & WILLIAMSON TOBACCO CORPORATION et al.

529 US —, 146 L Ed 2d 121, 120 S Ct 1291

[No. 98-1152]

Argued December 1, 1999.
Decided March 21, 2000.

Decision: Congress held to have precluded Food and Drug Administration from asserting jurisdiction to regulate tobacco products.

SUMMARY

Under the Food, Drug, and Cosmetic Act (FDCA) (21 USCS §§ 301 et seq.), the Food and Drug Administration (FDA) was granted the authority to regulate, among other items, "drugs" and "devices." In August 1996, the FDA asserted jurisdiction to regulate tobacco products in the United States after concluding that, under the FDCA, (1) nicotine was a "drug," (2) cigarettes and smokeless tobacco were "devices" that delivered nicotine to the body, and (3) therefore, the FDA had jurisdiction to regulate those tobacco products as customarily marketed, that is, without manufacturer claims of therapeutic benefit. Pursuant to this asserted authority, the FDA promulgated regulations governing tobacco products' advertising, promotion, labeling, and accessibility to children and adolescents. By reducing tobacco use by minors, the regulations aimed substantially to reduce the prevalence of addic-

107

tion and thus, the incidence of tobacco-related death and disease. A group of tobacco manufacturers, retailers, and advertisers (1) filed, in the United States District Court for the Middle District of North Carolina, a suit challenging the FDA's regulations, and (2) moved for summary judgment on the claimed grounds that (a) the FDA lacked jurisdiction to regulate tobacco products as customarily marketed, (b) the regulations exceeded the FDA's authority under 21 USCS § 360j(e), and (c) the advertising restrictions violated the Federal Constitution's First Amendment. Granting the respondents' motion in part and denying the motion in part, the District Court (1) ruled that (a) the FDCA authorized the FDA to regulate tobacco products as they were customarily marketed, (b) the FDA's access and labeling regulations were permissible, and (c) the FDA's advertising and promotion restrictions exceeded the agency's authority under § 360j(e); (2) stayed implementation of the regulations which the court found valid (except the prohibition on the sale of tobacco products to minors); and (3) certified the court's order for immediate interlocutory appeal (966 F Supp 1374). Without addressing whether the regulations exceeded the FDA's authority under § 360j(e) or violated the First Amendment, the United States Court of Appeals for the Fourth Circuit reversed, expressing the view that Congress had not granted the FDA jurisdiction to regulate tobacco products (153 F3d 155).

On certiorari, the United States Supreme Court affirmed. In an opinion by O'CONNOR, J., joined by REHNQUIST, Ch. J., and SCALIA, KENNEDY, and THOMAS, JJ., it was held that Congress had clearly precluded the FDA from asserting jurisdiction to regulate tobacco products as customarily marketed—that is, without manufacturer claims of therapeutic benefit—as such

FDA authority was inconsistent with (1) the intent that Congress had expressed in the regulatory scheme of the FDCA—requiring that any product regulated by the FDA that was to remain on the market ought to be safe and effective for the product's intended use—and (2) the tobacco-specific legislation that Congress—relying, in part, on the consistent and repeated representations of the FDA, prior to 1995, that the agency had no authority to regulate tobacco—had enacted subsequent to the FDCA.

BREYER, J., joined by STEVENS, SOUTER, and GINSBURG, JJ., dissenting, expressed the view that the FDA had authority to regulate tobacco products, since (1) tobacco products fit within the statutory language of the FDCA; (2) the FDCA's basic purpose—the protection of public health—supported the inclusion of cigarettes within the statute's scope; (3) the FDCA's legislative history established that the FDA had authority to regulate tobacco; (4) the statute-specific arguments against jurisdiction were based on erroneous assumptions; (5) the inferences drawn from later legislative history were not persuasive; (6) the fact that the FDA had changed the scope of the agency's own jurisdiction was legally insignificant; and (7) the degree of accountability that would likely have attached to the FDA's action in the case at hand ought to have alleviated any concern that Congress, rather than an administrative agency, ought to make this important regulatory decision.

COUNSEL

Seth P. Waxman argued the cause for petitioners.

Richard M. Cooper argued the cause for respondents.

CORTEZ BYRD CHIPS INC., Petitioner

v

BILL HARBERT CONSTRUCTION CO., A DIVISION OF BILL HARBERT INTERNATIONAL, INC.

529 US —, 146 L Ed 2d 171, 120 S Ct 1331

[No. 98-1960]

Argued January 10, 2000.
Decided March 21, 2000.

Decision: Venue provisions of Federal Arbitration Act (9 USCS §§ 9-11) held to allow motion to confirm, vacate, or modify to be brought in district where award was made or in any district proper under general venue statute.

SUMMARY

The venue provisions of the Federal Arbitration Act (FAA) (9 USCS §§ 9-11) provide that (1) if no court is specified in an agreement of the parties, application for an order confirming an arbitration award may be made to the United States court in and for the district within which the award was made, and (2) the United States court in and for the district wherein the award was made may (a) make an order vacating the award upon the application of any party to the arbitration in any of five enumerated situations, and (b) make an order modifying or correcting the award upon the application of any party to the arbitration. Two companies agreed that the first company would build a wood chip mill for the second company in Brookhaven, Mississippi. Under the agreement, (1) all disputes relating to the agreement, or a breach thereof, would be decided

111

by arbitration unless the parties mutually agreed otherwise, (2) an award rendered by an arbitrator or arbitrators would be final, (3) judgment could be entered upon it in accordance with applicable law in any court having jurisdiction thereof, (4) the agreement to arbitrate would be specifically enforceable under applicable law in any court having jurisdiction thereof, and (5) the law of the place where the project was located, Mississippi, would govern. After a dispute arose, the first company invoked the agreement by a filing with the Atlanta office of the American Arbitration Association, which conducted arbitration in November 1997 in Birmingham, Alabama. The next month, the arbitration panel issued an award in favor of the first company. In January 1998, the second company filed a complaint in the United States District Court for the Southern District of Mississippi, which complaint sought to vacate or modify the arbitration award. The first company then sought to confirm the award by filing an action 7 days later in the United States District Court for the Northern District of Alabama. The Alabama District Court (1) denied a motion by the second company to dismiss, transfer, or stay the Alabama action, (2) concluded that venue was proper only in the Northern District of Alabama, and (3) entered judgment for the first company. The United States Court of Appeals for the Eleventh Circuit, in affirming, expressed the view that (1) under the FAA's venue provisions, venue for motions to confirm, vacate, or modify awards was exclusively in the district in which the arbitration award was made, and (2) as the arbitration in the present case was held in Birmingham, the rule as so construed limited venue to the Northern District of Alabama (169 F3d 693).

On certiorari, the United States Supreme Court reversed the judgment of the Court of Appeals and remanded the case for further proceedings. In an opinion by SOUTER, J., expressing the unanimous view of the court, it was held that the motion to vacate or modify the award was properly laid in the District Court for the Southern District of Mississippi and, under principles of deference, the District Court for the Northern District of Alabama should have considered staying its hand as to the motion to confirm the award, because the venue provisions of the FAA are permissive, rather than restrictive, and permit a motion to confirm, vacate, or modify an award to be brought either in the district where the award was made or in any district proper under the general venue statute (28 USCS § 1391(a)(2)), as, among other matters, (1) the language of §§ 9-11 did not answer the question whether the provisions are restrictive or permissive, for there was language supporting both views, and (2) the history and function of the provisions confirmed that the provisions were meant to expand, not limit, venue choice.

COUNSEL

Daniel H. Bromberg argued the cause for petitioner. Susan S. Wagner argued the cause for respondent.

WAL-MART STORES, INC., Petitioner

v

SAMARA BROTHERS, INC.

529 US —, 146 L Ed 2d 182, 120 S Ct 1339

[No. 99-150]

Argued January 19, 2000.
Decided March 22, 2000.

Decision: In action for infringement of unregistered
trade dress under § 43(a) of Lanham Act (15 USCS
§ 1125(a)), product's design held to be distinctive,
and therefore protectible, only upon showing of
secondary meaning.

SUMMARY

A company that designed and manufactured children's clothing had as its primary product line a
particular line of spring/summer outfits. A retailer,
which contracted with a supplier to manufacture children's clothing, sent the supplier photographs of a
number of the designer's garments, many of which
contained copyrighted elements. The supplier copied
the garments, with only minor modifications, to produce so-called "knockoffs" that were sold by the retailer and four other retailers. After the designer
brought, against the supplier and the five retailers in
the United States District Court for the Southern
District of New York, an action that alleged, among
other matters, infringement of unregistered trade dress
under § 43(a) of the Lanham Act (15 USCS § 1125(a)),
the supplier and the four other retailers settled before
trial. The jury found in favor of the designer on all of its

claims. The retailer—alleging, among other matters, that there was insufficient evidence to support a conclusion that the copied designs could be legally protected as distinctive trade dress for purposes of § 43(a)—renewed a motion for judgment as a matter of law. However, the District Court denied the motion and awarded the designer damages, interest, costs, fees, and injunctive relief (969 F Supp 895). The United States Court of Appeals for the Second Circuit affirmed the denial of the retailer's motion (165 F3d 120).

On certiorari, the United States Supreme Court reversed and remanded. In an opinion by SCALIA, J., expressing the unanimous view of the court, it was held that a product's design was distinctive, and therefore protectible, in an action for infringement of unregistered trade dress under § 43(a), only upon a showing that the design had developed a secondary meaning, which occurred when the design, even if not inherently distinctive, had, in the minds of the public, the primary significance of identifying the source of the product rather than the product itself.

COUNSEL

William D. Coston argued the cause for petitioner.

Lawrence G. Wallace argued the cause for the United States, as amicus curiae, by special leave of court.

Stuart M. Riback argued the cause for respondent.

BOARD OF REGENTS OF THE UNIVERSITY OF
WISCONSIN SYSTEM, Petitioner

v

SCOTT HAROLD SOUTHWORTH et al.

529 US —, 146 L Ed 2d 193, 120 S Ct 1346

[No. 98-1189]

Argued November 9, 1999.
Decided March 22, 2000.

Decision: First Amendment held to permit public university to charge students mandatory fee to fund extracurricular student speech, where there was viewpoint neutrality in allocation of funding to student organizations engaging in such speech.

SUMMARY

The University of Wisconsin, a public university, required full-time students to pay a nonrefundable student activity fee which was segregated from the university's tuition charge. Part of the fee supported extracurricular activities of registered student organizations that engaged in various forms of political or ideological speech. Such organizations were able to apply for a portion of the fee moneys from (1) a student activity fund administered by the student government, or (2) a student services fund administered through the student government's finance committee. Alternatively, fee moneys could be allocated to such organizations by means of a student referendum. Some students and former students of the university (1) sought declaratory and injunctive relief by filing suit in the United States District Court for the Western District

of Wisconsin against members of the university's board
of regents; and (2) alleged, among other matters, that
(a) the imposition of the fee violated the rights of free
speech and free association under the Federal Constitution's First Amendment, and (b) the university had to
grant objecting students the choice not to fund those
organizations that engaged in political and ideological
expression which was offensive to the objectors' personal beliefs. The parties stipulated that the process for
reviewing and approving allocations from the student
activity fund and the student services fund had been
administered in a viewpoint-neutral fashion. The District Court (1) granted summary judgment to the
plaintiffs, and (2) entered a judgment declaring that
the mandatory segregated fee policy violated the First
Amendment (1996 US Dist LEXIS 20980, amd 1996 US
Dist LEXIS 20990). In a subsequent proceeding, the
District Court enjoined the board of regents from using
segregated fees to fund any student organization engaging in political or ideological speech. The United
States Court of Appeals for the Seventh Circuit (1)
affirmed the District Court's determination that forcing objecting students to fund private organizations
which engaged in political and ideological activities
violated the First Amendment, on the grounds that the
university's fee program (a) was not germane to the
university's mission, (b) did not further a vital policy of
the university, and (c) imposed too much of a burden
on the objecting students' free speech rights; but (2)
reversed and vacated portions of the District Court's
declaratory judgment and injunction (151 F3d 717, reh
den 157 F3d 1124).

On certiorari, the United States Supreme Court (1)
reversed the Court of Appeals' judgment, (2) remanded the case for further proceedings, and (3)
ordered the parties to bear their own costs in the

Supreme Court. In an opinion by KENNEDY, J., joined by REHNQUIST, Ch. J., and O'CONNOR, SCALIA, THOMAS, and GINSBURG, JJ., it was held that (1) the First Amendment permits a public university to charge students a mandatory student activity fee that is used to fund a program to facilitate the free and open exchange of extracurricular student speech, where (a) the university's mission is served by providing students with the means to engage in dynamic extracurricular discussions of philosophical, religious, scientific, social, and political subjects, and (b) there is viewpoint neutrality in the allocation of funding support to student organizations that engage in such speech; (2) the university's viewpoint-neutrality requirement in the process for reviewing and approving allocations from the student activity fund and the student services fund was sufficient, for First Amendment purposes, to protect the rights of objecting students; and (3) a remand was necessary and appropriate to resolve the question of the First Amendment validity of the student referendum mechanism, which appeared to permit the exaction of fees in violation of the viewpoint-neutrality principle.

SOUTER, J., joined by STEVENS and BREYER, JJ., concurring in the judgment, (1) agreed that the university's general disbursement scheme was permissible under the First Amendment; and (2) expressed the view that (a) the First Amendment interest claimed by the objecting students was insufficient to merit protection by anything more than the viewpoint neutrality already accorded by the university, and (b) it was not necessary to impose a cast-iron viewpoint-neutrality requirement to uphold the university's scheme.

COUNSEL

Susan K. Ullman argued the cause for petitioner.

Jordan W. Lorence argued the cause for respondents.

———————

J. WAYNE GARNER, Former Chairman of the State
Board of Pardons and Paroles of Georgia, et al., Petitioners

v

ROBERT L. JONES

529 US —, 146 L Ed 2d 236, 120 S Ct 1362

[No. 99-137]

Argued January 11, 2000.
Decided March 28, 2000.

Decision: Retroactive application of Georgia provision
permitting extension of intervals between parole
considerations held not to necessarily violate Federal Constitution's ex post facto law prohibition.

SUMMARY

An accused—who had (1) begun serving a life sentence after a Georgia conviction for murder, (2) es-
caped from prison, and (3) committed another
murder—was apprehended, convicted of the second
murder, and sentenced to a second life term. At the
time the accused committed his second offense, the
state's board of pardons and paroles required reconsid-
erations of parole to take place every 3 years following
an initial consideration after 7 years. After the accused
had begun serving his second life sentence, the parole
board, acting under statutory authority, amended its
rules to provide that reconsideration of those inmates
serving life sentences who have been denied parole
would take place at least every 8 years. The parole
board (1) considered the accused for parole 7 years
after the second conviction, (2) denied release, and (3)
120

consistent with the amended rule, set reconsideration for 8 years later. The United States Court of Appeals for the Eleventh Circuit, in another case, held that retroactive application of the amended rule violated the prohibition on ex post facto laws contained in Art I, § 10, cl 1 of the Federal Constitution. In compliance with that decision, the parole board reconsidered the accused's case in 3-year intervals, with parole being denied each time. Subsequently, the parole board (1) determined that the United States Supreme Court's decision in California Dep't of Corrections v Morales (1995) 514 US 499, 131 L Ed 2d 588, 115 S Ct 1597, had rejected the rationale underlying the Court of Appeals decision in the other case, and (2) set the accused's next consideration for 8 years after his most recent review. The accused brought an action in the United States District Court for the Northern District of Georgia against individual members of the parole board, which action claimed that the amended rule violated the Constitution's ex post facto law prohibition. The District Court (1) denied the accused's motion for leave to conduct discovery to support his claim, (2) entered summary judgment for the defendants, and (3) expressed the view that the amendment to the parole board rule changed only the timing between reconsideration hearings for inmates sentenced to life in prison, thereby relieving the board of the necessity of holding parole hearings for prisoners who had no reasonable chance of being released. The Court of Appeals for the Eleventh Circuit reversed the judgment of the District Court and expressed the view that (1) the amended rule's retroactive application was necessarily an ex post facto violation, and (2) a parole board policy which permitted inmates, upon a showing of a change in "their circumstance" or where the board received new information, to receive expedited reconsideration for parole was insufficient (164 F3d 589).

On certiorari, the Supreme Court reversed the judgment of the Court of Appeals and remanded the case for further proceedings. In an opinion by KENNEDY, J., joined by REHNQUIST, Ch. J., and O'CONNOR, THOMAS, and BREYER, JJ., it was held that the retroactive application of the amendment to the parole board's rule did not necessarily violate the Constitution's prohibition on ex post facto laws, as (1) the controlling inquiry was whether such a retroactive application created a sufficient risk of increasing the measure of punishment attached to the covered crimes; (2) the requisite risk (a) was not inherent in the framework of the amended rule, and (b) had not otherwise been demonstrated on the record; (3) the Court of Appeals erred in not considering the internal policy statement of the board; and (4) the board's stated policy—to provide reconsideration at 8-year intervals when it was not reasonable to expect that parole would be granted during the intervening years—enabled the board to (a) put its resources to better use, and (b) insure that those prisoners who ought to receive parole came to the board's attention.

SCALIA, J., concurring in part in the judgment, expressed the view that the change in frequency prescribed by the parole board would not violate the Constitution's prohibition on ex post facto laws even if the change posed a sufficient risk of decreasing the likelihood of parole, as (1) the state's statute required only that the board provide for automatic periodic reconsideration, and (2) the length of the period was entrusted to the board's discretion.

SOUTER, J., joined by STEVENS and GINSBURG, JJ., dissenting, expressed the view that (1) if the parole

board decided to make changes retroactive, it had to do
something to prevent those changes from increasing
punishment in violation of the Constitution's prohibition on ex post facto laws; and (2) because the parole
board's ability to reconsider—based on a change in an
accused's circumstance or where the board received
new information—was entirely discretionary, an 8-year
period before further consideration of parole made
solely upon review of an inmate's file had to create a
real risk of longer confinement.

COUNSEL

Christopher S. Brasher argued the cause for petitioners.

Elizabeth S. Kertscher argued the cause for respondent.

FLORIDA, Petitioner

v

J. L.

529 US —, 146 L Ed 2d 254, 120 S Ct 1375

[No. 98-1993]

Argued February 29, 2000.
Decided March 28, 2000.

Decision: Anonymous tip that person is carrying gun held to be, without more, insufficient, under Federal Constitution's Fourth Amendment, to justify police officer's stop and frisk of that person.

SUMMARY

An anonymous caller reported to local police in Florida that a young black male standing at a particular bus stop and wearing a plaid shirt was carrying a gun. Two police officers responded to the tip by going to the bus stop, where the officers saw three black males, one of whom, the accused, was wearing a plaid shirt. Apart from the tip, the officers had no reason to suspect any of the three of illegal conduct. The officers did not see a firearm, and the accused made no threatening or otherwise unusual movements. One of the officers told the accused to put his hands on the bus stop, frisked him, and seized a gun from the accused's pocket. The accused, who at the time of the frisk was 15 years old, was charged under Florida law with carrying a concealed firearm without a license and possessing a firearm while under the age of 18. After a trial court granted the accused's motion to suppress the gun as the fruit of an unlawful search, an intermediate appellate court reversed the trial court's decision. The Supreme Court of Florida, expressing the view that the search of the accused lacked sufficient indicia of reliability and violated the prohibition under the Federal Constitution's Fourth Amendment against unreasonable searches and seizures, quashed the intermediate appellate court's decision (727 So 2d 204).

On certiorari, the United States Supreme Court affirmed. In an opinion by GINSBURG, J., expressing the unanimous view of the court, it was held that the search of the accused violated the Fourth Amendment, because the anonymous tip did not exhibit sufficient indicia of reliability to provide reasonable suspicion to make an investigatory stop, as the anonymous call left the police without means to test the informant's knowledge or credibility, where the unknown and unaccountable informant neither (1) explained how the informant knew about the gun, nor (2) supplied any basis for believing that the informant had inside information.

KENNEDY, J., joined by REHNQUIST, Ch. J., concurring, expressed the view that, in some instances, a tip might be anonymous in some sense yet have certain other features, either supporting reliability or narrowing the likely class of informants, so that the tip did provide the lawful basis for some police action.

COUNSEL

Michael J. Neimand argued the cause for petitioner.

Irving L. Gornstein argued the cause for the United States, as amicus curiae, by special leave of court.

Harvey J. Sepler argued the cause for respondent.

CITY OF ERIE et al., Petitioners

v

PAP'S A. M., tdba "KANDYLAND"

529 US —, 146 L Ed 2d 265, 120 S Ct 1382

[No. 98-1161]

Argued November 10, 2000.
Decided March 29, 2000.

Decision: Pennsylvania city's public indecency ordinance, as applied to prohibit nude dancing, held not to violate free expression guarantee of Federal Constitution's First Amendment.

SUMMARY

The city of Erie, Pennsylvania enacted a public indecency ordinance that prohibited knowingly or intentionally appearing in public in a "state of nudity." In order to comply with this ordinance, dancers at an Erie establishment—that featured female nude dancing—had to wear, at a minimum, "pasties" and a "G-string." Two days after the ordinance went into effect, the corporation which operated the nude dancing establishment (1) filed a complaint against the city of Erie, the mayor of the city, and members of the city council, and (2) sought declaratory relief and a permanent injunction against the enforcement of the ordinance. The Court of Common Pleas of Erie County (1) granted the permanent injunction, and (2) struck down the ordinance as unconstitutional. On cross appeals, the Commonwealth Court reversed the trial court's order (674 A2d 338). The Pennsylvania Supreme Court granted review and reversed, reasoning that (1) the ordinance's public nudity provisions violated the corporation's right to freedom of expression as protected by the Federal Constitution's First and Fourteenth Amendments, (2) nude dancing was expressive conduct entitled to some quantum of protection under the First Amendment, (3) the ordinance was content based and subject to strict scrutiny, and (4) the ordinance failed the narrow tailoring requirement of strict scrutiny (553 Pa 348, 719 A2d 273). After the United States Supreme Court granted certiorari (526 US 1111, 143 L Ed 2d 786, 119 S Ct 1753), the corporation filed a motion to dismiss the case as moot, noting that (1) the establishment no longer operated as a nude dancing club, and (2) the corporation was not operating such a club at any other location. The Supreme Court denied the motion (527 US 1034, 144 L Ed 2d 792, 119 S Ct 2391).

On certiorari, the Supreme Court reversed and remanded. In those portions of the opinion of O'CONNOR, J., which constituted the opinion of the court and were joined by REHNQUIST, Ch. J., and KENNEDY, SOUTER, and BREYER, JJ., it was held that the case at hand had not been rendered moot, where (1) the corporation was still incorporated under state law, (2) the corporation had not mentioned a potential mootness issue in the corporation's brief in opposition to the city's petition for a writ of certiorari, (3) the city had an ongoing injury, and (4) the Supreme Court had an interest in preventing litigants from attempting to manipulate jurisdiction to insulate a favorable decision from review. Also, O'CONNOR, J., joined by REHNQUIST, Ch. J., and KENNEDY and BREYER, JJ., expressed the view that—even though nude dancing performed as entertainment was expressive conduct that was entitled to some protection under the First Amendment—(1) the city's interest in combating the negative secondary effects associated with nude dancing establishments—which effects assertedly included violence, sexual harassment, public intoxication, prostitution, and the spread of sexually transmitted diseases—was a legitimate government interest unrelated to the suppression of expression; (2) thus, the city's public indecency ordinance ought to be evaluated under a four-factor test from United States v O'Brien (1968) 391 US 367, 20 L Ed 2d 672, 88 S Ct 1673; and (3) the city's ordinance was a content-neutral regulation that satisfied the O'Brien test so as to be sufficiently justified under the First Amendment, where (a) the city's efforts to protect public health and safety were within the city's police powers, (b) the ordinance furthered the important government interests of regulating conduct through a public nudity ban and of combating the harmful secondary effects associated with nude dancing, (c) the government interest was unrelated to the suppression of free expression, and (d) the restriction was no greater than was essential to the furtherance of the government interest.

SCALIA, J., joined by THOMAS, J., concurring in the judgment, expressed the view that although the case at hand ought to have been dismissed for want of jurisdiction on the basis of mootness, (1) the city's ordinance—as a general law regulating the conduct of going nude in public and not specifically directed at expression—was not subject to First Amendment scrutiny at all; (2) when conduct other than speech is regulated, the First Amendment is violated only where the government prohibits conduct precisely because of conduct's communicative attributes; and (3) thus, even if the city had specifically singled out the activity of nude dancing, the ordinance did not violate the First Amendment unless—in a circumstance not demonstrated on the record—the communicative character of nude dancing had prompted the ban.

SOUTER, J., concurring in part and dissenting in part, expressed the view that (1) the city's stated interest in combating the secondary effects associated with nude dancing establishments was an interest unrelated to the suppression of expression, (2) the city's public indecency ordinance was thus properly considered under the four-factor test from United States v O'Brien, (3) the record did not provide a sufficient evidentiary showing—either for the seriousness of the threatened harm or for the efficacy of the chosen remedy—to sustain the city's ordinance, and (4) the decision of the Pennsylvania Supreme Court ought to have been vacated and remanded.

STEVENS, J., joined by GINSBURG, J., dissenting, expressed the view that the city's ordinance ought to have been ruled invalid, as, among other factors, (1) nude dancing performed as entertainment was expressive conduct that was entitled to some protection under the First Amendment; (2) the secondary effects of commercial enterprises featuring indecent entertainment had justified only the regulation of the location of these establishments through zoning; (3) the extension of secondary-effects cases to the total suppression of protected speech—in the form of nude dancing in the case at hand—was not supported by precedent or by persuasive reasoning; (4) the dispersal of establishments that simply limited the places where speech could occur was a minimal imposition, whereas a total ban was the most exacting of restrictions; and (5) the state's interest in fighting presumed secondary effects was sufficiently strong to justify the former, but far too weak to support the latter.

COUNSEL

Gregory A. Karle argued the cause for petitioners.
John W. Weston argued the cause for respondent.

———————

STEVEN DEWAYNE BOND, Petitioner

v

UNITED STATES

529 US —, 146 L Ed 2d 365, 120 S Ct 1462

[No. 98-9349]

Argued February 29, 2000.
Decided April 17, 2000.

Decision: Law enforcement officer's physical manipulation of bus passenger's carry-on luggage held to
violate Fourth Amendment's prohibition against
unreasonable searches.

SUMMARY

An accused had been a passenger on a bus that left
California bound for Little Rock, Arkansas. At a permanent border patrol checkpoint in Texas, a border patrol
agent (1) boarded the bus to check the immigration
status of its passengers, (2) squeezed the soft luggage
which passengers had placed in the overhead storage
space above the seats, including a green canvas bag,
and (3) noticed that the green bag contained a brick-
like object. The accused admitted that the bag was his
and agreed to allow the agent to open it. Upon opening
the bag, the agent discovered a "brick" of methamphetamine. The accused was indicted for conspiracy to
possess methamphetamine, and possession with intent
to distribute methamphetamine in violation of federal
law. In Federal District Court, the accused moved to
suppress the drugs and argued that the agent conducted an illegal search of his bag, in alleged violation
of the Federal Constitution's Fourth Amendment pro-

hibition against unreasonable searches and seizures. The District Court (1) denied the accused's motion to suppress, (2) found the accused guilty on both counts, and (3) sentenced the accused to 57 months in prison. On appeal, the accused conceded that other passengers had access to his bag, but contended that the agent had manipulated the bag in a way that other passengers would not have. The United States Court of Appeals for the Fifth Circuit (1) rejected this argument, (2) expressed the view that the agent's manipulation of the bag was not a search within the meaning of the Fourth Amendment, and (3) affirmed the denial of the motion to suppress (167 F3d 225).

On certiorari, the United States Supreme Court reversed the judgment of the Court of Appeals. In an opinion by REHNQUIST, Ch. J., joined by STEVENS, O'CONNOR, KENNEDY, SOUTER, THOMAS, and GINSBURG, JJ., it was held that the agent's physical manipulation of the accused's carry-on luggage violated the Fourth Amendment's prohibition against unreasonable searches, as (1) the accused's luggage was an effect protected by the Fourth Amendment; (2) cases in which the Supreme Court had held that matters open to public observation were not protected by the Fourth Amendment had involved only visual, as opposed to tactile, observation; (3) physically invasive inspection was more intrusive than purely visual inspection; (4) the accused had exhibited an actual expectation of privacy by using an opaque bag and placing that bag directly above his seat; and (5) the accused's expectation of privacy was one that society was prepared to recognize as reasonable.

BREYER, J., joined by SCALIA J., dissenting, expressed the view that the accused—in placing a soft-sided bag in the shared overhead storage compartment of a bus—did not have a reasonable expectation that strangers would not push, pull, prod, squeeze, or otherwise manipulate his luggage.

COUNSEL

Carolyn Fuentes argued the cause for petitioner.
Jeffrey A. Lamken argued the cause for respondent.

———————

NORFOLK SOUTHERN RAILWAY COMPANY, Petitioner

v

DEDRA SHANKLIN, Individually, and as Next Friend of Jessie Guy Shanklin

529 US —, 146 L Ed 2d 374, 120 S Ct 1467

[No. 99-312]

Argued March 1, 2000.
Decided April 17, 2000.

Decision: Federal Railroad Safety Act of 1970, along with federal regulations, held to pre-empt state tort claims concerning railroad's alleged failure to maintain adequate warning devices at crossings where federal funds were utilized in devices' installation.

SUMMARY

The Federal Railroad Safety Act of 1970 (FRSA), as amended (49 USCS §§ 20101 et seq.), authorizes the United States Secretary of Transportation (Secretary) to (1) promulgate regulations and issue orders for railroad safety, and (2) maintain a coordinated effort to solve railroad grade crossing problems. Also, the FRSA has an express pre-emption provision. 23 CFR § 646.214(b)—as promulgated by the Secretary through the Federal Highway Administration (FHWA)—addresses the adequacy of warning devices installed under the Federal Railway-Highway Crossings Program (Crossings Program) (see 23 USCS § 130), which provides funds to states for the construction of such devices. According to 23 CFR § 646.214(b)(3),
134

automatic gates and flashing lights are adequate warning devices installed using federal funds where any of several conditions are present. For crossings where those conditions are not present, a state's decision about what devices to install is subject to FHWA approval under 23 CFR § 646.214(b)(4). A widow's spouse was killed when a train operated by a railroad hit the spouse's vehicle at a crossing with advance warning signs and reflectorized crossbucks that Tennessee's department of transportation had installed using federal funds under the Crossings Program. The signs were installed and fully compliant with applicable federal standards. The widow (1) brought a diversity wrongful death action in the United States District Court for the Western District of Tennessee, and (2) alleged that the railroad was negligent in, among other things, failing to maintain adequate warning devices at the crossing. Reasoning that the FRSA did not pre-empt the widow's inadequate-warning-device claim, the District Court denied the railroad's summary judgment motion. The widow was awarded damages on this and other negligence issues. The United States Court of Appeals for the Sixth Circuit affirmed (173 F3d 386).

On certiorari, the United States Supreme Court reversed and remanded. In an opinion by O'CONNOR, J., joined by REHNQUIST, Ch. J., and SCALIA, KENNEDY, SOUTER, THOMAS, and BREYER, JJ., it was held that the FRSA, in conjunction with §§ 646.214(b)(3) and (4), pre-empted state tort claims concerning a railroad's alleged failure to maintain adequate warning devices at crossings where federal funds were utilized in the devices' installation, as §§ 646.214(b)(3) and (4) established a federal standard of adequacy that determined the railroad warning devices to be installed when federal funds participated in a crossing improvement project.

135

BREYER, J., concurring, expressed the view that the specific FHWA regulations at issue—when read in light of CSX Transp. v Easterwood (1993) 507 US 658, 123 L Ed 2d 387, 113 S Ct 1732—said that once federal funds were requested and spent to install warning devices at a grade crossing, the regulations' standards of adequacy (1) applied across the board, and (2) pre-empted state law seeking to impose an independent duty on a railroad with respect to the adequacy of the warning devices installed.

GINSBURG, J., joined by STEVENS, J., dissenting, expressed the view that (1) state negligence law was, in the case at hand, displaced with no substantive federal standard of conduct to fill the void; (2) federal funding was necessary to trigger pre-emption, but federal funding was not sufficient by itself to do so; and (3) §§ 646.214(b)(3) and (4) did not dictate that the FHWA's authorization of federal funding to install devices was tantamount to approval of each of those devices as adequate to protect safety at every crossing so funded.

COUNSEL

Carter G. Phillips argued the cause for petitioner.

Gregory S. Coleman argued the cause for the Texas, et al., as amici curiae, by special leave of the Court, supporting the petitioner.

Patricia A. Millett argued the cause for the United States, as amicus curiae, by special leave of court, supporting the respondent.

Thomas C. Goldstein argued the cause for respondent.

TERRY WILLIAMS, Petitioner

v

JOHN TAYLOR, Warden

529 US —, 146 L Ed 2d 389, 120 S Ct 1495

[No. 98-8384]

Argued October 4, 1999.
Decided April 18, 2000.

Decision: Accused's right to effective assistance of counsel held violated at Virginia sentencing hearing in which accused received death sentence; accused held entitled to federal habeas corpus relief under 28 USCS § 2254(d)(1).

SUMMARY

In Strickland v Washington (1984) 446 US 668, 80 L Ed 2d 674, 104 S Ct 2052, the United States Supreme Court held that, to establish ineffectiveness, an accused must show (1) that counsel's performance was so deficient that counsel was not functioning as the counsel guaranteed by the Federal Constitution's Sixth Amendment, and (2) prejudice, by showing that there is a reasonable probability that but for counsel's unprofessional errors, the result of the proceeding would have been different. Under 28 USCS § 2254(d)(1), a state prisoner's application for a writ of habeas corpus shall not be granted with respect to any claim that was adjudicated on the merits in state court proceedings unless the adjudication of the claim resulted in a decision that was "contrary to or involved an unreasonable application of clearly established Federal law, as determined by the Supreme Court of the United

137

States." A Virginia trial court convicted an accused of robbery and capital murder. At the accused's sentencing hearing, (1) the evidence offered by the accused's counsel consisted of the testimony of (a) the accused's mother and two neighbors to the effect that the accused was not violent, and (b) a psychiatrist to the effect that the accused had removed the bullets from the accused's gun in the course of earlier robberies; and (2) the weight of counsel's closing was devoted to explaining that it was difficult to find a reason why the jury should spare the accused's life. After the trial judge imposed the death sentence that had been fixed by the jury on the basis of a finding of the probability of future dangerousness, the Virginia Supreme Court affirmed the conviction and sentence (234 Va 168, 360 SE2d 361, cert den 484 US 1020, 98 L Ed 2d 681, 108 S Ct 733). Subsequently, the accused, alleging that he had received ineffective assistance of counsel at the sentencing hearing, filed for collateral relief in the state trial court. The trial court, finding that counsel had been ineffective, recommended that the accused be granted a rehearing concerning his sentencing. However, the Virginia Supreme Court—concluding that (1) there was no reasonable possibility that the mitigating evidence that was omitted by the accused's counsel would have affected the jury's sentencing recommendation, and (2) the accused had failed to demonstrate that the sentencing proceeding was fundamentally unfair—denied the accused's request for state habeas corpus relief (254 Va 16, 487 SE2d 194). The accused, having exhausted his state remedies, then sought a federal writ of habeas corpus pursuant to 28 USCS § 2254. The United States District Court for the Eastern District of Virginia granted the writ. The United States Court of Appeals for the Fourth Circuit, in reversing the District Court's judgment, construed § 2254(d)(1) as prohibiting a grant of habeas corpus relief, unless the state court decided the question by interpreting or applying the relevant precedent in a manner that reasonable jurists would all agree was unreasonable (163 F3d 860).

On certiorari, the United States Supreme Court reversed the judgment of the Court of Appeals and remanded the case for further proceedings. It was held, with different majorities of Justices for each holding, that (1) the accused had been deprived of the constitutional right to the effective assistance of counsel, as defined in Strickland v Washington; and (2) the Virginia Supreme Court's refusal to set aside the accused's death sentence was a decision that was contrary to or involved an unreasonable application of clearly established federal law, as determined by the United States Supreme Court.

In those portions (Parts I, III, and IV) of the opinion of STEVENS, J., which constituted the opinion of the court and were joined by O'CONNOR, KENNEDY, SOUTER, GINSBURG, and BREYER, JJ., it was held that (1) counsel, who did not begin to prepare for the sentencing phase of the trial until a week before the trial, did not fulfill the obligation to conduct a thorough investigation of the accused's background, (2) counsel's unprofessional service prejudiced the accused within the meaning of Strickland v Washington, where counsel failed to introduce a comparatively voluminous amount of evidence in the accused's favor, and (3) the Virginia Supreme Court's decision was both "contrary to" and "involved an unreasonable application of" clearly established federal law, as determined by the United States Supreme Court. Also, STEVENS, J., joined by SOUTER, GINSBURG, and BREYER, JJ., expressed the view that in § 2254(d)(1), the phrase (1) "clearly established" is not intended to modify the independent obligation of the federal courts, even on habeas corpus review, to say what the law is, and (2) "contrary to or an unreasonable application of" does not require federal courts to defer to the opinion of every reasonable state court judge on the content of federal law.

In that portion (Part II, except the footnote) of the opinion of O'CONNOR, J., which constituted the opinion of the court and was joined by REHNQUIST, Ch. J., and KENNEDY and THOMAS, JJ., and by SCALIA, J. (except as to the footnote), it was held that (1) under § 2254(d)(1)'s "contrary to" clause, a federal court may grant a writ of habeas corpus if a state court (a) applies a rule that contradicts the governing law set forth in the United States Supreme Court's cases, or (b) decides a case differently than the Supreme Court has on a set of materially indistinguishable facts; and (2) under § 2254(d)(1)'s "unreasonable application" clause, a federal court may grant a writ of habeas corpus if a state court identifies the correct governing legal principle from the Supreme Court's decisions but unreasonably applies that principle to the facts of a prisoner's case. Also, O'CONNOR, J., joined by KENNEDY, J., concurring in part and concurring in the judgment, (1) agreed with the majority that the Virginia Supreme Court's adjudication of the accused's claim of ineffective assistance of counsel resulted in a decision that was both contrary to and involved an unreasonable application of the United States Supreme Court's precedent, but (2) expressed disagreement with Justice Stevens concerning the standard that had to be applied under § 2254(d)(1) in evaluating the accused's claims on federal habeas corpus review.

REHNQUIST, Ch. J., joined by SCALIA and THOMAS, JJ., concurring in part and dissenting in part, (1) agreed with the United States Supreme Court's interpretation of § 2254(d)(1); but (2) expressed the view

140

that habeas corpus relief was barred by § 2254(d) in the instant case, as (a) the Virginia Supreme Court's adjudication was not "contrary to" the United States Supreme Court's clearly established precedent, because the Virginia Supreme Court appropriately relied on Strickland v Washington to make a decision, and (b) it was not unreasonable for the Virginia Supreme Court to decide that a jury would not have been swayed by some additional evidence to the effect that the accused had a terrible childhood and a low IQ, because there was strong evidence that the accused would continue to be a danger to society, both in and out of prison.

COUNSEL

John J. Gibbons argued the cause for petitioner.
Robert Q. Harris argued the cause for respondent.

MICHAEL WAYNE WILLIAMS, Petitioner

v

JOHN TAYLOR, Warden

529 US —, 146 L Ed 2d 435, 120 S Ct 1479

[No. 99-6615]

Argued February 28, 2000.
Decided April 18, 2000.

Decision: Federal habeas corpus petitioner held not to have "failed to develop" factual basis for claim in state court, so as to bar evidentiary hearing under 28 USCS § 2254(e)(2), absent lack of diligence or some greater fault.

SUMMARY

In a Virginia court, an individual was (1) convicted, partly on the basis of the testimony of an alleged confederate, on charges including murder, and (2) sentenced to death. After direct appeals and a state habeas corpus petition proved unsuccessful, the individual filed a habeas corpus petition in the United States District Court for the Eastern District of Virginia. This petition asserted, for the first time, that (1) state prosecutors had violated Brady v Maryland (1963) 373 US 83, 10 L Ed 2d 215, 83 S Ct 1194, by failing to disclose a report of a confidential pretrial psychiatric examination of the confederate; (2) the individual's trial had been rendered unfair by a juror's failure to disclose at voir dire that she had formerly been married to a prosecution witness and had been represented in her divorce by one of the prosecutors; and (3) this prosecutor had committed misconduct by failing to
142

reveal his knowledge of the juror's possible bias. The District Court initially granted the petitioner an evidentiary hearing on the latter two claims. However, the District Court vacated that order and dismissed the petition after being directed by the United States Court of Appeals for the Fourth Circuit to apply 28 USCS § 2254(e)(2), as amended by the Antiterrorism and Effective Death Penalty Act of 1996 (PL 104-132), which provided that if habeas corpus petitioners "failed to develop the factual basis" of their claims in state court proceedings, an evidentiary hearing could not be held unless (1) the claims relied on either a new rule of constitutional law or a factual predicate that could not have been previously discovered through the exercise of due diligence, and (2) the underlying facts were sufficient to establish by clear and convincing evidence that, but for the constitutional error, no reasonable factfinder would have found the petitioners guilty. The Court of Appeals, in subsequently affirming the dismissal, expressed the view that (1) § 2254(e)(2) would not apply if the petitioner had been diligent in attempting to develop his claims in state court; (2) the petitioner had not been diligent with respect to his claims of nondisclosure of evidence, juror bias, and prosecutorial misconduct; and (3) the petitioner could not satisfy the conditions for excusing a failure to develop claims under § 2254(e)(2) (189 F3d 421).

On certiorari, the United States Supreme Court affirmed in part, reversed in part, and remanded the case for further proceedings. In an opinion by KENNEDY, J., expressing the unanimous view of the court, it was held that (1) the "failed to develop" clause of § 2254(e)(2) did not apply in every case where a petitioner had not developed the factual basis for a claim in state court, but only where there had been a lack of diligence, or some greater fault, attributable to the petitioner or petitioner's counsel; and (2) in the case at hand, the individual (a) had not exercised the diligence required to preserve his federal habeas corpus claim regarding nondisclosure of the alleged confederate's psychiatric report, but (b) had met his burden of showing that he had been diligent in efforts to develop the facts supporting his claims of juror bias and prosecutorial misconduct.

COUNSEL

John H. Blume argued the cause for petitioner.
Donald R. Curry argued the cause for respondent.

RONALD D. EDWARDS, Warden, Petitioner

v

ROBERT W. CARPENTER

529 US —, 146 L Ed 2d 518, 120 S Ct 1587

[No. 98-2060]

Argued February 28, 2000.
Decided April 25, 2000.

Decision: Procedurally defaulted ineffective-assistance-of-counsel claim held to provide cause excusing procedural default of other claim in federal habeas corpus proceeding only if petitioner showed cause and prejudice with respect to counsel claim.

SUMMARY

An individual (1) was indicted by an Ohio grand jury on charges of aggravated murder and aggravated robbery, (2) pleaded guilty, and (3) was sentenced to life imprisonment, with parole possible after 30 years. On direct appeal, the individual challenged only the length of the minimum sentence, without success. After unsuccessfully pursuing state postconviction relief, the individual petitioned the Ohio Court of Appeals to reopen his direct appeal on the asserted ground that his original appellate counsel had been constitutionally ineffective in failing to challenge the sufficiency of the evidence. However, the Court of Appeals dismissed the application on the ground that the individual had not shown good cause for failing to file such a petition within the 90-day period established by a state appellate rule. The Supreme Court of Ohio affirmed. The individual thereafter filed a petition for a writ of habeas corpus in the United States District Court for the Southern District of Ohio, which petition alleged in part that (1) the evidence supporting his plea and sentence was insufficient in violation of the Federal Constitution's Fifth and Fourteenth Amendments, and (2) his former counsel had been constitutionally ineffective in failing to raise that claim on direct appeal. The District Court (1) determined that—while the sufficiency claim had been procedurally defaulted—the ineffective-assistance-of-counsel claim (a) could excuse that default, and (b) was not itself barred from review, because the state appellate rule had not been consistently applied by state courts; and (2) granted the petition, conditioned on the state courts reopening direct appeal of the sufficiency claim. On cross-appeals, the United States Court of Appeals for the Sixth Circuit (1) expressed the view that the ineffective-assistance-of-counsel claim could serve as cause to excuse the procedural default of the sufficiency claim, regardless of whether the ineffective-assistance-of-counsel claim had been procedurally defaulted; and (2) ordered that the writ be issued, conditioned on the state courts granting the individual a new culpability hearing (163 F3d 938).

On certiorari, the United States Supreme Court reversed and remanded. In an opinion by SCALIA, J., joined by REHNQUIST, Ch. J., and O'CONNOR, KENNEDY, SOUTER, THOMAS, and GINSBURG, JJ., it was held that in a federal habeas corpus proceeding in which the petitioner was a state prisoner, a procedurally defaulted ineffective-assistance-of-counsel claim could serve as cause to excuse the procedural default of another claim only if the petitioner could satisfy the "cause and prejudice" standard with respect to the ineffective-assistance-of-counsel claim, where—as in the case at

146

hand—there was not at issue the cause-and-prejudice standard's exception for a fundamental miscarriage of justice.

BREYER, J., joined by STEVENS, J., concurred in the judgment, expressing the view that (1) since the determination of cause to excuse a procedural default was a matter for the federal habeas corpus judge, the ineffective-assistance-of-counsel claim, when offered as such cause, ought not itself to be subject to procedural default; and (2) the case at hand was properly remanded for the individual to prove that (a) the assistance which he had received on direct appeal was constitutionally ineffective, and (b) his trial violated the Constitution.

COUNSEL

Edward B. Foley argued the cause for petitioner.

J. Joseph Bodine, Jr. argued the cause for respondent.

DONALD E. NELSON, Petitioner

v

ADAMS USA, INC., et al.

529 US —, 146 L Ed 2d 530, 120 S Ct 1579

[No. 99-502]

Argued March 27, 2000.
Decided April 25, 2000.

Decision: Amendment of attorney fees judgment in favor of corporation to join president of another corporation as party and to make president liable for fee award, without opportunity to contest personal liability, held to violate due process.

SUMMARY

A plaintiff, a corporation holding two patents relating to a method of manufacturing a foamed padding used in athletic equipment, sued another corporation for alleged patent infringement. The United States District Court for the Northern District of Ohio dismissed the plaintiff's claim and ordered the plaintiff to pay the second corporation's costs and attorney fees. In awarding costs and attorney fees, the District Court determined that (1) the plaintiff's president and sole shareholder had deceitfully withheld from the United States Patent and Trademark Office prior art that rendered the plaintiff's patents invalid, and (2) this behavior constituted inequitable conduct. The second corporation, afraid that the plaintiff might be unable to pay the fee, (1) moved under Rule 15 of the Federal Rules of Civil Procedure (FRCP) to amend the second corporation's pleading to add the plaintiff's president,
148

personally, as a party from whom fees could be collected; and (2) asked the District Court, under Rule 59(e) of the FRCP, to amend the judgment to make the president immediately liable for the fee award. The District Court granted the motion in full. In affirming the District Court's judgment against the president, the United States Court of Appeals for the Federal Circuit reasoned that the president had made no showing that anything different or additional would have been done to stave off the judgment had the president been a party, in his individual capacity, from the outset (175 F3d 1343).

On certiorari, the United States Supreme Court reversed and remanded. In an opinion by GINSBURG, J., expressing the unanimous view of the court, it was held that in the case at hand, the amendment of the attorney fees judgment to join the president as a party and to make the president liable for the fee award, without the opportunity to contest personal liability, violated due process under the Federal Constitution—as reflected in both Rules 12 and 15 of the FRCP—since due process required that the president be given an opportunity to respond and to contest personal liability for the award after being made a party and before the entry of judgment.

COUNSEL

Debra J. Dixon argued the cause for petitioner.
Jack A. Wheat argued the cause for respondents.

ANTONIO TONTON SLACK, Petitioner

v

ELDON McDANIEL, Warden, et al.

529 US —, 146 L Ed 2d 542, 120 S Ct 1595

[No. 98-6322]

Argued October 4, 1999.
Reargued March 29, 2000.
Decided April 26, 2000.

Decision: Federal habeas corpus petition filed by state prisoner, after initial petition was dismissed without adjudication on merits, held not to constitute "second or successive" petition subject to dismissal for abuse of writ.

SUMMARY

Under Rule 9(b) of the Rules Governing § 2254 Cases in the United States District Courts, a "second or successive petition" alleging new and different grounds for federal habeas corpus relief may be dismissed if the judge finds that the petitioner's failure to assert those grounds in a prior petition constituted an abuse of the writ. A prisoner who had been convicted, in a Nevada trial court, of second-degree murder—and whose direct appeals had been unsuccessful—filed a petition for a writ of habeas corpus in the United States District Court for the District of Nevada. Subsequently, the petitioner, having decided to raise claims not previously asserted in state proceedings, moved to hold his federal petition in abeyance while he exhausted his remedies as to those claims in state court. The District Court ordered the petition dismissed without prejudice and
150

with leave to file a motion to renew. However, when the petitioner, having pursued his claims unsuccessfully in state court, filed a new federal habeas corpus petition in 1995, the District Court eventually dismissed the petition, as amended in 1997, on the grounds that (1) the new petition was a "second or successive" petition; (2) claims not raised in the previous petition therefore ought to be dismissed for abuse of the writ; and (3) since one of the petitioner's remaining claims had not been presented in state court, all of the remaining claims ought to be dismissed, because they were in a "mixed" petition. The petitioner filed a notice of appeal on April 29, 1998. However, both the District Court and the United States Court of Appeals for the Ninth Circuit refused to issue certificates of probable cause—under the procedure in effect prior to the enactment of the Antiterrorism and Effective Death Penalty Act of 1996 (AEDPA) (PL 104-132)—thereby effectively barring the petitioner from appealing the dismissal.

On certiorari, the United States Supreme Court reversed and remanded. In an opinion by KENNEDY, J., joined in part (as to holding 1 below) by REHNQUIST, Ch. J., and O'CONNOR, SCALIA, THOMAS, and GINS-BURG, JJ., and joined in part (as to holdings 2 and 3 below) by REHNQUIST, Ch. J., and STEVENS, O'CONNOR, SOUTER, GINSBURG, and BREYER, JJ., it was held that (1) when a federal habeas corpus petitioner sought to initiate an appeal of the dismissal of a petition after April 24, 1996—the AEDPA's effective date—the petitioner's right to appeal was governed by the certificate of appealability (COA) provisions of the AEDPA (28 USCS § 2253(c)); (2) when District Court denied a state prisoner's habeas corpus petition on procedural grounds without reaching the prisoner's underlying federal constitutional claims, a COA ought to issue—and an appeal of the District Court's order might properly be taken—if the prisoner showed, at least, that jurists of reason would find it debatable both whether (a) the petition stated a valid claim of the denial of a constitutional right, and (b) the District Court was correct in its procedural ruling; and (3) in the case at hand, the District Court was not correct in its procedural ruling, because a federal habeas corpus petition which was filed by a state prisoner after an initial petition was dismissed without adjudication on the merits for failure to exhaust state remedies—and was further dismissed without condition and without prejudice—was not a second or successive petition within the meaning of Rule 9(b).

STEVENS, J., joined by SOUTER, J. and BREYER, J., concurred in part and concurred in the judgment, expressing the view that (1) the pre-AEDPA version of 28 USCS § 2253 governed the right to appeal with respect to an appeal noticed after the effective date of the AEDPA in a habeas corpus proceeding commenced prior to that date; and (2) the balance of the opinion of the court was correct.

SCALIA, J., joined by THOMAS, J., concurred in part and dissented in part, expressing the view that the petitioner's inclusion of new and unexhausted claims in his postexhaustion petition rendered it a second or successive petition which was properly dismissed by the District Court.

COUNSEL

Michael Pescetta argued and reargued the cause for petitioner.

Matthew D. Roberts argued the cause for the United States, as amicus curiae, by special leave of court.

David F. Sarnowski argued and reargued the cause for respondents.

———————

ROBERT A. BECK, II, Petitioner

v

RONALD M. PRUPIS

529 US —, 146 L Ed 2d 561, 120 S Ct 1608

[No. 98-1480]

Argued November 3, 1999.
Decided April 26, 2000.

Decision: Person injured by overt act done in furtherance of RICO conspiracy held not to have cause of
action under 18 USCS § 1964(c) where overt act
was not act of racketeering.

SUMMARY

The Racketeer Influenced and Corrupt Organizations Act (RICO) (18 USCS §§ 1961 et seq.) (1) makes
it unlawful to engage in certain activities through a
pattern of racketeering (18 USCS §§ 1962(a)-(c)); (2)
makes it unlawful for a person to conspire to violate any
of the provisions of §§ 1962(a)-(c) (18 USCS
§ 1962(d)); (3) states that a cause of action is available
to anyone injured by reason of a violation of § 1962 (18
USCS § 1964(c)); and (4) contains an exhaustive list of
acts of "racketeering" (18 USCS § 1961(1)). An individual who had been the president and chief executive
officer, as well as a director and shareholder, of a
corporation brought an action in the United States
District Court for the Southern District of Florida
under § 1964(c) against certain officers and directors
of the corporation, which action alleged that (1) the
officers and directors had engaged in a pattern of
racketeering in violation of §§ 1962(a), (b), and (c);
154

(2) the officers and directors had conspired to commit the aforementioned acts, in violation of § 1962(d); (3) the individual had discovered the officers' and directors' unlawful conduct and had contacted regulators; and (4) the officers and directors had then orchestrated a scheme to remove the individual from the company. The officers and directors filed a motion for summary judgment, whereupon the District Court dismissed the individual's RICO conspiracy claim. The United States Court of Appeals for the Eleventh Circuit (1) affirmed the judgment of the District Court, and (2) expressed the view that (a) a cause of action under § 1964(c) for a violation of § 1962(d) was not available to a person injured by an overt act in furtherance of a RICO conspiracy unless the overt act was an act of racketeering, and (b) the overt act that allegedly caused the individual's injury in the present case was not an act of racketeering under § 1961(1) (162 F3d 1090).

On certiorari, the United States Supreme Court affirmed the judgment of the Court of Appeals. In an opinion by THOMAS, J., joined by REHNQUIST, Ch. J., and O'CONNOR, SCALIA, KENNEDY, GINSBURG, and BREYER, JJ., it was held that (1) a person injured by an overt act done in furtherance of a RICO conspiracy did not have a cause of action under § 1964(c) where the overt act was not an act of racketeering or otherwise unlawful under the statute, as (a) the obvious source in the common law for the combined meaning of §§ 1964(c) and 1962(d) was the law of civil conspiracy, (b) the principle that a plaintiff could bring suit for civil conspiracy only if he or she had been injured by an act that was itself tortious was so widely accepted at the time of RICO's enactment in 1970 as to be incorporated in the common understanding of "civil conspiracy," and (c) consistency with the common law required that a RICO conspiracy plaintiff allege injury from an act that was analogous to an act of a tortious character; and (2) the alleged overt act in the present case was not independently wrongful under any substantive provision of RICO.

STEVENS, J., joined by SOUTER, J., dissenting, expressed the view that (1) the individual had alleged an injury proximately caused by an overt act in furtherance of a conspiracy that violated § 1962(d); and (2) the plain language of RICO made it clear that the individual therefore had a cause of action under § 1964(c), regardless of whether the overt act was a racketeering activity listed in § 1961(1).

COUNSEL

Jay Starkman argued the cause for petitioner.

Michael M. Rosenbaum argued the cause for respondents.

SCOTT LESLIE CARMELL, Petitioner

v

TEXAS

529 US —, 146 L Ed 2d 577, 120 S Ct 1620

[No. 98-7540]

Argued November 30, 1999.
Decided May 1, 2000.

Decision: Retrospective application of Texas statutory provision allowing alleged sexual offense victim's uncorroborated testimony to support conviction held to violate Federal Constitution's Art I, § 10, cl 1 prohibition against ex post facto laws.

SUMMARY

Before September 1993, a Texas statutory provision specified that (1) an alleged victim's testimony about an alleged sexual offense could not support a conviction unless (a) such testimony was corroborated by other evidence, or (b) the victim made an "outcry"—that is, informed another person of the alleged offense—within 6 months of the alleged offense's occurrence; but (2) such testimony alone could support a conviction if the alleged victim was under 14 at the time of the alleged offense. Effective September 1, 1993, an amendment to the provision allowed the victim's testimony alone to support a conviction if the victim was under 18. In 1997, an accused was convicted on 15 counts of committing sexual offenses against his stepdaughter from 1991 to 1995, when she was 12 to 16 years old. Before the Court of Appeals of Texas, the accused argued that four of the convictions—with

157

respect to offenses allegedly committed between June 1992 and July 1993—could not stand under the former version of the provision, because those convictions were based solely on the testimony of the victim, who was not under 14 at the time of the offenses and had not made a timely outcry. The Court of Appeals, in affirming the convictions, expressed the view that the amended version of the provision was applicable to the case, as this version (1) had not increased the punishment or changed the elements of the offense that the state had to prove, (2) had merely removed existing restrictions upon the competency of some classes of persons as witnesses, and (3) was thus a rule of procedure (963 SW2d 833). The Court of Criminal Appeals of Texas denied discretionary review.

On certiorari, the United States Supreme Court reversed the Court of Appeals' judgment and remanded the case for further proceedings. In an opinion by STEVENS, J., joined by SCALIA, SOUTER, THOMAS, and BREYER, JJ., it was held that the amended provision could not be applied in a trial for offenses that were committed before the amendment's effective date without violating the Federal Constitution's Art I, § 10, cl 1 prohibition against ex post facto laws, for the amended provision was (1) a law that altered the legal rules of evidence so as to receive less or different testimony than the law had required at the time of the commission of the offense in order to convict the offender; and (2) not a witness-competency rule that simply (a) enlarged the class of persons who might be competent to testify, or (b) removed existing restrictions upon the competency of certain classes of persons as witnesses.

GINSBURG, J., joined by REHNQUIST, Ch. J., and O'CONNOR and KENNEDY, JJ., dissenting, expressed the view that the amended statute (1) was not a sufficiency-of-the-evidence rule, but rather a witness-competency rule dictating the circumstances under which the jury could credit victim testimony in sexual offense prosecutions; and (2) such a witness-competency rule could be applied—without violating the ex post facto prohibition—to offenses committed before the rule's enactment.

COUNSEL

Richard D. Bernstein argued the cause for petitioner.

Beth S. Brinkmann argued the cause for the United States, as amicus curiae, by special leave of court.

John Cornyn argued the cause for respondent.

EDWARD CHRISTENSEN, et al., Petitioners

v

HARRIS COUNTY et al.

529 US —, 146 L Ed 2d 621, 120 S Ct 1655

[No. 98-1167]

Argued February 23, 2000.
Decided May 1, 2000.

Decision: Fair Labor Standards Act of 1938 (29 USCS §§ 201 et seq.) and its implementing regulations held not to prohibit public employer from compelling use of compensatory time.

SUMMARY

A Fair Labor Standards Act of 1938 (FLSA) provision (29 USCS § 207(*o*)) authorizes states and their political subdivisions to compensate employees for overtime by granting the employees compensatory time, which entitles the employees to take time off work with full pay. Under §§ 207(*o*)(3) and (4), if employees do not use their accumulated compensatory time, then the employer must pay cash compensation under certain circumstances. A Texas county, which was seeking to reduce accrued compensatory time, asked the United States Department of Labor's Wage and Hour Division whether the county sheriff would be allowed to scheduled nonexempt employees to use compensatory time. The Division's Acting Administrator replied with an opinion letter expressing the view that (1) a public employer could schedule its nonexempt employees to use their accrued compensatory time as directed, if a prior agreement specifically contained such a provi-
160

sion, but (2) absent such an agreement, neither the FLSA (29 USCS §§ 201 et seq.) nor its implementing regulations permitted an employer to require an employee to use accrued compensatory time. Subsequently, the county adopted a policy under which its employees could be ordered to schedule compensatory time at specified times. A group of deputy sheriffs (1) sued defendants including the county, and (2) alleged that the county's policy violated the FLSA, on the theory that § 207(*o*)(5), which required that an employer reasonably accommodate employee requests to use compensatory time, provided the exclusive means of utilizing accrued time, in the absence of an agreement or understanding permitting some other method. The United States District Court for the Southern District of Texas granted summary judgment for the deputies and entered a declaratory judgment that the county's policy violated the FLSA (945 F Supp 1067). The United States Court of Appeals for the Fifth Circuit, in reversing, expressed the view that the FLSA did not speak to the issue in question and thus did not prohibit the county from implementing its compensatory time policy (158 F3d 341).

On certiorari, the United States Supreme Court affirmed. In an opinion by THOMAS, J., joined by REHNQUIST, Ch. J., and O'CONNOR, KENNEDY, and SOUTER, JJ., and joined in pertinent part by SCALIA, J., it was held that the deputies could not, as they were required to do by 29 USCS § 216(b), prove that the county had violated § 207, as (1) nothing in the FLSA or its implementing regulations prohibited an employer from compelling the use of compensatory time, and (2) the county's policy was compatible with § 207(*o*)(5).

SOUTER, J., concurring, expressed the view that the court's opinion did not foreclose a reading of the FLSA that allowed the Secretary of Labor to issue regulations limiting forced use of compensatory time.

SCALIA, J., concurring in part and concurring in the judgment, expressed the view that (1) the fact that the Solicitor General of the United States, as an amicus curiae in the instant case, had filed a brief cosigned by the United States Solicitor of Labor, which brief represented the position set forth in the opinion letter to be the position of the Secretary of Labor, would, even in the absence of the opinion letter, have entitled that position to deference under Chevron U. S. A. Inc. v Natural Resources Defense Council (1984) 437 US 837, 81 L Ed 2d 694, 104 S Ct 2778—which held that a court must give effect to an administrative agency's regulation containing a reasonable interpretation of an ambiguous statute—but (2) the Secretary's position was not a reasonable interpretation of the statute.

STEVENS, J., joined by GINSBURG and BREYER, JJ., dissenting, expressed the view that under the FLSA, an employer had no right to impose compensatory overtime payments upon its employees, except in accordance with the terms of an agreement authorizing the use of compensatory time.

BREYER, J., joined by GINSBURG, J., dissenting, expressed the view that (1) when thoroughly considered and consistently observed, an administrative agency's views, particularly in a rather technical case such as the instant case, merited the court's respect; and (2) the Labor Department's position on the matter in question was reasonable and hence, persuasive.

COUNSEL

Michael T. Leibig argued the cause for petitioners.

Matthew D. Roberts argued the cause for the United States, as amicus curiae, by special leave of court.

Michael P. Fleming argued the cause for respondents.

UNITED STATES, Petitioner

v

ANTONIO J. MORRISON et al. (No. 99-5)

CHRISTY BRZONKALA, Petitioner

v

ANTONIO J. MORRISON et al. (No. 99-29)

529 US —, 146 L Ed 2d 658, 120 S Ct 1740

Argued January 11, 2000.
Decided May 15, 2000.

Decision: Congress held to have no authority under either Federal Constitution's commerce clause or § 5 of Constitution's Fourteenth Amendment to enact 42 USCS § 13981, providing federal civil remedy for victims of gender-motivated violence.

SUMMARY

A woman who had been a student at a Virginia university (1) filed suit in the United States District Court for the Western District of Virginia against defendants including two male individuals; and (2) alleged, among other matters, that (a) she had been raped by the two individuals while she and they had been attending the university, and (b) this attack violated 42 USCS § 13981, which provided a federal civil remedy for the victims of gender-motivated violence. The United States intervened to defend § 13981's validity under the Federal Constitution. Although the District Court decided that the complaint stated a claim against the two alleged attackers under § 13981, the District Court, in dismissing the complaint, reasoned that Congress lacked authority to enact § 13981 under either the Constitution's commerce clause (Art I, § 8, cl 3) or § 5 of the Constitution's Fourteenth Amendment (935 F Supp 779). A panel of the United States Court of Appeals for the Fourth Circuit initially reversed the District Court (132 F3d 949). However, on rehearing en banc, the Court of Appeals, among other matters, instead affirmed the District Court's determination that Congress lacked authority under the Constitution to enact § 13981's civil remedy (169 F3d 820).

On certiorari, the United States Supreme Court affirmed. In an opinion by REHNQUIST, Ch. J., joined by O'CONNOR, SCALIA, KENNEDY, and THOMAS, JJ., it was held that Congress had no authority to enact § 13981 under either the commerce clause or § 5 of the Fourteenth Amendment, as, among other matters, (1) gender-motivated crimes of violence were not—in any sense of the phrase—economic activity; (2) § 13981 contained no jurisdictional element establishing that a federal cause of action was in pursuance of Congress' power to regulate interstate commerce; (3) the Constitution required a distinction between what was truly national and what was truly local; (4) there was no better example of state police power than the suppression of violent crime and the vindication of victims; and (5) § 13981 was directed at individuals who had committed criminal acts motivated by gender bias, rather than at a state or state actor.

THOMAS, J., concurring, expressed the view that while the decision in United States v Lopez (1995) 514 US 549, 131 L Ed 2d 626, 115 S Ct 1624, was correctly applied to the case at hand, (1) the notion of a "substantial effects" test under the commerce clause was inconsistent with the original understanding of Congress' powers and with the Supreme Court's early commerce clause cases; and (2) by continuing to apply this standard, the Supreme Court encouraged the Federal Government to persist in the view that the commerce clause had virtually no limits.

SOUTER, J., joined by STEVENS, GINSBURG, and BREYER, JJ., dissenting, expressed the view that (1) some claims by the Supreme Court in the case at hand—that (a) the court's commerce clause precedent was left undisturbed, and (b) § 13981 exceeded Congress's power under that clause—were irreconcilable; (2) Congress had the power to legislate with regard to activity that, in the aggregate, had a substantial effect on interstate commerce; and (3) the sufficiency of the evidence assembled by Congress—showing the effects of violence against women on interstate commerce—could not seriously be questioned under a rational-basis standard.

BREYER, J., joined by STEVENS, J., and joined in part (as to points 1 and 2 below) by SOUTER and GINSBURG, JJ., dissenting, expressed the view that (1) virtually every kind of activity in the nation—due to centuries of scientific, technological, commercial, and environmental change—could affect commerce outside a specific state; (2) Congress—representing state and local district interests—could reflect state concerns for autonomy in the details of sophisticated statutory schemes better than the judiciary; (3) § 13981's enactment by Congress represented state and federal efforts to cooperate in order to help solve a mutually acknowledged national problem; and (4) § 13981 was a necessary and proper exercise of legislative power granted to Congress by the commerce clause.

COUNSEL

Julie Goldscheid argued the cause for petitioner in No. 99-29.

Seth P. Waxman argued the cause for the United States in No. 99-5.

Michael E. Rosman argued the cause for respondents.

JEFFREY ALLAN FISCHER, Petitioner

v

UNITED STATES

529 US —, 146 L Ed 2d 707, 120 S Ct 1780

[No. 99-116]

Argued February 22, 2000.
Decided May 15, 2000.

Decision: Medicare payments received by health care providers held to constitute "benefits" within meaning of federal bribery statute (18 USCS § 666), prohibiting fraud and other offenses against organizations receiving federal benefits.

SUMMARY

A federal bribery statute (18 USCS § 666) prohibits various offenses, including fraud, against or involving parties defined in 18 USCS § 666(b) as organizations, governments, or agencies which receive, in any 1-year period, more than $10,000 in "benefits" under a federal program involving a grant, contract, subsidy, loan, guarantee, insurance, or other federal assistance. The president and part owner of a medical consulting firm was tried and convicted in a Federal District Court on the charge, among others, that he had violated § 666 by defrauding a municipal agency, which (1) operated two local hospitals, and (2) had received more than $10 million in Medicare funds during the year when the alleged fraud occurred. On appeal, the president asserted that the prosecution had failed to prove that the municipal agency had received benefits from a federal program, as required by § 666(b).
168

However, the convictions were affirmed by the United States Court of Appeals for the Eleventh Circuit, which expressed the view that funds received by an organization constituted such benefits if the source of the funds was a federal program, such as Medicare, that provided aid or assistance to participating organizations (168 F3d 1273).

On certiorari, the United States Supreme Court affirmed. In an opinion by KENNEDY, J., joined by REHNQUIST, Ch. J., and STEVENS, O'CONNOR, SOUTER, GINSBURG, and BREYER, JJ., it was held that Medicare payments to health care providers such as the one allegedly defrauded in the case at hand were benefits within the meaning of § 666.

THOMAS, J., joined by SCALIA, J., dissented, expressing the view that (1) the only persons who received benefits under Medicare, for purposes of § 666, were individual patients, and (2) payments made by the Federal Government to a Medicare health care provider as reimbursement for the cost of services rendered, rather than as financial aid to a hospital, were not such benefits.

COUNSEL

Mark L. Horwitz argued the cause for petitioner.
Lisa S. Blatt argued the cause for respondent.

CORNELL JOHNSON, Petitioner

v

UNITED STATES

529 US —, 146 L Ed 2d 727, 120 S Ct 1795

[No. 99-5153]

Argued February 22, 2000.
Decided May 15, 2000.

Decision: Prior version of 18 USCS § 3583(e)(3) held to authorize Federal District Court to impose additional term of supervised release after revocation of initial term and reimprisonment; 18 USCS § 3583(h) held not retroactively applicable.

SUMMARY

In the Sentencing Reform Act of 1984 (18 USCS §§ 3551 et seq.), Congress eliminated most forms of parole in favor of supervised release, which was a form of postconfinement monitoring overseen by the sentencing court, rather than the United States Parole Commission. Under 18 USCS § 3583, (1) the sentencing court was authorized to impose a term of supervised release to follow imprisonment, with the maximum length of the term varying according to the severity of the initial offense (18 USCS §§ 3583(a) and 3583(b)); (2) an offender, while on supervised release, was required to abide by certain conditions, some specified by statute and some imposable at the court's discretion (18 USCS § 3583(d)); and (3) upon violation of a condition, the sentencing court was authorized to revoke a term of supervised release and to require the person to serve in prison all or part of the
170

term of supervised release without credit for time previously served on postrelease supervision (18 USCS § 3583(e)(3)). In 1994, an accused was convicted in a Federal District Court of violating a federal criminal statute and was sentenced to imprisonment followed by a term of supervised release. After beginning supervised release in 1995, the accused violated two conditions of his release. The District Court revoked his release and ordered him to serve an 18-month prison term to be followed by an additional 12 months of supervised release. The accused appealed his sentence and argued that (1) § 3583(e)(3) did not give the District Court power to order a new supervised release term following reimprisonment, and (2) the application of 18 USCS § 3583(h)—a provision, added after the accused's conviction, that explicitly gave District Courts the power to impose another term of supervised release following revocation and reimprisonment—violated the Federal Constitution's Art I, § 9, cl 3 prohibition against ex post facto laws. However, the United States Court of Appeals for the Sixth Circuit, in affirming, expressed the view that the application of § 3583(h) to the accused did not violate the ex post facto prohibition (181 F3d 105, reported in full 1999 US App LEXIS 8558).

On certiorari, the United States Supreme Court affirmed the judgment of the Court of Appeals. In an opinion by SOUTER, J., joined by REHNQUIST, Ch. J., and STEVENS, O'CONNOR, GINSBURG, and BREYER, JJ., and joined in pertinent part by KENNEDY, J., it was held that the District Court did not exceed the court's authority by ordering the accused to be placed on an additional term of supervised release, because (1) § 3583(h) did not apply retroactively; (2) therefore, no issue concerning a violation of the Art I, § 9, cl 3 ex post facto prohibition arose in the accused's case; and (3) under

171

the version of § 3583 in effect at the time of the accused's conviction, § 3583(e)(3) permitted the District Court to impose supervised release following revocation and reimprisonment, as, among other matters, (a) the more plausible textual reading of § 3583(e)(3) left open the possibility of supervised release after reincarceration, (b) such a reading served the evident congressional purpose to improve the odds of a successful transition from the prison to liberty, and (c) the traditional rule of lenity in interpreting criminal statutes did not demand a contrary result.

KENNEDY, J., concurring in part, expressed the view that the opinion of the Supreme Court was correct, except with respect to (1) a discussion concerning District Court authority under 18 USCS § 3583(e)(2), and (2) a "dictum" regarding § 3583(a).

THOMAS, J., concurring in the judgment, expressed the view that the Supreme Court's textual analysis of § 3583(e)(3) was (1) correct, and (2) sufficient to resolve the case without relying on any apparent congressional purpose supporting the court's reading of that provision.

SCALIA, J., dissenting, expressed the view that (1) the Supreme Court was correct as to holdings 1 and 2 above; but (2) § 3583(e)(3) did not authorize a District Court to impose additional supervised release, as (a) the term "revoke" should have been construed in accordance with its ordinary or natural meaning, (b) under this reading, the revoked term of supervised release was canceled, and (c) since there was no authorization in the statute for a new term of supervised release, additional supervised release was unavailable.

COUNSEL

Rita La Lumia argued the cause for petitioner.
Paul R.Q. Wolfson argued the cause for respondent.

PUBLIC LANDS COUNCIL et al., Petitioners

v

BRUCE BABBITT, Secretary of the Interior, et al.

529 US —, 146 L Ed 2d 753, 120 S Ct 1815

[No. 98-1991]

Argued March 1, 2000.
Decided May 15, 2000.

Decision: Interior Department regulations (43 CFR §§ 4100.0-5, 4110.1(a), 4120.3-2(b)) concerning livestock grazing on federal public rangelands held not to exceed authority of Secretary of Interior under Taylor Grazing Act of 1934 (43 USCS §§ 315 et seq.)

SUMMARY

The Taylor Grazing Act of 1934 (43 USCS §§ 315 et seq.) granted the United States Secretary of the Interior authority to (1) divide the federal public rangelands into grazing districts, (2) specify the amount of grazing permitted in each district, (3) issue leases or permits to graze livestock, and (4) charge reasonable fees for use of the land. In 43 USCS § 315b, the Act (1) gave preference, in respect to permits, to (a) landowners engaged in the livestock business, (b) bona fide occupants or settlers, or (c) owners of water or water rights; and (2) provided that (a) grazing privileges would be adequately safeguarded, but (b) the creation of a grazing district or the issuance of a permit did not create any right, title, interest, or estate in or to the lands. A group of nonprofit ranching-related organizations with members who held grazing permits brought,
174

against defendants including the Secretary, an action challenging 10 of the new federal grazing regulations issued by the Secretary in 1995. The United States District Court for the District of Wyoming found 4 of the 10 regulations unlawful (929 F Supp 1436). As to the four regulations, the United States Court of Appeals for the Tenth Circuit, reversing in part, upheld three—(1) 43 CFR § 4100.0-5, which changed the definition of "grazing preference;" (2) 43 CFR § 4110.1(a), which permitted those who were not "engaged in the livestock business" to qualify for grazing permits; and (3) 43 CFR § 4120.3-2(b), which granted the United States title to all future range improvements (167 F3d 1287).

On certiorari, the United States Supreme Court affirmed. In an opinion by BREYER, J., expressing the unanimous view of the court, it was held that neither § 4100.0-5, § 4110.1(a), nor § 4120.3-2(b) exceeded the authority that the Act granted to the Secretary, as (1) the new definition, in § 4100.0-5, of "grazing preference" did not violate the § 315b requirement that recognized grazing privileges be adequately safeguarded, where § 4100.0-5 referred to "permitted use," which was defined as the forage, expressed in animal unit months (AUMs), allocated under an applicable land use plan, whereas earlier regulations had referred to (a) grazing privileges as "apportioned," or (b) a specific number of AUMs attached to a base property; (2) the omission, in § 4110.1(a), of a requirement—that eligibility for grazing permits be limited to those engaged in the livestock business—did not cause § 4110.1(a) to violate the § 315b provision for the issuance of grazing permits to only settlers, residents, and other stock owners; and (3) the § 4120.3-2(b) provision concerning title to range improvements in the name of the United States did not violate 43

175

USCS § 315c, which provided that no permit would entitle the permittee to the use of range improvements constructed and owned by a prior occupant, until the permit applicant had paid the prior occupant the reasonable value of such improvements.

O'CONNOR, J., joined by THOMAS, J., concurring, expressed the view that the court's decision did not foreclose permit holders from bringing (1) an as-applied challenge to the Secretary's specific application of the regulations, or (2) a challenge to the regulations under the Administrative Procedures Act (5 USCS § 706(2)(A)).

COUNSEL

Timothy S. Bishop argued the cause for petitioners.
Edwin S. Kneedler argued the cause for respondents.

MARIA SUZUKI OHLER, Petitioner

v

UNITED STATES

529 US —, 146 L Ed 2d 826, 120 S Ct 1851

[No. 98-9828]

Argued March 20, 2000.
Decided May 22, 2000.

Decision: Federal criminal defendant who pre-emptively introduced evidence of prior conviction on direct examination held not entitled to challenge admission of such evidence on appeal.

SUMMARY

An individual, who had entered the United States in a van which was found to contain large amounts of marijuana, was charged in Federal District Court with importation of marijuana and possession of marijuana with intent to distribute. The government (1) filed, among other items, a motion in limine seeking to introduce, for impeachment purposes, evidence of the individual's previous felony conviction for possession of methamphetamine; and (2) obtained an order allowing the government to do so if the individual testified on her own behalf. The individual then chose to admit to the prior conviction on direct examination before the prosecution could introduce it. On appeal from her ensuing conviction, the individual challenged the District Court's in limine ruling, but the United States Court of Appeals for the Ninth Circuit, in affirming,

177

ruled that the individual had waived her objection by introducing evidence of the conviction on direct examination (169 F3d 1200).

On certiorari, the United States Supreme Court affirmed. In an opinion by REHNQUIST, Ch. J., joined by O'CONNOR, SCALIA, KENNEDY, and THOMAS, JJ., it was held that a federal criminal defendant who preemptively introduces evidence of a prior conviction on direct examination may not claim on appeal that the admission of such evidence was error.

SOUTER, J., joined by STEVENS, GINSBURG, and BREYER, JJ., dissented, expressing the view that defendants who oppose admission of prior-conviction evidence—and who introduce such evidence themselves only to mitigate the evidence's effect—do not thereby waive the right to challenge an order allowing the prosecution to use such evidence.

COUNSEL

Benjamin L. Coleman argued the cause for petitioner.

Barbara B. McDowell argued the cause for respondent.

VERMONT AGENCY of NATURAL RESOURCES,
Petitioner

v

UNITED STATES ex rel. STEVENS

529 US —, 146 L Ed 2d 836, 120 S Ct 1858

[No. 98-1828]

Argued November 29, 1999.
Decided May 22, 2000.

Decision: Private individual held to have standing to
bring action on behalf of United States under False
Claims Act (FCA) (31 USCS §§ 3729-3733), but
FCA held not to subject state or state agency to
liability in such actions.

SUMMARY

Under the False Claims Act (FCA) (31 USCS §§ 3729-
3733), a private person—known as a "relator"—was
empowered to bring a qui tam civil action, on behalf of
the relator and on behalf of the Federal Government,
in the name of the government against any person who
allegedly knowingly presented, or caused to be presented, a false or fraudulent claim for payment or
approval to an officer or employee of the Federal
Government. When such an action was initiated, the
government had 60 days to intervene and to assume
primary responsibility for prosecuting the action. If the
government declined to intervene, then the relator had
the exclusive right to conduct the action. Also, regardless of whether the government intervened, the relator
would receive a share of any proceeds from the action,
plus attorneys' fees and costs. An individual brought

such a qui tam action as a relator in the United States District Court for the District of Vermont against the relator's former employer—the state of Vermont's agency of natural resources—which action alleged that the state agency had submitted false claims to the Environmental Protection Agency (EPA) in connection with various federal grant programs administered by the EPA by overstating the amount of time spent by the state agency's employees on the federally funded projects. The United States declined to intervene in the action. The state agency then moved to dismiss the action and argued that (1) a state or a state agency was not a "person" subject to liability under the FCA, and (2) a qui tam action in federal court against a state was barred by the Federal Constitution's Eleventh Amendment. The District Court denied the motion. The state agency then filed an interlocutory appeal in the United States Court of Appeals for the Second Circuit and the District Court stayed the proceedings pending the outcome of the state's appeal. The Court of Appeals affirmed the District Court's denial of the state's motion to dismiss the action (162 F3d 195).

On certiorari, the United States Supreme Court reversed the judgment of the Court of Appeals. In an opinion by SCALIA, J., joined by REHNQUIST, Ch. J., and O'CONNOR, KENNEDY, THOMAS, and BREYER, JJ., it was held that (1) the relator had standing under Article III of the Constitution to maintain a suit brought under the FCA, as (a) an adequate basis for the relator's suit for his bounty was to be found in the doctrine that the assignee of a claim had standing to assert the injury in fact suffered by the assignor, and (b) therefore, the United States' injury in fact sufficed to confer standing on the qui tam relator; (2) the court would address the statutory question whether a state or a state agency was a person subject to qui tam liability under the FCA before the question whether the Eleventh Amendment barred such a suit against a state or state agency; (3) the relator could not bring suit in a federal court on behalf of the United States against the state agency under the FCA, as, among other matters, (a) the Supreme Court had to apply to the FCA's text the court's longstanding interpretive presumption that "person" did not include the sovereign, (b) the FCA's liability provisions, as originally enacted, bore no indication that states were subject to the FCA's penalties, (c) although the liability provisions of the original FCA had undergone various changes, none of them suggested a broadening of the term "person" to include states, and (d) several features of the current statutory scheme supported the conclusion that states were not subject to qui tam liability; and (4) the court would express no view whether such a qui tam action ran afoul of the Eleventh Amendment.

BREYER, J., concurring, expressed the view that he joined the opinion of the Supreme Court in full and also joined the opinion of GINSBURG, J.

GINSBURG, J., joined by BREYER, J., concurring in the judgment, expressed the view that (1) the Supreme Court properly resolved the statutory question whether Congress had authorized qui tam suits against the states under the FCA, and (2) the court's opinion ought to be read as having left open the question whether the word "person" encompassed states when the United States itself sued under the FCA.

STEVENS, J., joined by SOUTER, J., dissenting, expressed the view that (1) Congress intended states to be included within the meaning of the word "person" in § 3729; (2) this view was supported by (a) the legislative history of some 1986 amendments to the FCA, (b) the Supreme Court's construction of statutes in cases de-

181

cided before the 1986 amendments were enacted, and (c) the FCA's text; (3) qui tam actions were cases or controversies within the meaning of Article III; and (4) the claim of sovereign immunity from suit also ought to fail, in view of factors including Congress' clear intent to subject states to qui tam actions under the FCA.

COUNSEL

J. Wallace Malley, Jr. argued the cause for petitioner.

Edwin S. Kneedler argued the cause for the United States.

Theodore B. Olson argued the cause for respondent Jonathan Stevens.

UNITED STATES, et al., Appellants

v

PLAYBOY ENTERTAINMENT GROUP, INC.

529 US —, 146 L Ed 2d 865, 120 S Ct 1878

[No. 98-1682]

Argued November 30, 1999.
Decided May 22, 2000.

Decision: First Amendment's free speech guarantee held violated by § 505 of Telecommunications Act of 1996 (47 USCS § 561), restricting transmission of cable television channels primarily dedicated to sexually oriented programming.

SUMMARY

Cable television operators use signal "scrambling" to insure that only paying customers have access to some programming. Out of a concern that scrambling might be insufficient to prevent "signal bleed"—a phenomenon under which audio or visual portions of the scrambled programs might be heard or seen—with respect to sexually oriented programming, Congress enacted § 505 of the Telecommunications Act of 1996 (47 USCS § 561), which required cable television operators who provided channels primarily dedicated to sexually oriented programming to (1) fully scramble or otherwise fully block those channels, or (2) "time channel," that is, limit transmission to hours when children were unlikely to be viewing. To comply with § 505, the majority of cable operators ultimately adopted the time channeling approach, with the result that for two-thirds of the day, no viewers in the operators' service areas could receive the programming in question. An entity that owned and prepared such programming and transmitted the programming to cable television operators brought suit against the Federal Government in the United States District Court for the District of Delaware, in which suit the entity sought (1) a declaration that § 505 violated the Federal Constitution's First Amendment, and (2) an injunction prohibiting the enforcement of § 505. For purposes of the litigation, the programming in question was not alleged to be obscene. A three-judge panel of the District Court denied a preliminary injunction (945 F Supp 772), and the United States Supreme Court summarily affirmed (520 US 1141, 137 L Ed 2d 473, 117 S Ct 1309). After a full trial, however, the District Court (1) observed that § 505 imposed a content-based restriction on speech; (2) concluded that although the interests that § 505 advanced were compelling, the government might further those interests in a less restrictive way by means of § 504 of the Telecommunications Act (47 USCS § 560)—which required cable operators to block undesired channels at individual households upon request—provided that adequate notice of the availability of § 504 blocking devices were given to cable subscribers; (3) declared § 505 unconstitutional and enjoined § 505's enforcement; and (4) required the entity to insure, in the entity's contractual arrangements with cable operators, that the operators would provide adequate notice of § 504 (30 F Supp 2d 702).

On direct appeal, the Supreme Court affirmed. In an opinion by KENNEDY, J., joined by STEVENS, SOUTER, THOMAS, and GINSBURG, JJ., it was held that § 505 violated the First Amendment's free speech guarantee, as (1) § 505 was a content-based regulation of a form of speech that enjoyed First Amendment protection; (2)

§ 505 singled out particular programmers for regulation; (3) the only reasonable way for a substantial number of cable operators to comply with the letter of § 505 was to time channel; (4) to prohibit this much speech was a significant restriction of communication between speakers and willing adult listeners; (5) the evidence was inadequate to show that signal bleed was a pervasive problem; (6) no support for such a restriction could be found in the legislative record; (7) the government's interest was thus not sufficiently compelling to justify such a widespread restriction on speech; and (8) § 505 had not been shown to be the least restrictive means for addressing the problem in question, for a less restrictive alternative was provided by § 504, which—if publicized in an adequate manner—might possibly be an effective means to achieve the government's goals.

STEVENS, J., concurring, expressed the view that the programs in question ought not to be treated as obscene, and thus unprotected by the First Amendment, merely because of the way that the programs were advertised.

THOMAS, J., concurring, expressed the view that (1) some of the programming at issue might have met the Supreme Court's test of obscenity, but (2) under the litigants' assumption that the programming was merely indecent and thus protected speech, § 505 could not be upheld under the First Amendment on the theory argued by the government.

SCALIA, J., dissenting, expressed the view that even under the assumption that the individual programs at issue were not obscene, § 505 could be upheld under the First Amendment on the ground that § 505 (1) was supported by a compelling state interest and was narrowly tailored, or (2) regulated the business of obscenity.

BREYER J., joined by REHNQUIST, Ch. J., and O'CONNOR and SCALIA, JJ., dissenting, expressed the view that § 505 was valid under the First Amendment, because (1) the government had not failed to prove the seriousness of the problem addressed by § 505, namely, the receipt of adult channels by children whose parents did not request the broadcast of such channels; and (2) the record had made clear that § 504 did not provide a similarly effective alternative to § 505.

COUNSEL

James A. Feldman argued the cause for appellants. Robert Corn-Revere argued the cause for appellee

---

DEWEY J. JONES, Petitioner

v

UNITED STATES

529 US —, 146 L Ed 2d 902, 120 S Ct 1904

[No. 99-5739]

Argued March 21, 2000.
Decided May 22, 2000.

Decision: Arson of owner-occupied residence not currently used for any commercial purpose held not to be subject to prosecution under 18 USCS § 844(i), because residence was not "used" in commerce or commerce-affecting activity.

SUMMARY

A private residence that was being used by its owner for everyday living was severely damaged by a fire that resulted when an accused tossed a Molotov cocktail into the residence. The accused was convicted, in the United States District Court for the Northern District of Indiana, on three federal counts, including violation of 18 USCS § 844(i), which made it a federal crime to maliciously damage, by means of fire, any building used in interstate or foreign commerce or in any activity affecting interstate or foreign commerce. The United States Court of Appeals for the Seventh Circuit—rejecting the accused's contention that § 844(i), when applied to the arson of a private residence, exceeded the authority vested in Congress under the Federal Constitution's commerce clause (Art I, § 8, cl 3)—affirmed the District Court judgment (178 F3d 479).

On certiorari, the United States Supreme Court reversed and remanded. In an opinion by GINSBURG, J., expressing the unanimous view of the court, it was held that arson of an owner-occupied residence that—like the residence involved in the case at hand—was not currently used for any commercial purpose was not subject to prosecution under 18 USCS § 844(i), because such a residence was not "used" in commerce or commerce-affecting activity, as, among other matters, "used" was most sensibly read to mean active employment for commercial purposes.

STEVENS, J., joined by THOMAS, J., concurring, expressed the view that the court should interpret narrowly federal criminal laws that overlap with state authority, unless congressional intention to assert its jurisdiction is plain.

THOMAS, J., joined by SCALIA, J., concurring, expressed no view on the question whether § 844(i), as construed in the court's opinion, was constitutional in its application to all buildings used for commercial activities.

COUNSEL

Donald M. Falk argued the cause for petitioner.
Michael R. Dreeben argued the cause for respondent.

———————

ALEXIS GEIER, et al., Petitioners

v

AMERICAN HONDA MOTOR CO., INC., et al.

529 US —, 146 L Ed 2d 914, 120 S Ct 1913

[No. 98-1811]

Argued , December 7, 1999.
Decided May 22, 2000.

Decision: National Traffic and Motor Safety Act of
1966—when taken together with relevant regulatory standard—held to pre-empt common-law tort
action claiming that car manufacturer, compliant
with standard, ought to have equipped car with
airbags.

SUMMARY

Under the National Traffic and Motor Vehicle Safety
Act of 1966 (the 1966 Act) (15 USCS §§ 1381 et seq.,
later recodified at 49 USCS §§ 30101 et seq.), the
United States Department of Transportation promulgated Federal Motor Vehicle Safety Standard (FMVSS)
208 (49 CFR § 571.208), which, among other matters,
required auto manufacturers to equip some but not all
of their 1987 vehicles with passive restraints. In 1992, a
driver of a 1987 automobile that did not have such
restraints was injured in an accident. The driver and the
parents of the driver (1) sought damages under the
District of Columbia's tort law, (2) filed suit in the
United States District Court for the District of Columbia against the automobile's manufacturer and the
manufacturer's affiliates, and (3) alleged, among other
matters, that the manufacturer and its affiliates had

been negligent in not equipping the driver's automobile with a driver's side airbag. In dismissing the suit, the District Court (1) noted that FMVSS 208 gave car manufacturers a choice as to whether to install airbags, and (2) concluded that the suit in question—as it sought to establish an airbag requirement—was expressly pre-empted by a provision of the 1966 Act (15 USCS § 1392(d), later recodified at 49 USCS § 30103(b)) that pre-empted any safety standard that was not identical to a federal safety standard applicable to the same aspect of performance. In affirming the District Court's dismissal, the United States Court of Appeals for the District of Columbia Circuit reasoned that (1) the driver's state-law tort claims posed an obstacle to the accomplishment of the objectives of FMVSS 208, (2) for that reason, those claims conflicted with FMVSS 208, and (3) under ordinary pre-emption principles, the 1966 Act consequently pre-empted the suit (166 F3d 1236).

On certiorari, the United States Supreme Court affirmed. In an opinion by BREYER, J., joined by REHNQUIST, Ch. J., and O'CONNOR, SCALIA, and KENNEDY, JJ., it was held that the 1966 Act, when read in conjunction with FMVSS 208, pre-empted a state common-law tort action claiming that an auto manufacturer, who was in compliance with the standard, ought to have equipped a 1987 automobile with airbags, as—even though § 1392(d) did not expressly pre-empt the suit—(1) the 1966 Act's saving clause (15 USCS § 1397(k), later recodified at 49 USCS § 30103(e)), like § 1392(d), did not bar the ordinary working of conflict pre-emption principles by suggesting an intent to save state-law tort actions that were inconsistent with federal regulations; and (2) the common-law action in the case at hand presented an obstacle to, among other matters, (a) the variety and mix of passive restraint devices that

190

the federal regulation sought, (b) the gradual phase-in of passive restraints that the federal regulation deliberately imposed, and (c) quite possibly, the adoption of a law mandating that automobile seat belts be buckled up.

STEVENS, J., joined by SOUTER, THOMAS, and GINSBURG, JJ., dissenting, expressed the view that, among other matters, (1) the rule that the Supreme Court enforced in the case at hand was not enacted by Congress and was not found in the text of any Executive Order or regulation; (2) the term "safety standard," as used in §§ 1392(d) and 1397(k), referred to an objective rule prescribed by a legislature or an administrative agency and did not encompass case-specific decisions by judges and juries that resolved common-law claims; and (3) a pre-emption argument—that if the manufacturers had known that they would be held liable for failure to install airbags, then that risk would have led manufacturers to install airbags in all cars, thereby allegedly frustrating the Secretary of Transportation's safety goals and interfering with the methods designed to achieve them—was flawed.

COUNSEL

Arthur H. Bryant argued the cause for petitioners.

Lawrence G. Wallace argued the cause for the United States, as amicus curiae, by special leave of court.

Malcolm E. Wheeler argued the cause for respondents.

———

HARTFORD UNDERWRITERS INSURANCE COM-
PANY, Petitioner

v

UNION PLANTERS BANK, N. A.

530 US —, 147 L Ed 2d 1, 120 S Ct 1942

[No. 99-409]

Argued March 20, 2000.
Decided May 30, 2000.

Decision: 11 USCS § 506(c) held not to empower
administrative claimant of bankruptcy estate to
seek payment of claim from estate property encumbered by secured creditor's lien.

SUMMARY

A corporation which operated restaurants and other
businesses filed a voluntary petition for reorganization
under Chapter 11 of the Bankruptcy Code (11 USCS
§§ 1101 et seq.) in the United States Bankruptcy Court
for the Eastern District of Missouri. During the reorganization attempt, the corporation obtained workers'
compensation insurance from an underwriting company, but repeatedly failed to pay the premiums. When
the reorganization failed, the Bankruptcy Court con-
verted the case into a liquidation under Chapter 7 of
the Bankruptcy Code (11 USCS §§ 701 et seq.). The
underwriting company, learning of the bankruptcy
proceedings, sought to recover its premiums as an
administrative expense under 11 USCS § 503. Since
essentially all of the corporation's assets were subject to
a bank's security interest, which would ordinarily have
priority over administrative expenses, the underwriting

company sought to invoke 11 USCS § 506(c), which provides that "[t]he trustee may recover" from property subject to an allowed secured claim the reasonable and necessary costs of preserving or disposing of such property. The Bankruptcy Court ruled in favor of the underwriting company. This ruling was affirmed (1) by the United States District Court for the Eastern District of Missouri, and (2) subsequently, by a panel of the United States Court of Appeals for the Eighth Circuit (150 F3d 868). However, the Court of Appeals granted rehearing en banc and reversed, on the ground that § 506(c) could not be invoked by an administrative claimant (177 F3d 719).

On certiorari, the United States Supreme Court affirmed. In an opinion by SCALIA, J., expressing the unanimous view of the court, it was held that § 506(c) did not provide administrative claimants—such as the underwriting company in the case at hand—with an independent right to seek payment of their claims from property subject to secured claims.

COUNSEL

G. Eric Brunstad, Jr. argued the cause for petitioner.

Robert H. Brownlee argued the cause for respondent.

THOMAS E. RALEIGH, Chapter 7 trustee for the
ESTATE OF WILLIAM J. STOECKER, Petitioner

v

ILLINOIS DEPARTMENT OF REVENUE

530 US —, 147 L Ed 2d 13, 120 S Ct 1951

[No. 99-387]

Argued April 17, 2000.
Decided May 30, 2000.

Decision: Burden of proof on state tax claim in bankruptcy court held to be on trustee in bankruptcy,
where substantive state law creating tax obligation
put burden on taxpayer.

SUMMARY

When a debtor was president of an Illinois corporation, the corporation purchased an airplane out of state
and moved the plane to Illinois. Illinois law (1) required, with respect to planes purchased out of state
and moved to Illinois, that the buyer file a state use tax
return and pay the use tax within 30 days after the
plane entered the state, and (2) provided that any
corporate officer responsible for the tax payment who
failed to file a return or make the payment was personally liable for a penalty equal to the total unpaid tax
amount. By the time the state's department of revenue,
having discovered that the corporation had failed to file
a use tax return or pay the tax on the plan, issued a
notice of tax liability against the corporation and a
notice of penalty liability against the debtor, the corporation was defunct and the debtor was in bankruptcy.
There was no affirmative proof that the debtor was
194

responsible for payment of the tax. However, Illinois law shifted the burden of proof, both on production and persuasion, to the purportedly responsible officer—in this case, the trustee in bankruptcy—once a notice of penalty liability was issued. As to the department's claim against the debtor's estate for the penalty, the United States Court of Appeals for the Seventh Circuit ruled in favor of the department, as the court expressed the view that the burden of proof remained on the trustee, just as the burden would have been on the debtor if the proceedings had taken place outside of bankruptcy (179 F3d 546).

On certiorari, the United States Supreme Court affirmed. In an opinion by SOUTER, J., expressing the unanimous view of the court, it was held that when—as in the case at hand—the substantive law creating a tax obligation put the burden of proof on a taxpayer, the burden of proof on the tax claim in bankruptcy court remained where the substantive law put it, as among other matters, tax law was no candidate for exception to the general rule that one who asserts a claim is entitled to the burden of proof that normally comes with the claim.

COUNSEL

Robert Radasevich argued the cause for petitioner.

Lawrence G. Wallace argued the cause for the United States, as amicus curiae, by special leave of court.

Benjamin Goldgar argued the cause for respondent.

UNITED STATES, Petitioner

v

WEBSTER L. HUBBELL

530 US —, 147 L Ed 2d 24, 120 S Ct 2037

[No. 99-166]

Argued February 22, 2000.
Decided June 5, 2000.

Decision: Accused's federal indictment held required to be dismissed, where evidence used to obtain indictment was not derived from sources independent of documents produced under grant of immunity.

SUMMARY

In 1994, upon the request of the United States Attorney General, an Independent Counsel was appointed to investigate possible criminal violations relating to, among other matters, the President's relationships with various business entities. In the course of this investigation, a former United States Associate Attorney General was charged with mail fraud and tax evasion arising out of his billing practices as a member of an Arkansas law firm from 1989 to 1992. In a guilty-plea agreement, the former official promised to provide the Independent Counsel with information about matters relating to the investigation. In 1996, the Independent Counsel obtained a subpoena duces tecum that called on the former official to produce documents before a federal grand jury sitting in Little Rock, Arkansas. The former official appeared before the grand jury and invoked the Federal Constitution's Fifth Amendment
196

privilege against self-incrimination. However, the independent counsel produced a federal court order which (1) directed the former official to respond to the subpoena; and (2) granted him immunity, under 18 USCS § 6002, against the use and derivative use of compelled testimony. The former official then delivered the specified documents. Subsequently, a federal grand jury in the District of Columbia returned an indictment which charged the former official with various tax-related crimes and mail and wire fraud. However, the United States District Court for the District of Columbia, in dismissing the indictment, relied in part on the ground that the independent counsel's use of the subpoenaed documents violated § 6002, as the District Court concluded that all of the evidence that would have been offered against the former official at trial derived either directly or indirectly from the testimonial aspects of the former official's immunized act of producing those documents (11 F Supp 2d 25). The United States Court of Appeals for the District of Columbia Circuit, in vacating the District Court's judgment and in remanding for further proceedings, expressed the view that (1) the District Court had incorrectly relied on the fact that the Independent Counsel had not had prior knowledge of the contents of the subpoenaed documents; (2) the District Court ought to have addressed the question of the extent of the Independent Counsel's independent knowledge of (a) the documents' existence and authenticity, and (b) the former official's possession or control of the documents; and (3) if the Independent Counsel could not demonstrate with reasonable particularity a prior awareness that the documents existed and were in the former official's possession, then the indictment would be tainted (334 US App DC 315, 167 F3d 552). The Independent Ccounsel—having acknowledged, on remand, that he could not satisfy the reasonable-particularity standard—entered into a conditional plea agreement providing for (1) dismissal of the indictment, unless the United States Supreme Court's disposition of the case were to make it reasonably likely that the former official's immunity would not pose a significant bar to his prosecution; and (2) the entry of a guilty plea and a sentence if the Supreme Court were to reverse the Court of Appeals' judgment.

On certiorari, the Supreme Court affirmed. In an opinion by STEVENS, J., joined by O'CONNOR, SCALIA, KENNEDY, SOUTER, THOMAS, GINSBURG, and BREYER, JJ., it was held that the former official's indictment had to be dismissed, where the Federal Government could not prove that the evidence that it used to obtain the indictment—and proposed to use at trial—was derived from legitimate sources that were entirely independent of the testimonial aspect of the former official's immunized conduct in producing the subpoenaed documents, as, among other matters, (1) § 6002's guarantee of use-and-derivative-use immunity was as broad as the Fifth Amendment's privilege against self-incrimination; (2) the former official's production of the catalog of existing documents fitting within any of the 11 broadly worded subpoena categories could have provided the Independent Counsel with (a) a lead to incriminating evidence, or (b) a link in the chain of evidence needed to prosecute; (3) the testimonial aspect of the former official's act of production was the first step in the chain of evidence leading to prosecution; and (4) the Independent Counsel had shown no prior knowledge of either the existence or the whereabouts of the documents ultimately produced.

THOMAS, J., joined by SCALIA, J., concurring, expressed the view that although the Supreme Court properly applied the act-of-production doctrine, (1) that doctrine could be inconsistent with the original meaning of the Fifth Amendment's self-incrimination clause, (2) a substantial body of evidence suggested that the Fifth Amendment privilege protected against the compelled production not just of incriminating testimony, but of any incriminating evidence, and (3) the scope and meaning of the self-incrimination clause ought to be reconsidered in a future case.

REHNQUIST, Ch. J., dissenting, would have reversed the Court of Appeals' judgment in part for the reasons expressed by a dissenting Court of Appeals judge, to the effect that the inquiry about the subpoenaed documents ought to have been limited to verifying that the Independent Counsel, in securing the former official's indictment, had only used information that would have been used if the documents had appeared in the Independent Counsel's office, unsolicited and without explanation.

COUNSEL

Ronald J. Mann argued the cause for petitioner.

Michael R. Dreeben argued the cause for the United States Department of Justice, as amicus curiae, by special leave of court.

John W. Nields, Jr. argued the cause for respondent.

JENIFER TROXEL, et vir, Petitioners

v

TOMMIE GRANVILLE

530 US —, 147 L Ed 2d 49, 120 S Ct 2054

[No. 99-138]

Argued January 12, 2000.
Decided June 5, 2000.

Decision: Application of Washington state child-visitation-rights statute to allow visitation rights to paternal grandparents held to violate mother's Fourteenth Amendment due process right to bring up her children.

SUMMARY

A Washington state statute (1) permitted any person to petition a state court for child visitation rights at any time, and (2) authorized the court to order visitation rights for any person when visitation might serve the best interest of the child. Pursuant to the statute, paternal grandparents filed a petition to obtain visitation rights with their deceased son's children. After the Washington Superior Court for Skagit County granted the grandparents more visitation time than the children's mother desired, the mother appealed. While the appeal was pending, the mother, who had never married the children's father, was married to a father of six, who adopted the two children. The Washington Court of Appeals reversed the visitation order and dismissed the petition for visitation (87 Wash App 131, 940 P2d 698). The Washington Supreme Court, affirming the judgment of the Court of Appeals, expressed the view that the statute infringed on the fundamental right, under the Federal Constitution, of parents to rear their children (137 Wash 2d 1, 969 P2d 21).

On certiorari, the United States Supreme Court affirmed. Although unable to agree on an opinion, six members of the court agreed that application of the state statute to allow visitation rights to the paternal grandparents violated the mother's right, under the due process clause of the Constitution's Fourteenth Amendment, to bring up her children.

O'CONNOR, J., announced the judgment of the court and, in an opinion joined by REHNQUIST, Ch. J., and GINSBURG and BREYER, JJ., expressed the view that (1) the Fourteenth Amendment's due process clause protected the fundamental right of parents to make decisions concerning the care, custody, and control of their children; and (2) as applied to the mother and her family in the instant case, the state statute unconstitutionally infringed on that fundamental right, as (a) the grandparents did not allege, and no court had found, that the mother was an unfit parent, (b) there was a traditional presumption that fit parents acted in the best interests of their children, and (c) there was no allegation that the mother ever sought to cut off visitation entirely.

SOUTER, J., concurring in the judgment, expressed the view that there should be a simple affirmance of the facial invalidation, by the Supreme Court of Washington, of its own state statute.

THOMAS, J., concurring in the judgment, expressed the view that (1) the appropriate standard of review for the alleged infringement of fundamental constitutional rights was strict scrutiny, and (2) in the case at hand, the state lacked even a legitimate interest in second-guessing a fit parent's decision regarding visitation with third parties.

STEVENS, J., dissenting, expressed the view that (1) certiorari should have been denied, because there was no pressing need to review a decision of a state's highest court that merely required the state legislature to draft a better statute; and (2) the due process clause left room for states to consider the impact on a child of possibly arbitrary parental decisions that neither served nor were motivated by the best interests of the child.

SCALIA, J., dissenting, expressed the view that the power that the Constitution conferred upon a judge, as a judge, did not entitle the judge to deny legal effect to laws that, in the judge's view, infringed upon what was, in the judge's view, parents' unenumerated constitutional right to rear their children.

KENNEDY, J., dissenting, expressed the view that the Washington Supreme Court's judgment ought to be vacated and the case ought to be remanded for further proceedings, because the Washington Supreme Court had erred in its central conclusion that the best-interests-of-the-child standard was never appropriate in third-party visitation cases.

COUNSEL

Mark D. Olson argued the cause for petitioners.
Catherine W. Smith argued the cause for respondent.

JUATASSA SIMS, Petitioner

v

KENNETH S. APFEL, Commissioner of Social Security

530 US —, 147 L Ed 2d 80, 120 S Ct 2080

[No. 99-9537]

Argued March 28, 2000.
Decided June 5, 2000.

Decision: Social Security claimant—who had (1) exhausted administrative remedies, and (2) obtained judicial review—held not to have waived any issues that were not raised in request for review by Social Security Appeals Council.

SUMMARY

In 1994, an individual applied for disability benefits under Title II of the Social Security Act (SSA) (42 USCS §§ 401 et seq.) and for Supplemental Security Income benefits under Title XVI of the SSA (42 USCS §§ 1381 et seq.). After a state agency denied the claims, the claimant obtained a hearing before a Social Security Administrative Law Judge (ALJ). The ALJ (1) also denied the claims, and (2) concluded that although the claimant did have some medical impairments, the claimant had not been and was not under a "disability" as defined in the SSA (42 USCS §§ 423(d) and 1382c(a)(3)). The claimant then requested review by the Social Security Appeals Council, which denied review. Next, the claimant (1) filed suit in the United States District Court for the Northern District of Mississippi, and (2) contended that (a) the ALJ had made selective use of the record, (b) the questions which the ALJ had posed to a vocational expert to determine the claimant's ability to work were defective because they had omitted several of the claimant's ailments, and (c) in light of certain peculiarities in the medical evidence, the ALJ should have ordered a consultative examination. The District Court rejected the claimant's contentions. The United States Court of Appeals for the Fifth Circuit (1) affirmed on the merits with regard to the claimant's first contention; and (2) concluded that—with regard to the second and third contentions—the Court of Appeals lacked jurisdiction because the contentions were not included in the claimant's request for review by the Appeals Council (162 F3d 1160, reported in full 200 F3d 229).

On certiorari, the United States Supreme Court reversed and remanded. THOMAS, J., announced the judgment of the court, and in the portion of his opinion which constituted the opinion of the court and which was joined by STEVENS, O'CONNOR, SOUTER, and GINSBURG, JJ., it was held that the claimant had not waived any issues that the claimant had not included in the request to the Appeals Council, as, among other matters, (1) nothing in 42 USCS § 405(g) or the regulations implementing the section barred judicial review of the issues; (2) while it was common for an agency's regulations to require issue exhaustion in administrative appeals, the SSA regulations did not; and (3) where an administrative proceeding was not adversarial—as in the case at hand—the reasons for a federal court to require issue exhaustion were much weaker. Also, THOMAS, J., joined by STEVENS, SOUTER, and GINSBURG, JJ., expressed the view that—although many agency systems of adjudication were based to a significant extent on the judicial model of decisionmaking—the differences between courts and agencies were nowhere more pronounced than in Social Security proceedings, as (1) Social Security proceedings were inquisitorial rather than adversarial, (2) the duty to investigate the facts and develop the arguments both for and against granting benefits was placed upon the ALJ, (3) the Appeals Council's review was similarly broad, and (4) the Commissioner of Social Security had no representative before the ALJ and the Appeals Council to oppose the claim for benefits.

O'CONNOR, J., concurring in part and concurring in the judgment, expressed the view that (1) the SSA's failure to notify claimant of an issue exhaustion requirement was a sufficient basis for the Supreme Court's decision; and (2) requiring issue exhaustion was particularly inappropriate in the case at hand, where the regulations and procedures of the SSA affirmatively suggested that specific issues need not be raised before the Appeals Council.

BREYER, J., joined by REHNQUIST, Ch. J., and SCALIA and KENNEDY, JJ., dissenting, expressed the view that (1) under ordinary principles of administrative law, a reviewing court would not consider arguments that a party failed to raise in timely fashion before an administrative agency; (2) although the rule had exceptions, it applied with particular force where resolution of the claim significantly depended upon specialized agency knowledge or practice; and (3) in the present case, the claimant asked the reviewing court to consider arguments of the kind that clearly fell within the general rule, that is, whether the ALJ ought to have ordered a further medical examination or asked different questions of a vocational expert.

COUNSEL

Sarah H. Bohr argued the cause for petitioner.

Malcolm L. Stewart argued the cause for respondent.

JAIME CASTILLO, et al., Petitioners

v

UNITED STATES

530 US —, 147 L Ed 2d 94, 120 S Ct 2090

[No. 99-658]

Argued April 24, 2000.
Decided June 5, 2000.

Decision: Provision of 18 USCS § 924(c)(1) imposing stiffer penalty for using "machinegun" in crime of violence held to state element of separate offense, rather than sentencing factor.

SUMMARY

It was provided in 18 USCS § 924(c)(1) (later amended) that (1) anyone who used or carried a "firearm" during or in relation to a crime of violence would, in addition to the sentence for that crime, be sentenced to 5 years' imprisonment; and (2) if the firearm was of certain particular types, including a "machinegun," the additional sentence would be 30 years. Some individuals who had engaged in a violent confrontation with federal officers were tried in the United States District Court for the Western District of Texas on charges of conspiring to murder those officers. The jury determined that the individuals had violated § 924(c)(1) by using firearms in connection with the alleged conspiracy. The District Court then imposed the mandatory 30-year sentence, partly on the basis of the District Court's determination that the individuals had actually or constructively possessed machineguns and hand grenades. The United States

Court of Appeals for the Fifth Circuit (1) remanded for a determination whether the individuals had used, rather than merely possessed, machineguns and other enhanced weapons; (2) determined that statutory terms such as "machinegun" did not state elements of a crime separate from that of using a firearm, but instead established factors enhancing a sentence; and (3) concluded that (a) no jury determination as to the use of machineguns was required, and (b) the District Court could reimpose the 30-year sentence if the District Court found that enhanced weapons had been actively used (91 F3d 699). The District Court reimposed the 30-year sentence, and the Court of Appeals affirmed (179 F3d 321).

On certiorari, the United States Supreme Court reversed the judgment of the Court of Appeals and remanded the case for further proceedings. In an opinion by BREYER, J., joined by REHNQUIST, Ch. J., and STEVENS, O'CONNOR, KENNEDY, SOUTER, THOMAS, and GINSBURG, JJ., and joined in pertinent part by SCALIA, J., it was held that § 924(c)(1) used words such as "machinegun" to state the elements of a separate offense, whose existence had to be determined by a jury, rather than to state sentencing factors to be determined by a judge.

COUNSEL

Stephen P. Halbrook argued the cause for petitioners.

James K. Robinson argued the cause for respondent.

ROGER REEVES, Petitioner

v

SANDERSON PLUMBING PRODUCTS, INC.

530 US —, 147 L Ed 2d 105, 120 S Ct 2097

[No. 99-536]

Argued March 21, 2000.
Decided June 12, 2000.

Decision: Prima facie case under Age Discrimination in Employment Act (29 USCS §§ 621 et seq.), together with sufficient evidence to disbelieve employer's justification, held potentially sufficient to support finding of discrimination.

SUMMARY

A former employee of a manufacturing company, who had been terminated from his supervisory position at age 57 and replaced with persons in their thirties, (1) filed an action against the company in the United States District Court for the Northern District of Mississippi, and (2) alleged that he had been fired because of his age in violation of the Age Discrimination in Employment Act (29 USCS §§ 621 et seq.). At trial, the company contended that it had fired the employee due to his failure to maintain accurate attendance records. However, the employee (1) argued that this was a pretext, and (2) introduced evidence that (a) he had accurately recorded the attendance of the employees under his particular supervision, and (b) the company's director of manufacturing had demonstrated age-related animus in dealing with him. The company unsuccessfully moved for judgment as a matter of law, under Rule 50 of the Federal Rules of Civil Procedure. The case went to the jury, which returned a verdict in favor of the employee. After the company, among other items, unsuccessfully renewed its motion for judgment as a matter of law, the United States Court of Appeals for the Fifth Circuit reversed on the ground that the employee had not presented sufficient evidence to sustain a finding of age-based discrimination, as the Court of Appeals expressed the view that (1) while the employee might have offered sufficient evidence for a reasonable jury to find that the company's proffered reason for the firing was pretextual, this circumstance was not dispositive of the ultimate issue whether the employee had sufficiently shown that he had been discharged because of his age; and (2) the employee's additional evidence of discrimination, when weighed against other circumstances surrounding the firing, was not sufficient for a rational jury to make such a finding (197 F3d 688).

On certiorari, the United States Supreme Court reversed. In an opinion by O'CONNOR, J., expressing the unanimous view of the court, it was held that—if it were assumed for the sake of argument that the evidentiary framework developed in McDonnell Douglas Corp. v Green (1973) 411 US 792, 36 L Ed 2d 668, 93 S Ct 1817, and subsequent decisions, for discriminatory-treatment claims under § 703(a)(1) of the Civil Rights Act of 1964 (42 USCS § 2000e-2(a)(1)), applied to the ADEA case at hand—then (1) in such an ADEA action, (a) a plaintiff's prima facie case of age discrimination, combined with sufficient evidence to find that the employer's asserted justification for its action was false, may permit the trier of fact to conclude that the employer unlawfully discriminated, and (b) the plaintiff need not always introduce additional and independent evidence of discrimination; and (2) in the case at hand, the company was not entitled to judgment as a matter of law, where the employee had (a) established a prima facie case of discrimination, (b) created a jury issue concerning the falsity of the company's claim as to why the employee had been fired, and (c) introduced additional evidence that the company's director of manufacturing had been motivated by age-related animus and had been principally responsible for the firing. GINSBURG, J., concurred, expressing the view that the Supreme Court might be required, in a future case, to define more precisely the circumstances in which plaintiffs would be required to submit evidence beyond a prima facie case and a showing of pretext in order to survive a motion under Rule 50.

COUNSEL

Jim Waide argued the cause for petitioner.

Patricia A. Millett argued the cause for the United States, as amicus curiae, by special leave of court.

Taylor B. Smith argued the cause for respondent.

———

BOBBY LEE RAMDASS, Petitioner

v

RONALD J. ANGELONE, Director, Virginia Department of Corrections

530 US —, 147 L Ed 2d 125, 120 S Ct 2113

[No. 99-7000]

Argued April 18, 2000.
Decided June 12, 2000.

Decision: Accused held not entitled to federal habeas corpus relief under capital sentencing rule of Simmons v South Carolina (1994) 512 US 154, 129 L Ed 2d 133, 114 S Ct 2187, where accused was not ineligible for parole at time of sentencing.

SUMMARY

Under Virginia criminal law, a conviction did not become final until (1) the jury returned a verdict, and (2) the trial judge entered a final judgment of conviction. An accused was convicted, in a Virginia trial court, of capital murder. At the time of the sentencing phase of this trial, (1) a final judgment had been entered against the accused for an armed robbery, and (2) a jury had found the accused guilty of a second armed robbery, but (3) no final judgment had been entered for the second armed robbery. At the sentencing phase of the accused's capital murder trial, the prosecution (1) submitted the case to the jury using an aggravating circumstance of future dangerousness, and (2) argued that the death penalty ought to be imposed because the accused would commit criminal acts of violence that would constitute a continuing serious threat to society.

The jury recommended death. Virginia law permitted the trial judge to give a life sentence despite the jury's recommendation. Two months after the jury's death-sentence recommendation, the judge conducted a hearing to decide whether the recommended sentence would be imposed. During the interval between the jury trial and this hearing, final judgment had been entered on the second armed robbery conviction. At the sentencing hearing in the capital murder case, the accused, in arguing for a life sentence, claimed that his prior convictions made him ineligible for parole under Virginia's three-strikes law, which law denied parole to a person convicted of three separate felony offenses of murder, rape, or armed robbery that were not part of a common act, transaction, or scheme. However, the trial judge sentenced the accused to death, and Virginia's highest court affirmed the sentence (246 Va 413, 437 SE2d 566). The accused (1) filed a petition for a writ of certiorari in the United States Supreme Court, and (2) in such petition argued, among other things, that the trial judge should have instructed the jury that the accused was ineligible for parole. While the petition for certiorari was pending, the Supreme Court decided Simmons v South Carolina (1994) 512 US 154, 129 L Ed 2d 133, 114 S Ct 2187, which held that under the due process clause of the Federal Constitution's Fourteenth Amendment, where a defendant had been parole ineligible under state law at the time of a jury's death penalty deliberations, the jury should have been informed of that fact. The Supreme Court granted the accused's petition for certiorari in the case at hand and, in light of Simmons v South Carolina, remanded the case for reconsideration (512 US 1217, 129 L Ed 2d 830, 114 S Ct 2701). On remand, Virginia's highest court affirmed the accused's death sentence, as the state's highest court (1) concluded that the rule of

213

Simmons v South Carolina applied only if the accused had been ineligible for parole when the jury considered his sentence; and (2) determined that in the case at hand, the accused had not been parole ineligible when the jury had considered his sentence in the capital murder case, on the basis that the murder conviction had not been his third conviction for purposes of the three-strikes law, as (a) the second armed robbery did not count as a conviction because no final judgment had been entered on the verdict, and (b) thus, the only conviction which had counted for such purposes, at the time of the capital murder sentencing trial, had been the conviction for the first armed robbery (248 Va 518, 450 SE2d 360). The accused (1) sought habeas corpus relief in the United States District Court for the Eastern District of Virginia, and (2) argued that Virginia's highest court had erred in not applying the rule of Simmons v South Carolina. The District Court granted such relief (28 F Supp 2d 343). However, the United States Court of Appeals for the Fourth Circuit reversed in pertinent part (187 F3d 396).

On certiorari, the United States Supreme Court affirmed the judgment of the Court of Appeals. Although unable to agree on an opinion, a majority of five Justices agreed that the accused was not entitled to federal habeas corpus relief, as (1) whether the accused could obtain relief under the holding in Simmons v South Carolina was governed by 28 USCS § 2254(d)(1), which forbade federal habeas corpus relief unless a state-court adjudication of a federal claim resulted in a decision that was contrary to, or involved an unreasonable application of, clearly established federal law as determined by the Supreme Court; and (2) the decision of Virginia's highest court was not (a) contrary to the Supreme Court's holding in Simmons v South

Carolina, or (b) an unreasonable application of that holding. KENNEDY, J., announced the judgment of the court and, in an opinion joined by REHNQUIST, Ch. J., and SCALIA and THOMAS, JJ., expressed the view that (1) material differences existed between the accused's case and the case in Simmons v South Carolina, as the defendant in the Simmons case had conclusively established his parole ineligibility at the time of sentencing, whereas the accused in the present case had not; (2) the accused did not refute the critical point that he was not parole ineligible as a matter of state law at the time of his capital murder sentencing trial; (3) extending the rule of Simmons v South Carolina to cover situations where it looked like an accused would have turned out to be parole ineligible was neither necessary nor workable; (4) Virginia's highest court was not unreasonable in refusing to do so; and (5) while state courts remained free to adopt rules that went beyond the Constitution's minimum requirements, (a) the Constitution did not require the instruction that the accused had requested, and (b) the sentencing proceeding was not invalid by reason of the omission of such an instruction.

O'CONNOR, J., concurring in the judgment, expressed the view that (1) whether the accused was entitled to inform the jury that he was parole ineligible was ultimately a federal-law question, but the Supreme Court looked to state law to determine the accused's parole status; (2) if the entry of judgment were a purely ministerial act under Virginia law, then the facts in this case would have been materially indistinguishable from those in Simmons v South Carolina; and (3) however, under Virginia law, a guilty verdict did not inevitably lead to the entry of a judgment order.

STEVENS, J., joined by SOUTER, GINSBURG, and BREYER, JJ., dissenting, expressed the view that (1) the prosecution had relied upon the second armed robbery to establish the accused's future dangerousness; (2) there was an acute unfairness in permitting the state to engage in such reliance while simultaneously permitting the state to deny that there was such a conviction when the accused attempted to argue that he was parole ineligible and therefore not a future danger; (3) even the most miserly reading of Simmons v South Carolina supported the conclusion that the accused had been denied the right to meet the state's case against him; (4) the question in the present case turned on whether the hypothetical possibility that the trial judge might have failed to sign a piece of paper entering judgment on a guilty verdict should have meant that the accused was precluded from arguing his parole ineligibility to the jury; and (5) that hypothetical possibility did not distinguish the present case from Simmons v South Carolina.

COUNSEL

David I. Bruck argued the cause for petitioner.

Katherine P. Baldwin argued the cause for respondent.

———————

LORI PEGRAM, et al., Petitioners

v

CYNTHIA HERDRICH

530 US —, 147 L Ed 2d 164, 120 S Ct 2143

[No. 98-1949]

Argued February 23, 2000.
Decided June 12, 2000.

Decision: Mixed treatment-and-eligibility decisions made by health maintenance organization, acting through its physician employees, held not to be fiduciary acts within meaning of ERISA (29 USCS §§ 1001 et seq.).

SUMMARY

A proprietary health maintenance organization (HMO) was owned by physicians who provided prepaid medical services to participants in health care plans when the participants' employers contracted with the HMO to provide such coverage. One of the HMO's physicians, upon discovering an inflammation in a participant's abdomen, decided that the participant would have to wait 8 days for an ultrasound of her abdomen. Before the 8 days passed, the participant's appendix ruptured. The participant sued the physician and the HMO in state court for two counts of malpractice and two counts of state-law fraud. The physician and the HMO (1) asserted that the Employee Retirement Income Security Act of 1974, as amended (ERISA) (29 USCS §§ 1001 et seq.) pre-empted the fraud counts, (2) removed the case to a Federal District Court, and (3) moved for summary judgment on the fraud counts. The District Court granted the motion as to one fraud count, but granted the participant leave to amend her complaint as to the other. Her amended complaint alleged that (1) the physician and the HMO were (a) fiduciaries with respect to the plan in question, and (b) under 29 USCS § 1109(a), were obligated to discharge their duties with respect to the plan solely in the interests of plan participants and beneficiaries; and (2) the HMO's provision of medical services under terms rewarding physician owners for limiting medical care violated § 1109(a) by creating an incentive to make decisions in the physicians' self-interests, rather than in the exclusive interests of plan participants. The District Court granted the HMO's motion to dismiss on the ground that the HMO was not an ERISA fiduciary. The United States Court of Appeals for the Seventh Circuit, reversing, expressed the view that the participant's allegations were sufficient to state a claim (154 F3d 362).

On certiorari, the United States Supreme Court reversed. In an opinion by SOUTER, J., expressing the unanimous view of the court, it was held that the participant's ERISA count failed to state an ERISA claim, because mixed treatment-and-eligibility decisions—that is, decisions, such as the ones assertedly involved in the case at hand, about both (1) how to diagnose or treat a patient's condition, and (2) whether the patient's medical plan covered the condition or its treatment procedure—made by an HMO, acting through its physician employees, were not fiduciary acts within meaning of ERISA.

COUNSEL

Carter G. Phillips argued the cause for petitioner.

James A. Feldman argued the cause for the United States, as amicus curiae, by special leave of court.

James P. Ginzkey argued the cause for respondent.

HARRIS TRUST AND SAVINGS BANK, as TRUSTEE
for the AMERITECH PENSION TRUST, et al., Petitioners

v

SALOMON SMITH BARNEY INC. et al.

530 US —, 147 L Ed 2d 187, 120 S Ct 2180

[No.99-579]

Argued April 17, 2000.
Decided June 12, 2000.

Decision: Authorization, under § 502(a)(3) of Employee Retirement Income Security Act of 1974
(ERISA) (29 USCS § 1132(a)(3)), of civil action
for "appropriate equitable relief" held to extend
to suit against nonfiduciary party in interest to
transaction barred by § 406(a) of ERISA (29 USCS
§ 1106(a)).

SUMMARY

Under the Employee Retirement Income Security
Act of 1974 (ERISA) (29 USCS §§ 1001 et seq.), (1)
§ 406(a) of ERISA (29 USCS § 1106(a)) bars a fiduciary
of an employee benefit plan from causing the plan to
engage in certain transactions with a "party in interest"; and (2) § 502(a)(3) of ERISA (29 USCS
§ 1132(a)(3)) authorizes a "participant, beneficiary, or
fiduciary" of a plan to bring a civil action to obtain
"appropriate equitable relief" to redress some ERISA
violations. After an ERISA pension plan and a
nonfiduciary—allegedly a party in interest—assertedly
entered into a transaction that was prohibited by
§ 406(a), the plan's trustee and its administrator sued

the nonfiduciary under § 502(a)(3). The nonfiduciary moved for summary judgment, arguing that § 502(a)(3), when used to remedy a transaction prohibited by § 406(a), authorized a suit only against the fiduciary who caused the plan to enter the transaction. The District Court denied the summary judgment motion, but granted the nonfiduciary's subsequent motion for certification of the issue for interlocutory appeal. On interlocutory appeal, the United States Court of Appeals for the Seventh Circuit in reversing, expressed the view that a nonfiduciary could not be liable under § 502(a)(3) for participating in a § 406 transaction (184 F3d 646).

On certiorari, the United States Supreme Court—accepting the case on the assumption that the plan and the nonfiduciary had entered into a transaction that was prohibited by § 406(a)—reversed and remanded. In an opinion by THOMAS, J., expressing the unanimous view of the court, it was held that the authorization, under § 502(a)(3), of a civil action for "appropriate equitable relief" extended to a suit against a nonfiduciary party in interest to a transaction barred by § 406(a), as, among other matters, (1) § 502(a)(3) itself imposed certain duties, and (2) therefore, liability under § 502(a)(3) did not depend on whether ERISA's substantive provisions imposed a specific duty on the party being sued.

COUNSEL

Robert A. Long argued the cause for petitioners.

Beth S. Brinkmann argued the cause for the United States, as amicus curiae, by special leave of court.

Peter C. Hein argued the cause for respondents.

FLOYD J. CARTER, Petitioner

v

UNITED STATES

530 US —, 147 L Ed 2d 203, 120 S Ct 2159

[No. 99-5716]

Argued April 19, 2000.
Decided June 12, 2000.

Decision: Accused held not entitled to lesser-included-offense instruction, as offense described in 18 USCS § 2113(b) held not to be lesser included offense of offense described in 18 USCS § 2113(a).

SUMMARY

An accused was indicted by a federal grand jury and was charged with violating 18 USCS § 2113(a), which punished whoever, by force and violence, or by intimidation, took from the person or presence of another any thing of value which belonged to, or was in the possession of, any bank. The accused (1) did not contest the alleged facts of the episode, but (2) pleaded not guilty in the United States District Court for the District of New Jersey, on the theory that he had not taken the bank's money by force and violence or by intimidation. The accused moved, under Rule 31(c) of the Federal Rules of Criminal Procedure, that the District Court instruct the jury on the offense described by 18 USCS § 2113(b)—which punished, among other matters, whoever took and carried away, with intent to steal or purloin, any thing of value exceeding $1,000 which belonged to, or was in the possession of, any bank—as a lesser included offense of the offense
222

described by § 2113(a). The District Court denied the motion in a preliminary ruling. At the close of the prosecution's case, the accused moved for a judgment of acquittal. The District Court denied the accused's motion and indicated that the preliminary ruling which had denied the lesser-included-offense instruction would stand. The jury (1) was instructed on the offense described in § 2113(a) alone, and (2) returned a guilty verdict. The District Court entered judgment pursuant to the jury's guilty verdict. The United States Court of Appeals for the Third Circuit affirmed the judgment of the District Court (185 F3d 863, 1999 US App LEXIS 16056).

On certiorari, the United States Supreme Court affirmed the judgment of the Court of Appeals. In an opinion by THOMAS, J., joined by REHNQUIST, Ch. J., and O'CONNOR, SCALIA, and KENNEDY, JJ., it was held that the offense described in § 2113(b) was not a lesser included offense of the offense described § 2113(a)—and therefore, the accused was prohibited as a matter of law from obtaining a lesser-included-offense instruction on the offense described by § 2113(b)—as, among other matters, (1) a textual comparison of the elements of the offenses described in §§ 2113(a) and 2113(b) suggested that § 2113(b) required three elements—(a) specific intent to steal, (b) asportation, and (c) valuation exceeding $1,000—which were not required by § 2113(a); and (2) normal principles of statutory construction did not counsel a departure from what was indicated by a straightforward reading of the statutory text.

GINSBURG, J., joined by STEVENS, SOUTER, and BREYER, JJ., dissenting, expressed the view that (1) the accused was not barred as a matter of law from obtaining a jury instruction on bank larceny as defined in § 2113(b); and (2) in reaching the opposite conclusion, the Supreme Court gave short shrift to the common-law origin and statutory evolution of 18 USCS § 2113.

COUNSEL

Donald McCauley argued the cause for petitioner.
David C. Frederick argued the cause for respondent.

SANTA FE INDEPENDENT SCHOOL DISTRICT, Petitioner

v

JANE DOE, individually and as next friend for her minor children, JANE and JOHN DOE, et al.

530 US —, 147 L Ed 2d 295, 120 S Ct 2266

[No. 99-62]

Argued March 29, 2000.
Decided June 19, 2000.

Decision: Texas school district's policy authorizing high school student's delivery of "invocation and/or message" before home varsity football games held to violate establishment of religion clause of Federal Constitution's First Amendment.

SUMMARY

In April 1995, two sets of current or former students at a Texas public high school brought suit, together with the students' mothers, for damages and declaratory and injunctive relief in the United States District Court for the Southern District of Texas against a public school district, in which action it was alleged that (1) the school district had maintained various policies and practices that violated the establishment of religion clause of the Federal Constitution's First Amendment, and (2) in particular, the school district had allowed students to read overtly Christian prayers at graduation ceremonies and home football games. The District Court entered an interim order which provided, among other matters, that a nondenominational prayer could be presented by students at graduation. In August 1995, in response to the order, the school district adopted a policy, titled "Prayer at Football Games," which authorized two student elections, the first to determine whether "invocations" ought to be delivered at home games, and the second to select the student spokesperson to deliver such invocations. Pursuant to the August policy, the high school students voted to allow such invocations and chose a spokesperson. In October 1995, the school district adopted a revised football game policy that was essentially the same as the August policy, although the title omitted the word "prayer." The October policy (1) authorized the student spokesperson to deliver an "invocation and/or message" during pregame ceremonies; (2) mandated that the spokesperson's "statement or invocation" be consistent with the policy's stated goals and purposes, which were to (a) solemnize the event, (b) promote good sportsmanship and student safety, and (c) establish the appropriate environment for the competition; (3) did not require, as an initial matter, that the content of the invocations be nonsectarian and nonproselytizing; (4) provided that such a limitation would be automatically added—by means of a fallback provision—only if the policy were to be enjoined by a court; and (5) incorporated a two-step student election system as in the August policy. However, the school did not conduct new elections to replace the results of the August policy elections. The District Court, although denying injunctive relief, ordered the school district to implement the fallback provision that required the invocations to be nonsectarian and nonproselytizing. The United States Court of Appeals for the Fifth Circuit, in reversing in pertinent part, concluded that the October policy, even in the fallback version, violated the establishment of religion clause (168 F3d 806).

226

On certiorari, the United States Supreme Court affirmed. In an opinion by STEVENS, J., joined by O'CONNOR, KENNEDY, SOUTER, GINSBURG, and BREYER, JJ., it was held that (1) under the circumstances presented, a student invocation pursuant to the October policy violated the establishment of religion clause, as (a) such invocations were not private student speech, but rather public speech, (b) the student election did nothing to protect minority views, (c) the policy involved perceived and actual endorsement of religion, (d) the student election mechanisms did not insulate the school from the coercive element of the message, (e) the elections encouraged divisiveness along religious lines in a public school setting, and (f) even if every high school student's decision to attend a home football game were regarded as purely voluntary, the delivery of a pregame prayer had the improper effect of coercing those present to participate in an act of religious worship; and (2) the simple enactment of the policy was a facial constitutional violation, even if no student ever offered a religious message pursuant to the policy.

REHNQUIST, Ch. J., joined by SCALIA and THOMAS, JJ., dissenting, expressed the view that although the policy might possibly be applied in an unconstitutional manner, the policy was not facially invalid, for (1) the students might vote not to have a pregame speaker; (2) the election might not focus on prayer; (3) any speech that might occur as a result of the election process would be private; and (4) the policy had plausible secular purposes.

COUNSEL

Jay A. Sekulow argued the cause for petitioner.

John Cornyn argued the cause for Texas, et al., as amici curiae, by special leave of court.

Anthony P. Griffin argued the cause for respondents.

_____

CHARLES B. MILLER, Superintendent, Pendleton
Correctional Facility, et al., Petitioners

v

RICHARD A. FRENCH et al. (No. 99-224)

UNITED STATES, Petitioner

v

RICHARD A. FRENCH et al. (No. 99-582)

530 US —, 147 L Ed 2d 326, 120 S Ct 2246

Argued April 18, 2000.
Decided June 19, 2000.

Decision: Prison Litigation Reform Act provision (18
USCS § 3626(e)(2)) staying existing prospective
relief upon filing of motion to terminate held (1)
mandatory, and (2) not violative of separation-of-
powers principles.

SUMMARY

In 1975, inmates at a state correctional facility
brought a class action in the United States District
Court for the Southern District of Indiana, which
eventually (1) held that living conditions at the facility
violated the Federal Constitution's Eighth Amendment
prohibition against cruel and unusual punishment
clause, and (2) ordered ongoing injunctive relief that
remained in effect, with modifications, over the next 20
years. In 1996, Congress enacted the Prison Litigation
Reform Act (including 18 USCS § 3626), which (1) in
§ 3626(a)(1), barred the issuance of new prospective
relief that was not found to be narrowly drawn and the
least intrusive means possible to correct the violations

229

of federal rights; (2) in § 3626(b)(2), allowed defendants or intervenors to seek modification or termination of pre-existing prospective relief, where such findings had not been made; (3) in § 3626(b)(3), barred termination of relief if a court subsequently made such findings; and (4) in § 3626(e)(2), provided that any motion for modification or termination "shall" operate as a stay from the 30th day after the filing of the motion until the date the court enters a final order ruling on the motion, with entry of the stay postponable up to 60 days for good cause shown. The state subsequently filed a motion to terminate the prospective relief ordered in the 1975 action, but the District Court granted a motion by prisoners to enjoin the operation of § 3626(e)(2)'s automatic stay. The United States Court of Appeals for the Seventh Circuit, in affirming that injunction, expressed the view that (1) § 3626(e)(2) was to be construed to bar courts from exercising their equitable powers to enjoin operation of the automatic stay; but (2) the statute, as so construed, violated constitutional principles of separation of powers, by directly suspending a court order (178 F3d 437).

On certiorari, the United States Supreme Court reversed the judgment of the Court of Appeals and remanded the case for further proceedings. In an opinion by O'CONNOR, J., joined by REHNQUIST, Ch. J., and SCALIA, KENNEDY, and THOMAS, JJ., and joined in part (as to holding 1 below) by SOUTER and GINSBURG, JJ., it was held that (1) the automatic stay under § 3626(e)(2) was mandatory throughout the specified time period, so as to bar courts from excercising their equitable authority to suspend the operation of the stay; and (2) § 3626(e)(2), as so interpreted, did not violate separation-of-powers principles by legislatively suspending final court judgments, as, among other matters, (a) the automatic stay merely reflected changed legal circumstances which rendered a judgment no longer enforceable unless and until it was found to meet the standards imposed by § 3626, and (b) § 3626(e)(2)'s imposition of a time limit on judicial decisionmaking did not in itself offend the structural concerns of protecting the role of the independent judiciary.

SOUTER, J., joined by GINSBURG, J., concurred in part and dissented in part, expressing the view that (1) § 3626(e)(2) unambiguously made the stay mandatory, and (2) the question whether § 3626(e)(2) violated separation-of-powers principles by setting a deadline for judicial action could not be decided in the absence of a determination by the District Court as to whether the time allowed was sufficient to make the findings required by § 3626(b)(3) in this particular case.

BREYER, J., joined by STEVENS, J., dissented, expressing the view that § 3626(e)(2) ought to be interpreted as maintaining the equitable power of District Courts to modify or suspend the operation of the stay if it were shown that (1) the stay would cause irreparable injury, (2) the motion to terminate prospective relief was likely to be defeated, and (3) the merits of that motion could not be resolved before the stay took effect.

COUNSEL

Jon Laramore argued the cause for petitioners in No. 99-224.

Barbara D. Underwood argued the cause for the United States.

Kenneth J. Falk argued the cause for respondents.

STEPHEN P. CROSBY, Secretary of Administration
and Finance of Massachusetts, et al., Petitioners

v

NATIONAL FOREIGN TRADE COUNCIL

530 US —, 147 L Ed 2d 352, 120 S Ct 2288

[No. 99-474]

Argued March 22, 2000.
Decided June 19, 2000.

Decision: Massachusetts provision restricting authority
of state agencies to purchase goods or services
from companies doing business with Burma (Myanmar) held pre-empted under supremacy clause
of Federal Constitution (Art VI, cl 2).

SUMMARY

In June 1996, Massachusetts adopted a provision
which generally barred state entities from buying goods
or services from any person identified on a restricted
purchase list of those doing business with Burma
(Myanmar). The state provision permitted an exception to the ban where, among other matters, a procurement effort elicited no offer that was no more than 10
percent greater than the bid of a company on the
restricted list. Three months after the Massachusetts
provision was enacted, Congress passed an act which
imposed a set of mandatory and conditional sanctions
on Burma (110 Stat 3009-166). The federal act (1)
imposed sanctions directly on Burma; (2) authorized
the President to impose further sanctions subject to
certain conditions; (3) directed the President to work
to develop a comprehensive and multilateral strategy to

bring democracy to, and improve human rights practices and the quality of life in, Burma; (4) required the
President to report periodically to certain congressional committee chairpersons on (a) the progress toward
democratization and better living conditions in Burma,
and (b) the development of the required strategy; and
(5) authorized the President to waive, temporarily or
permanently, any sanction under the federal act if the
President determined and certified to Congress that
the application of such sanction would have been
contrary to the national security interests of the United
States. Three companies represented by a nonprofit
corporation, which represented companies engaged in
foreign commerce, withdrew from Burma after the
passage of the state provision. In addition, one company represented by the nonprofit corporation had its
bid for a procurement contract increased by 10 percent
under the state provision's allowance of the acceptance
of a low bid from a listed bidder only if the next-to-
lowest bid was more than 10 percent higher. The
nonprofit corporation (1) filed suit in the United States
District Court for the District of Massachusetts, which
suit sought declaratory and injunctive relief against the
state officials charged with administering and enforcing
the state provision; and (2) argued that the state
provision (a) infringed on the foreign affairs power of
the Federal Government in violation of the Federal
Constitution, (b) violated the Constitution's foreign
commerce clause (in Art I, § 8, cl 3), and (c) was
pre-empted by the federal act. The District Court
permanently enjoined enforcement of the state provision, as the court expressed the view that the state
provision unconstitutionally impinged on the Federal
Government's exclusive authority to regulate foreign
affairs (26 F Supp 2d 287). The United States Court of

Appeals for the First Circuit affirmed the judgment of the District Court (181 F3d 38).

On certiorari, the United States Supreme Court affirmed the judgment of the Court of Appeals. In an opinion by SOUTER, J., joined by REHNQUIST, Ch. J., and STEVENS, O'CONNOR, KENNEDY, GINSBURG, and BREYER, JJ., it was held that the state provision was invalid under the Federal Constitution's supremacy clause (Art VI, cl 2), as a result of the state provision's threat of frustrating federal statutory objectives, as, among other matters, (1) Congress clearly intended the federal act to provide the President with flexible and effective authority over economic sanctions against Burma; (2) Congress manifestly intended to limit economic pressure against the Burmese government to a specific range; (3) the state provision conflicted with federal law at a number of points by penalizing individuals and conduct that Congress had explicitly exempted or excluded from sanctions; (4) the state provision was at odds with the President's intended authority to speak for the United States among the world's nations in developing a comprehensive and multilateral strategy to bring democracy to, and improve human rights practices and the quality of life in, Burma; and (5) the failure of Congress expressly to pre-empt the state provision did not imply approval of the state sanctions.

SCALIA, J., joined by THOMAS, J., concurring in the judgment, expressed the view that (1) it was "perfectly obvious" on the face of the federal act that (a) Congress intended to provide the President with flexibility in implementing Congress' Burma sanctions policy, (b) Congress expected the President to use his discretionary authority over sanctions to move the Burmese regime in the democratic direction, (c) Congress' Burma policy was a calibrated one, which limited economic pressure against the Burmese government to a specific range, and (d) Congress intended the President to develop a multilateral strategy in cooperation with other countries; (2) from the record, the inflexibility produced by the Massachusetts provision had in fact (a) caused difficulties with the nation's allies, and (b) impeded a multilateral strategy; (3) the Supreme Court's invocations of legislative history were irrelevant; and (4) neither the statements of individual members of Congress, nor Executive statements and letters addressed to congressional committees, nor the nonenactment of other proposed legislation, was a reliable indication of what a majority of both houses of Congress intended when they voted for the federal act.

COUNSEL

Thomas A. Barnico argued the cause for petitioners.

Seth P. Waxman argued the cause for the United States, as amicus curiae, by special leave of court.

Timothy B. Dyk argued the cause for respondent.

STATE OF ARIZONA, Complainant

v

STATE OF CALIFORNIA, et al.

530 US —, 147 L Ed 2d 374, 120 S Ct 2304

[No. 8, Orig.]

Argued April 25, 2000.
Decided June 19, 2000.

Decision: Quechan Tribe, and United States on behalf
of tribe, held not precluded from asserting some
claims for increased rights to water from Colorado
River by (1) 1963 decision in same original proceeding, or (2) 1983 Claims Court judgment.

SUMMARY

The Fort Yuma (Quechan) Indian Reservation was
located along the Colorado River. Two proceedings
arose which involved the effect of an 1893 agreement
whereby the Quechan Tribe ceded about 25,000 acres
of reservation boundary lands to the United States,
which cession was arguably conditioned on the performance by the United States of certain obligations that
arguably were not performed. However, in 1936, the
then Solicitor of the Department of the Interior issued
an opinion to the effect that the cession had been
unconditional. With respect to the first proceeding at
issue, which became known as "Docket No. 320," (1) in
1951, the Quechan Tribe filed an action before the
Indians Claims Commission that challenged the validity
and effect of the 1893 agreement; (2) in 1976, the
action was transferred to the United States Court of
Claims (later renamed the Claims Court); (3) in 1978,

a successor Solicitor issued a new opinion to the effect
that (a) the 1893 Agreement provided for a conditional
cession, (b) those conditions had not been met, and (c)
title in the disputed lands was held by the United States
in trust for the Quechan Tribe; (4) a 1978 order by the
then Secretary of the Interior adopted the 1978 opinion; and (5) in 1983, the Claims Court entered a
judgment approving a settlement between the United
States and the tribe, which settlement provided, among
other matters, that (a) the United States would pay the
tribe $15 million in full satisfaction of all rights, claims,
or demands which the tribe had asserted or could have
asserted with respect to the claims in Docket No. 320,
and (b) the tribe would be barred thereby from asserting any further rights, claims, or demands against the
United States "and any further action" on the claims
encompassed in Docket No. 320. The second proceeding at issue began in 1952, when the state of Arizona
invoked the United States Supreme Court's original
jurisdiction to settle a dispute with the state of California over rights to use water from the Colorado River.
Various other states or state-related entities eventually
became parties. In addition, the United States intervened and sought water rights on behalf of some
federal establishments including the Fort Yuma reservation. The Supreme Court appointed the first of
several successive Special Masters. In a 1963 decision
("Arizona I"), the Supreme Court held, among other
matters, that (1) the Fort Yuma reservation and four
other reservations had present perfected water rights
which ought to be apportioned in accordance with a
formula based on the amount of practicably irrigable
acreage on each reservation, and (2) the then Special
Master's findings as to the relevant acreage would be
sustained (373 US 546, 10 L Ed 2d 542, 83 S Ct 1468).
About 15 years later, some tribes including the

Quechan Tribe filed motions to intervene, while the United States ultimately joined the tribes in moving for additional water rights for the five reservations. In 1979, the Supreme Court entered a supplemental decree which (1) set out water rights for the five reservations, but (2) added that the rights for all five reservations would continue to be subject to appropriate adjustment by agreement or by decree of the Supreme Court in the event that the boundaries of the respective reservations were finally determined (439 US 419, 58 L Ed 2d 627, 99 S Ct 995). Such "finally determined" language was also used in a 1984 supplemental decree (466 US 144, 80 L Ed 2d 194, 104 S Ct 1900). Meanwhile, in a 1983 decision, the Supreme Court permitted the tribes to intervene, but held, among other matters, that some administrative actions, including the 1978 Secretarial order, did not qualify as "final determinations" of reservation boundaries (460 US 605, 75 L Ed 2d 318, 103 S Ct 1382). In 1989, the Supreme Court granted a motion by the state parties that asked the court to determine whether the Fort Yuma reservation and two other reservations were entitled to claim additional boundary lands and, if so, additional water rights (493 US 886, 107 L Ed 2d 180, 110 S Ct 227). Eventually, another Special Master issued a report which, among other matters, (1) rejected the state parties' assertion that the Arizona I decision precluded the United States and the Quechan Tribe from seeking water rights for the disputed boundary lands, but (2) concluded that the United States and the tribe were precluded from pursuing those claims by operation of the 1983 Claims Court judgment.

On exceptions to the report of the Special Master, the Supreme Court (1) remanded the outstanding water-rights claims associated with the disputed boundary lands of the Fort Yuma reservation to the Special

Master for a determination on the merits, (2) accepted the Special Master's recommendations to approve the parties' proposed settlements of the disputes involving the other two reservations, and (3) issued some directions concerning a proposed supplemental decree with respect to those two reservations. In an opinion by GINSBURG, J., joined by STEVENS, SCALIA, KENNEDY, SOUTER, GINSBURG, and BREYER, JJ., it was held that (1) the boundary-lands claims concerning the Fort Yuma reservation were not precluded by the Arizona I decision, because—even though the 1978 Secretarial order did not qualify as a "later and then unknown circumstance" that could overcome otherwise applicable preclusion principles—the Supreme Court would not reach the merits of the state parties' late-asserted defense of preclusion, in view of the state parties' failure to raise the defense at an earlier stage, despite ample opportunity and cause to do so; and (2) these boundary-lands claims were not precluded the 1983 consent judgment entered by the Claims Court, as, among other matters, the United States and the tribe had not intended their settlement to have the effect of issue preclusion, sometimes called collateral estoppel.

REHNQUIST, Ch. J., joined by O'CONNOR and THOMAS, JJ., concurring in part and dissenting in part, expressed the view that—while the Supreme Court correctly approved the proposed settlements concerning the other two reservations and correctly concluded that the 1978 Secretarial order was not a new fact justifying an exception to the application of preclusion—(1) the Supreme Court erred in refusing to reach the merits of the state parties' preclusion defense with respect to the Arizona I decision, and (2) under that decision, the claims by the United States and the Quechan Tribe for additional water rights ought to be barred by principles of res judicata.

COUNSEL

Jeffrey P. Minear argued the cause for the United States.

Mason D. Morisset argued the cause for the Quechan Indian Tribe.

Jerome C. Muys argued the cause for the State parties.

———————

CHARLES THOMAS DICKERSON, Petitioner

v

UNITED STATES

530 US —, 147 L Ed 2d 405, 120 S Ct 2326

[No. 99-5525]

Argued April 19, 2000.
Decided June 26, 2000.

Decision: Miranda v Arizona (1966) 384 US 436, 16 L
Ed 2d 694, 86 S Ct 1602, reaffirmed as governing
admissibility, in federal and state courts, of statements made during custodial interrogation; con-
flicting statute (18 USCS § 3501) held invalid.

SUMMARY

In Miranda v Arizona (1966) 384 US 436, 16 L Ed 2d
694, 86 S Ct 1602, the United States Supreme Court
held that the admissibility in evidence of any statement
given during custodial interrogation of a suspect depended on whether the police provided the suspect
with four specific warnings. However, in 1968, Congress
enacted 18 USCS § 3501, which (1) provided that in a
federal criminal prosecution, the admissibility of a
suspect's statement made during custodial interrogation turned on whether the statement was voluntarily
made under the totality of the circumstances; (2)
omitted any requirement that the suspect be given
pre-interrogation warnings; and (3) instructed trial
courts to consider a nonexclusive list of factors relevant
to the circumstances of a confession. A person who had
been accused of committing various federal crimes
moved, in the United States District Court for the

Eastern District of Virginia, to suppress a statement that he had made at a Federal Bureau of Investigation field office, on the grounds that he had not received Miranda warnings before being interrogated. The District Court, although finding that the accused's statement had been voluntary for purposes of the Federal Constitution's Fifth Amendment, nevertheless suppressed the statement on the ground that the statement had been obtained in technical violation of Miranda. On interlocutory appeal, the United States Court of Appeals for the Fourth Circuit, in reversing and in ordering a remand for further proceedings, (1) agreed that the accused had not received Miranda warnings before making his statement, but (2) expressed the view that (a) § 3501 had been satisfied in the case at hand, (b) Miranda was not a constitutional holding, and (c) the admissibility of confessions in federal court was therefore governed by § 3501 rather than by Miranda (166 F3d 667).

On certiorari, the Supreme Court reversed. In an opinion by REHNQUIST, Ch. J., joined by STEVENS, O'CONNOR, KENNEDY, SOUTER, GINSBURG, and BREYER, JJ., it was held that (1) Miranda was a constitutional decision which could not be in effect overruled by an act of Congress; (2) the Supreme Court itself would decline to overrule Miranda, on the ground that the principles of stare decisis weighed heavily against doing so; (3) § 3501, which conflicted with Miranda and was intended to overrule that decision, could not be sustained under the Constitution; and (4) Miranda and Miranda's progeny in the Supreme Court thus governed the admissibility of statements made during custodial interrogation in both state and federal courts.

SCALIA, J., joined by THOMAS, J., dissenting, expressed the view that (1) a violation of Miranda's rules was a violation not of the Constitution, but of prophylactic rules that went beyond the constitutional right against compelled self-incrimination; (2) Miranda ought to have been overruled by the Supreme Court; and (3) § 3501 ought to have been upheld.

COUNSEL

James W. Hundley argued the cause for petitioner.

Seth P. Waxman argued the cause for respondent.

Paul F. Cassell argued the cause as amicus curiae, at the invitation of the Court, in support of the judgment below.

——————————

CHARLES C. APPRENDI, Jr., Petitioner

v

NEW JERSEY

530 US —, 147 L Ed 2d 435, 120 S Ct 2348

[No. 99-478]

Argued March 28, 2000.
Decided June 26, 2000.

Decision: Due process held, in case involving New Jersey "hate crime" statute, to require that any fact that increased penalty for state crime beyond prescribed statutory maximum—other than fact of prior conviction—had to be submitted to jury and proven beyond reasonable doubt.

SUMMARY

An accused fired several shots into the home of an African-American family and made a statement—which was later retracted—that the accused did not want the family in the neighborhood because of the family's race. After a New Jersey grand jury returned a 23-count indictment charging the accused with shootings on four different dates—as well as the unlawful possession of various weapons—the accused entered into a plea agreement which provided, among other matters, that (1) the accused would plead guilty to (a) two counts of possession of a firearm for an unlawful purpose in the second degree, and (b) one count of unlawful possession of an antipersonnel bomb in the third degree; (2) the sentence on the sole third-degree offense would run concurrently with the other sentences; and (3) the accused and the state reserved rights with respect to the state's "hate crime" statute, which (b) provided for an enhanced prison sentence of 10 to 20 years if a trial judge found, by a preponderance of the evidence, that a defendant committed a crime with a purpose to intimidate a person or group on the basis of specified characteristics including race, and (b) had not been referred to in the indictment. Moreover, none of the indictment's counts had alleged that the accused had acted with a racially biased purpose. Under New Jersey law, a second-degree offense carried a penalty range of 5 to 10 years' imprisonment. After the trial judge accepted the three guilty pleas, the prosecutor filed a motion to enhance the sentence. The trial judge (1) found by a preponderance of the evidence that the shooting was racially motivated; and (2) sentenced the accused to (a) a 12-year term on one firearms count, and (b) shorter concurrent sentences on the other two counts. In upholding the sentence, the Appellate Division of the Superior Court of New Jersey rejected the accused's claim to the effect that the due process clause of the Federal Constitution's Fourteenth Amendment required that a bias finding be proved to a jury beyond a reasonable doubt, as the Appellate Division expressed the view that (1) the state legislature's decision to make the hate-crime enhancement a sentencing factor, rather than an element of an underlying offense, was within the state's established power; (2) the hate-crime statute did not create a presumption of guilt; and (3) while the hate-crime statute exposed criminal defendants to greater and additional punishment, this one factor, standing alone, was not sufficient to render the statute unconstitutional (304 NJ Super 147, 698 A2d 1265). The New Jersey Supreme Court, in affirming, expressed the view that the hate-crime statute (1) did not (a) allow impermissible burden shifting, or (b) create a separate offense calling for a separate penalty;

and (2) served as an appropriate balance between (a) concerns of punishing "thought itself," and (b) the state's compelling interest in vindicating the right to be free of invidious discrimination (159 NJ 7, 731 A2d 485).

On certiorari, the United States Supreme Court reversed and remanded. In an opinion by STEVENS, J., joined by SCALIA, SOUTER, THOMAS, and GINSBURG, JJ., it was held that (1) the Fourteenth Amendment's due process clause required that any fact that increased the penalty for a state crime beyond the prescribed statutory maximum—other than the fact of a prior conviction—had to be submitted to a jury and proved beyond a reasonable doubt; and (2) accordingly, the New Jersey statutory scheme at issue could not stand under the due process clause, as, among other matters, (a) the constitutional question was whether the 12-year sentence that was imposed on the accused in the case at hand was permissible, given that this sentence was above the 10-year maximum for the weapon offense charged, and (b) the adequacy of the state's procedure, not the substantive basis for the state's enhancement, was at issue.

SCALIA, J., concurring, expressed the view, among other matters, that (1) the nation's founders had not been not prepared to leave criminal justice to the state, (2) this was why the jury-trial guarantee had been one of the least controversial provisions of the Constitution's Bill of Rights; (3) the dissenters in the case at hand were unable to say what the right to trial by jury did guarantee if, as they asserted, the right did not guarantee—what it had been assumed to guarantee throughout the nation's history—the right to have a jury determine those facts that determined the maximum sentence the law allowed; and (4) under the Constitution, all the facts which existed in order to subject a defendant to a legally prescribed punishment ought to be found by the jury.

THOMAS, J., joined in part (as to point 2 below) by SCALIA, J., concurring, expressed the view, among other matters, that (1) the Constitution required a broader rule than the Supreme Court adopted; (2) American courts had readily applied to new laws the common-law understanding that a fact that was by law the basis for imposing or increasing punishment—including the fact of a prior conviction—was an element of a crime; (3) it was irrelevant, to the question of which facts were elements of a crime, that legislatures allowed sentencing judges discretion in determining punishment; (4) it was erroneous to attempt to discern whether a particular fact was traditionally a basis for a sentencing court to increase an offender's sentence; and (5) the common-law rule would cover the situation of a mandatory minimum sentence.

O'CONNOR, J., joined by REHNQUIST, Ch. J., and KENNEDY and BREYER, JJ., dissenting, expressed the view, among other matters, that (1) it had long recognized that not every fact that bore on a criminal defendant's punishment needed to be charged in an indictment, submitted to a jury, and proved by the government beyond a reasonable doubt; (2) the Supreme Court marshaled virtually no authority to support the extraordinary general rule which the court announced in the case at hand; and (3) the New Jersey statutory scheme in question ought to be held constitutional, where (a) the state scheme did not shift the burden of proof on an essential ingredient of the offense by presuming this ingredient upon proof of other elements of the offense, (b) the magnitude of the sentence enhancement was constitutionally permissible, and (c) the state scheme gave no impression of

247

having been enacted to evade the constitutional requirements that attached when a state made a fact an element of the charged offense.

BREYER, J., joined by REHNQUIST, Ch. J., dissenting, expressed the view that the impractical nature of the requirement that the Supreme Court recognized in the case at hand supported the proposition that the Constitution was not intended to embody that requirement.

COUNSEL

Joseph D. O'Neill argued the cause for petitioner.

Edward C. DuMont argued the cause for the United States, as amicus curiae, by special leave of court.

Lisa S. Gochman argued the cause for respondent.

CALIFORNIA DEMOCRATIC PARTY, et al., Petitioners

v

BILL JONES, Secretaty of State of California, et al.

530 US —, 147 L Ed 2d 502, 120 S Ct 2402

[No. 99-401]

Argued April 24, 2000.
Decided June 26, 2000.

Decision: California's "blanket" primary election system held to violate political parties' right to freedom of association under Federal Constitution's First Amendment.

SUMMARY

The state of California formerly had a "closed" primary system, under which only persons who were registered members of a particular political party could vote to determine that party's nominees for office. In 1996, the state amended its election laws so as to eliminate the former system in favor of a "blanket" primary system, under which (1) any person who was entitled to vote, including persons who were not registered members of any party, could vote for any candidate of any party for a given office, and (2) the candidate of each party who won the greatest number of votes would become that party's nominee. The state organizations of four political parties, each of which had party rules prohibiting persons who were not registered members of the parties from voting in their primaries, brought an action against a state official in the United States District Court for the Eastern District of California, which action (1) alleged that the blanket primary system violated the parties' right to freedom of association under the Federal Constitution's First Amendment, and (2) sought declaratory and injunctive relief. However, the District Court, in ruling in favor of the state, expressed the view that the burden on the parties' rights of association was not severe and was justified by state interests in enhancing (1) the democratic nature of the election process, and (2) the representativeness of elected officials (984 F Supp 1288). The United States Court of Appeals for the Ninth Circuit, adopting the District Court's opinion as its own, affirmed (169 F3d 646).

On certiorari, the United States Supreme Court reversed. In an opinion by SCALIA, J., joined by REHN-QUIST, Ch. J., and O'CONNOR, KENNEDY, SOUTER, THOMAS, and BREYER, JJ., it was held that the state's blanket primary system violated political parties' First Amendment right to freedom of association, a corollary of which was the right not to associate, as, among other matters, (1) while elections were a public matter subject to state regulation, when an election determined a party's nominee, the election was a party affair as well; (2) the blanket primary system imposed a heavy burden on parties' associational freedom, since the system forced parties to adulterate their candidate selection process; (3) the state's asserted interests were not compelling in the circumstances of the case at hand; and (4) even if those interests were compelling, the blanket primary system was not the most narrowly tailored means of furthering those interests.

KENNEDY, J., concurred, expressing the view that (1) the blanket primary law had the avowed purpose of (a) forcing the parties to accept candidates which the parties might not want, and (b) thereby changing the parties' doctrines on major issues; and (2) recent

Supreme Court decisions indicated that the parties' ability to spend their funds and resources to support preferred candidates, as suggested by the state as a means for parties to protect their associational rights, could be barred by state or federal regulation.

STEVENS, J., joined in part (as to points 1 and 2 below) by GINSBURG, J., dissented, expressing the view that (1) the First Amendment right not to associate, though properly applied to a political party's internal processes, was inapplicable to participation in a state election, which was a public affair; (2) even if the right not to associate were applicable, the interests asserted in the case at hand by the state in support of the blanket primary law were compelling; and (3) while a primary system adopted not through legislation but through referendum, as was the system at issue, was arguably invalid, under the elections clause in Art I, § 4, cl 1 of the Constitution, as applied to elections for Congress, that issue had not been raised in the case at hand.

COUNSEL

George Waters argued the cause for petitioners.
Thomas F. Gede argued the cause for respondent.

MOBIL OIL EXPLORATION & PRODUCING
SOUTHEAST, INC., Petitioner (No. 99-244)

v

UNITED STATES

MARATHON OIL COMPANY, Petitioner (No. 99-
253)

v

UNITED STATES

530 US —, 147 L Ed 2d 528, 120 S Ct 2423

Argued March 22, 2000.
Decided June 26, 2000.

Decision: Oil companies held entitled to restitution of
more than $150 million which companies paid
Federal Government in return for lease contracts
giving companies rights to explore for and develop
oil, because government repudiated contract
through enactment of new statute.

SUMMARY

In 1981, two oil companies paid the Federal Government more than $150 million in return for lease
contracts. The contracts gave the companies the rights
to explore for and develop oil off the coast of North
Carolina, provided that the companies received exploration and development permissions in accordance
with various statutes and regulations to which the lease
contracts were made subject, among which were (1) the
Outer Continental Shelf Lands Act (OCSLA) (43 USCS
§§ 1331 et seq.), (2) the Coastal Zone Management Act
of 1972 (CZMA) (16 USCS §§ 1451 et seq.), and (3)

regulations promulgated pursuant OCSLA and CZMA. Under OCSLA and CZMA, the companies were required, among other things, to (1) prepare, and obtain Department of the Interior approval for, a plan of exploration (43 USCS § 1340(c)), and (2) obtain an exploratory well-drilling permit. The Department of the Interior was required to approve any submitted exploration plan within 30 days of a company's submission unless the Department of the Interior found that the proposed exploration would probably cause serious harm or damage to life, to property, to any mineral, to the national security or defense, or to the marine, coastal, or human environment (43 USCS § 1334(a)(2)(A)(i)). To obtain a well-drilling permit, the companies were required to certify, under CZMA, that the exploration plan was consistent with the coastal zone management program of North Carolina. If North Carolina objected, then (1) the certification would fail, unless the Secretary of Commerce overrode North Carolina's objection, and (2) if the Secretary of Commerce ruled against the North Carolina, then the Department of the Interior could have granted the permit. In 1990, the companies submitted an exploration plan and CZMA consistency certification to the Department of the Interior. Two days prior to this submission, the Outer Banks Protection Act (OBPA) (104 Stat 555, later repealed) came into effect. OBPA prohibited the Secretary of the Interior from approving any plan until, among other things, (a) an OBPA-created Environmental Sciences Review Panel reported to the Secretary of the Interior, and (b) the Secretary of the Interior certified to Congress that that he or she had sufficient information to make approval decisions required by OSCLA. In addition, OPBA provided that the Secretary of the Interior could not approve any plan for 13 months. The Department of the Interior

253

then (1) told one of the companies that (a) its plan met OCSLA requirements, but (b) the Department of the Interior would not approve the plan until the OBPA requirements were met; (2) suspended all North Carolina offshore leases; (3) after the panel had made its report, made the requisite certification to Congress; and (4) said that the plan would not be considered until the department received further studies recommended by the panel. North Carolina objected to the CZMA certification. The Secretary of Commerce rejected a request by the company to override North Carolina's objection. After North Carolina objected to the certification, but before the Secretary of Commerce rejected the override request, the two companies joined a breach-of-contract lawsuit in the Court of Federal Claims. This court granted summary judgment in favor the companies, as the court found that (1) the Federal Government had broken its contractual promise to follow OCSLA's requirement to approve an exploration plan that satisfied OCSLA's requirements within 30 days of the plan's submission, (2) the government thereby had repudiated the contract, and (3) this repudiation entitled the companies to restitution of the payments (35 Fed Cl 309). The United States Court of Appeals for the Federal Circuit, in reversing, expressed the view that the Federal Government's refusal to consider the companies' final exploration plan was not the operative cause of any failure to carry out the contracts' terms, because North Carolina's objection to the company's CZMA consistency statement would have prevented the companies from exploring (177 F3d 1331).

On certiorari, the United States Supreme Court reversed the judgment of the Court of Appeals and remanded the case for further proceedings. In an opinion by BREYER, J., joined by REHNQUIST, Ch. J., and

O'CONNOR, SCALIA, KENNEDY, SOUTER, THOMAS, and GINSBURG, JJ., it was held that the companies were entitled to restitution of more than $150 million, because the government had broken its promise and repudiated its contracts with the companies, as, among other matters, (1) the government had breached the contracts, for none of the provisions incorporated into the contracts granted the Department of the Interior the legal authority to refuse to approve the companies' plan while suspending the leases instead; (2) the government had communicated an intent to breach, for (a) OBPA required the Department of the Interior to impose a contract-violating delay, and (b) therefore, it was made clear to the department and to the company that the United States had to violate the contract's terms and would continue to do so; and (3) the government's contract breach was substantial, for it deprived the companies of the benefit of their bargain.

STEVENS, J., dissenting, expressed the view that—while the government had committed breach of contract in failing to approve, within 30 days of receipt, the plan of exploration which the companies had submitted—(1) the remedy ordered by the Supreme Court was excessive, and (2) the companies were entitled at best to damages which resulted from the delay caused by the government's failure to approve the plan within the requisite time.

COUNSEL

Carter G. Phillips argued the cause for petitioners.
Kent L. Jones argued the cause for the United States.

BOY SCOUTS OF AMERICA AND MONMOUTH
COUNCIL, et al., Petitioners

v

JAMES DALE

530 US —, 147 L Ed 2d 554, 120 S Ct 2446

[No. 99-699]

Argued April 26, 2000.
Decided June 28, 2000.

Decision: Application of New Jersey's public accommodations law to require Boy Scouts of America to
admit avowed homosexual assistant scoutmaster
held to violate Boy Scouts' First Amendment right
of expressive association.

SUMMARY

The Boy Scouts of America (1) was a private and
not-for-profit organization engaged in instilling the Boy
Scouts' system of values in young people, and (2)
asserted that homosexual conduct was inconsistent with
those values. An individual's position as assistant scoutmaster of a New Jersey troop was revoked after a
division of the Boy Scouts learned that the individual
was an avowed homosexual and gay rights activist. The
assistant scoutmaster (1) filed suit in the New Jersey
Superior Court, and (2) alleged, among other matters,
that the Boy Scouts had violated a state law prohibiting
discrimination in places of public accommodation on
the basis of sexual orientation. The Superior Court's
Chancery Division granted summary judgment for the
Boy Scouts, but the Superior Court's Appellate
Division—in reversing in pertinent part and in order-

ing a remand—(1) rejected the Boy Scouts' constitutional claims, and (2) ruled that (a) the state's public accommodations law applied to the Boy Scouts, and (b) the Boy Scouts had violated the law (308 NJ Super 516, 706 A2d 270). The New Jersey Supreme Court, in affirming, expressed the view that (1) the Boy Scouts had violated the public accommodations law by revoking the assistant scoutmaster's membership on the basis of his avowed homosexuality; and (2) this application of the public accommodations law did not violate the Boy Scouts' right of expressive association under the Federal Constitution's First Amendment (160 NJ 562, 734 A2d 1196).

On certiorari, the United States Supreme Court reversed and remanded. In an opinion by REHNQUIST, Ch. J., joined by O'CONNOR, SCALIA, KENNEDY, and THOMAS, JJ., it was held that the application of New Jersey's public accommodations law to require the Boy Scouts to admit the assistant scoutmaster violated the Boy Scouts' First Amendment right of expressive association, as, among other matters, (1) the Boy Scouts (a) engaged in expressive activity, and (b) sincerely asserted the view that homosexual conduct was inconsistent with the Boy Scouts' values; (2) requiring the Boy Scouts to accept the assistant scoutmaster would significantly affect the Boy Scouts' expression, by interfering with the Boy Scouts' choice not to propound a point of view contrary to the Boy Scouts' beliefs; and (3) the state interests embodied in the public accommodations law did not justify such a severe intrusion.

STEVENS, J., joined by SOUTER, GINSBURG, and BREYER, JJ., dissenting, expressed the view that New Jersey's public accommodations law (1) did not impose any serious burdens on the Boy Scouts' collective effort on behalf of shared goals, (2) did not force the Boy Scouts to communicate any message that the Boy

Scouts did not wish to endorse, and (3) therefore, abridged no right of the Boy Scouts under the Constitution.

SOUTER, J., joined by GINSBURG and BREYER, JJ., dissenting, expressed the view, among other matters, that the Boy Scouts did not make out an expressive-association claim under the First Amendment, not because of what the Boy Scouts might espouse, but because the Boy Scouts—using the channels customarily employed to state the Boy Scouts' message—had failed to make sexual orientation the subject of any unequivocal advocacy.

COUNSEL

George A. Davidson argued the cause for petitioners. Evan Wolfson argued the cause for respondent.

———————

LEILA JEANNE HILL, AUDREY HIMMELMANN,
and EVERITT W. SIMPSON, Jr., Petitioners

v

COLORADO et al.

530 US —, 147 L Ed 2d 597, 120 S Ct 2480

[No.98-1856]

Argued January 19, 2000.
Decided June 28, 2000.

Decision: Colorado statute regulating speech-related
activities within 100 feet of health care facility
entrances held not to violate free speech guarantee of Federal Constitution's First Amendment.

SUMMARY

A Colorado statute made it unlawful, within 100 feet
of the entrance to any health care facility, for any
person to "knowingly approach" within 8 feet of another person, without that person's consent, for the
purpose of passing a leaflet or handbill to, displaying a
sign to, or engaging in oral protest, education, or
counseling with such other person. Individuals who
had previously engaged in antiabortion "sidewalk
counseling" within the areas now regulated by the
statute filed an action against the state in the District
Court for Jefferson County, Colorado, and sought (1) a
declaration that the statute was facially invalid, in part
because it violated the rights of free speech and press
under the Federal Constitution's First Amendment,
and (2) an injunction barring the statute's enforcement. The District Court, dismissing the complaint,
found that the statute permissibly imposed content-

neutral "time, place, and manner" restrictions that were narrowly tailored to serve significant state interests and left open ample alternative means of communication. The Colorado Court of Appeals affirmed. After the United States Supreme Court, vacated and remanded for reconsideration in the light of an intervening decision (519 US 1145, 137 L Ed 2d 213, 117 S Ct 1077), (1) the Court of Appeals reinstated its judgment (949 P2d 1107), and (2) the Colorado Supreme Court affirmed (973 P2d 1246).

On certiorari, the United States Supreme Court affirmed. In an opinion by STEVENS, J., joined by REHNQUIST, Ch. J., and O'CONNOR, SOUTER, GINSBURG, and BREYER, JJ., it was held that the statute did not violate the First Amendment's free speech guarantees, as (1) the statute was content neutral, because it did not restrict either a particular viewpoint or any subject matter; (2) the statute sufficiently met the requirement of being narrowly tailored to serve significant and legitimate state interests; (3) the fact that the statute's coverage was broader than the specific concern that led to its enactment did not make it unconstitutionally overbroad; (4) the statutory phrases relating to "protest, education, or counseling," "consent," and "approaching" were not unconstitutionally vague; and (5) the statute did not impose an unconstitutional prior restraint on speech.

SOUTER, J., joined by O'CONNOR, GINSBURG, and BREYER, JJ., concurred, expressing the view that (1) a restriction on speech is content based only if it is imposed because of the content of the speech and not because of offensive behavior identified with its delivery; (2) the fact that the statute did not apply to speech by a stationary speaker showed that the reason for its restriction went to the "approaching" rather than to the content of the speech; (3) there was no evident danger of the substantial overbreadth needed before a statute could be struck down out of concern for the rights of those not before the court; and (4) whether a "floating bubble zone" of speech restriction was so inherently difficult to administer as to be invalid was an issue neither before the court nor appropriate for decision on a facial challenge.

SCALIA, J., joined by THOMAS, J., dissented, expressing the view that (1) the Colorado statute was a content-based regulation of speech, because it applied only to persons approaching to deliver messages of protest, education, or counseling, and was clearly aimed at antiabortion protests; (2) the supposed state interest in protecting citizens' right to be let alone—which was repudiated by the state in question as a basis for its statute—was not an interest that could be legitimately weighed against speakers' First Amendment rights, nor was the statute narrowly tailored to protect such an interest; and (3) the statute was far broader than necessary to protect the state's asserted interest in preserving unimpeded access to health care facilities.

KENNEDY, J., dissented, expressing the view that (1) Justice Scalia's First Amendment analysis was correct; (2) the statute was invalid because it (a) was content based in the terms and categories it used, and the conditions for enforcement, and (b) was not viewpoint neutral but would apply only to antiabortion advocacy; (3) there was no constitutional right to avoid unpopular speech in a public forum; and (4) the statute was (a) unconstitutionally vague and overbroad in its use of terms such as "protest," "counseling," and "education," and (b) not a proper time, place and manner regulation leaving open ample alternative channels of communication, because it foreclosed the only venue where the attempt to dissuade women from abortion could take place.

COUNSEL

Jay A. Sekulow argued the cause for petitioners.

Barbara D. Underwood argued the cause for the United States, as amicus curiae, by special leave of court.

Michael E. McLachlan argued the cause for respondents.

GUY MITCHELL, et al., Petitioners

v

MARY L. HELMS et al.

530 US —, 147 L Ed 2d 660, 120 S Ct 2530

[No. 98-1648]

Argued December 1, 1999.

Decided June 28, 2000.

Decision: As applied in Louisiana parish, Chapter 2 of Education Consolidation and Improvement Act of 1981 (20 USCS §§ 7301-7373), under which educational materials were loaned to private schools, held not to violate First Amendment's establishment of religion clause.

SUMMARY

Under Chapter 2 of the Education Consolidation and Improvement Act of 1981 (20 USCS §§ 7301-7373), the Federal Government distributed funds to state and local governmental agencies that, in turned, loaned educational materials and equipment, such as library books and computer software and hardware, to elementary and secondary schools. Participating private schools received Chapter 2 aid based on the number of students enrolled in each school. Chapter 2 provided that (1) Chapter 2 assistance had to be offered to both public and private schools; (2) Chapter 2 funds could only supplement—and could not supplant—funds from nonfederal sources; (3) the services, materials, and equipment provided to private schools had to be secular, neutral, and nonideological; and (4) private schools could not acquire control of Chapter 2 funds or title to Chapter 2 materials, equipment, or property. In an average year in the mid-1980's, about 30 percent of Chapter 2 funds spent in Jefferson Parish, a local governmental unit in Louisiana, were allocated for private schools, most of which were Catholic or otherwise religiously affiliated. In 1985, some taxpayers brought suit in the United States District Court for the Eastern District of Louisiana against various state and local agencies and officials, in which suit it was alleged, among other matters, that Chapter 2, as applied in Jefferson Parish, violated the establishment of religion clause of the Federal Constitution's First Amendment. In 1990, the District Court granted summary judgment in favor of the taxpayers, on the ground that Chapter 2 had the primary effect of advancing religion, as (1) the materials and equipment loaned to the Catholic schools were direct aid to those schools, and (2) the Catholic schools were "pervasively sectarian." In 1994, the District Court issued an order permanently excluding pervasively sectarian schools in Jefferson Parish from receiving any Chapter 2 materials or equipment. However, on postjudgment motions in 1997, the District Court reversed the finding of unconstitutionality and granted the defendants' motion for summary judgment, on the ground that the reasoning behind the previous finding had been undermined by subsequent United States Supreme Court cases. The United States Court of Appeals for the Fifth Circuit, in reversing the District Court's 1997 judgment in pertinent part, concluded that (1) the Supreme Court's precedents as to the loan of instructional materials to religious schools had not been overruled; and (2) pursuant to such precedents, Chapter 2 was unconstitutional as applied in Jefferson Parish, to the extent that the program permitted the loaning of educational or instructional equipment to religious schools (151 F3d 347).

On certiorari, the Supreme Court reversed. Although unable to agree on an opinion, six members of the court agreed that (1) Chapter 2, as applied, did not violate the establishment of religion clause, for (a) it had not been contended that Chapter 2 lacked a secular purpose, and Chapter 2 did not have the effect of advancing religion and could not reasonably be viewed as an endorsement of religion, as (i) Chapter 2 did not result in religious indoctrination by the government, (ii) the recipients of Chapter 2 aid were not defined by reference to religion, and (iii) it had not been contended that Chapter 2 created an excessive entanglement between government and religion; and (2) two prior Supreme Court decisions—Meek v Pittenger (1975) 421 US 349, 44 L Ed 2d 217, 95 S Ct 1753, and Wolman v Walter (1977) 433 US 229, 53 L Ed 2d 714, 97 S Ct 2593—would be overruled to the extent that they were inconsistent with the judgment in the case at hand.

THOMAS, J., announced the judgment of the court and, in an opinion joined by REHNQUIST, Ch. J., and SCALIA and KENNEDY, JJ., expressed the view that (1) some direct and nonincidental government aid to religious schools was permissible under the establishment of religion clause, where such aid was made available neutrally, that is, to both religious and secular beneficiaries on a nondiscriminatory basis; and (2) with respect to governmental aid to religious schools, neither the divertibility nor the actual diversion of such aid to religious indoctrination violated the establishment of religion clause, where (a) the aid was not itself unsuitable for use in the public schools because of

265

religious content, and (b) eligibility for aid was determined in a constitutionally permissible manner.

O'CONNOR, J., joined by BREYER, J., concurring in the judgment, expressed the view that (1) neutrality—that is, generality or evenhandedness of distribution—although relevant in judging whether governmental aid to schools should be seen as aiding a sectarian school's religious mission, is not alone sufficient to qualify the aid as constitutional; (2) actual diversion of such aid to religious indoctrination is inconsistent with the establishment of religion clause; (3) to establish a violation of the establishment of religion clause with respect to any government aid to religious schools, the Supreme Court ought to follow the rule applied in the context of textbook lending programs, namely, that plaintiffs must prove that the aid actually is, or has been, used for religious purposes; and (4) evidence of actual diversion in the case at hand was de minimis.

SOUTER, J., joined by STEVENS and GINSBURG, JJ., dissenting, expressed the view that Chapter 2, as applied, violated the establishment of religion clause, because (1) the aid in question was divertible to religious indoctrination, and (2) substantial evidence of actual diversion existed.

COUNSEL

Michael W. McConnell argued the cause for petitioners.

Barbara D. Underwood argued the cause for the respondent United States in support of the petitioners.

Lee Boothby argued the cause for respondents Mary L. Helms, et al.

DON STENBERG, Attorney General of Nebraska, et al., Petitioners

v

LEROY CARHART

530 US —, 147 L Ed 2d 743, 120 S Ct 2597

[No. 99-830]

Argued April 25, 2000.
Decided June 28, 2000.

Decision: Nebraska statute that criminalized performance of any "partial birth abortion" that was not necessary to save life of mother held to violate Federal Constitution.

SUMMARY

A Nebraska statute criminalized the performance of any "partial birth abortion" that was not necessary to save the life of the mother. The statute defined (1) "partial birth abortion" as a procedure in which one "partially delivers vaginally a living unborn child before killing the unborn child and completing the delivery," and (2) "partially delivers vaginally a living unborn child" as intentionally delivering into the vagina a living unborn child, or a substantial portion thereof. A live delivery procedure known as dilation and extraction (D&X) was ordinarily associated with the term "partial birth abortion." However, the most common abortion procedure, which was known as dilation and evacuation (D&E), sometimes involved live delivery of at least some bodily part. A Nebraska physician who performed abortions in a clinical setting brought in the United States District Court for the District of Nebraska a lawsuit (1) seeking a declaration that the statute violated the Federal Constitution, and (2) asking for an injunction forbidding enforcement of the statute. The District Court held that the statute was unconstitutional (11 F Supp 2d 1099), and the United States District Court for the Eighth Circuit affirmed (192 F3d 1142).

On certiorari, the United States Supreme Court affirmed. In an opinion by BREYER, J., joined by STEVENS, O'CONNOR, SOUTER, and GINSBURG, JJ., it was held that the Nebraska statute violated the Constitution, because the statute (1) lacked any exception for the preservation of the health of the mother; and (2) imposed an undue burden on a woman's ability to choose a D&E abortion, thereby unduly burdening the right to choose an abortion itself.

STEVENS, J., joined by GINSBURG, J., concurring, expressed the view that it was an irrational notion that (1) either D&E or D&X was more akin to infanticide than the other, or (2) the state furthered any legitimate interest by banning one but not the other.

O'CONNOR, J., concurring, (1) agreed that the statute violated the Constitution, but (2) expressed the view that a ban on partial birth abortion that proscribed only D&X and included an exception to preserve the life and health of the mother would be constitutional.

GINSBURG, J., joined by STEVENS, J., concurring, expressed the view that the statute did not save any fetus from destruction, for the statute targeted only a method of performing abortion.

REHNQUIST, Ch. J., dissenting, expressed the view that Planned Parenthood of Southeastern Pennsylvania v Casey (1992) 505 US 833, 120 L Ed 2d 674, 112 S Ct 2791—which served as a precedent for the decision in the instant case—was wrongly decided.

SCALIA, J., dissenting, expressed the view that (1) Planned Parenthood had to be overruled, and (2) the court ought to return the abortion issue to the people, where the Constitution, by its silence on the issue, left it.

KENNEDY, J., joined by REHNQUIST, Ch. J., dissenting, expressed the view that (1) the court's decision invalidated a statute that advanced critical state interests, even though the statute (a) denied no woman the right to choose an abortion, and (b) placed no undue burden upon the right; and (2) the statute was well within the state's competence to enact.

THOMAS, J., joined by REHNQUIST, Ch. J., and SCALIA, J., dissenting, expressed the view that (1) the decision in Roe v Wade (1973) 410 US 113, 35 L Ed 2d 147, 93 S Ct 705, which served as a precedent for the decision in the instant case, was wrong; (2) although a state may permit abortion, nothing in the Constitution dictates that a state must do so; and (3) even if it were assumed that Planned Parenthood was correctly decided, the Nebraska statute ought to pass constitutional muster.

COUNSEL

Donald B. Stenberg argued the cause for petitioners. Simon Heller argued the cause for respondent.

GLOSSARY OF COMMON LEGAL TERMS

Abatement
The extinguishment of a lawsuit.

Abstention doctrine
The doctrine whereby a federal court may decline to exercise, or may postpone the exercise of, its jurisdiction, where a case involves a controlling question of state law.

Action
A lawsuit.

Administrative determination
A decision by a government board, agency or official, rather than by a court.

Administrator
One appointed by a court to settle the estate of a deceased person. The feminine form is "administratrix."

Admiralty
The body of law governing maritime cases.

Affidavit
A sworn written statement.

Amicus curiae
One who, not being a party to a lawsuit, assists the court in deciding the case.

Antitrust laws
Laws prohibiting restrictions on competition.

Appealable
That which may be taken to a higher court for review.

Appellant
One who appeals to a superior court from the order of an inferior court.

Appellee
A party against whom a case is appealed from an inferior court to a superior court.

Arbitration
The submission of a dispute to a selected person—not a court—for decision.

Arraign
To call a person before a judge or commissioner to answer criminal charges made against him.

Array
The whole body of persons, summoned to attend court, from whom a jury will be selected.

Assignee
One to whom property or a right is transferred.

Assignor
The transferor of property or a right.

Bill of Rights
The first ten amendments to the United States Constitution.

Brief
A written legal argument submitted to the court deciding the case.

Calendar
A list of cases awaiting decision in a court.

Capital crime
An offense punishable by death.

Cause of action
A right to legal redress.

Cease-and-desist order
An order to stop doing specified acts.

Certiorari
A superior court's order to a lower court to send up the record of a case for review by the superior court.

Choice of remedies
An election of which form of legal redress to seek.

Civil
Not criminal, as a civil lawsuit.

Class action
A lawsuit on behalf of persons too numerous to participate actively therein.

Commerce clause
The provision of the United States Constitution giving Congress power to regulate commerce with foreign nations, among the states.

Common law
The body of the law apart from constitutions, treaties, statutes, ordinances, and regulations.

Contempt
An exhibition of scorn or disrespect toward a judicial or legislative body.

Continuance
A postponement of proceedings.

Copyright
The exclusive privilege of publishing literary or artistic productions.

Coram nobis
A means of challenging a court's judgment, especially in criminal cases.

273

Court of Appeals
See United States Court of Appeals.

Cross Appeal
An appeal filed by the person against whom an appeal is taken.

De novo
Anew or over again, such as a trial de novo.

Devise
A will provision making a gift of land.

Disputes clause
A provision in a government contract for the settlement of disputes between the contractor and the government by decision of a government board or official.

District court
See United States District Court.

Diversity case
A case decided by a federal court because the parties are citizens of different states.

Double jeopardy
Placing a person twice in jeopardy of conviction for the same offense.

Due process clause
The provision of the United States Constitution that no person shall be deprived of life, liberty, or property without due process of law.

En banc
With all the judges of the court sitting.

Equal protection
The guaranty of the United States Constitution that no person or class of persons shall be denied the same protection of the laws that is enjoyed by other persons or classes of persons in like circumstances.

Establishment clause
The provision of the United States Constitution that Congress shall make no law respecting an establishment of religion.

Federal District Court
See District court.

Federal question jurisdiction
The jurisdiction of federal courts over cases presenting questions of federal law.

Felony
A crime punishable by death or by imprisonment in a state prison.

Forma pauperis
Without the payment of legal fees in advance.

Full faith and credit clause
The provision of the United States Constitution that full faith and credit shall be given in each state to the public acts, records, and judicial proceedings of every other state.

Habeas corpus
A judicial inquiry into the legality of the restraint of a person.

Indictment
A grand jury's accusation of crime.

Interlocutory
That which settles an intervening matter but does not decide a case.

Intestate
One who dies without leaving a valid will.

Jurisdiction of subject matter
The power to decide a certain type of case.

Just compensation clause
The provision of the United States Constitution that no private property may be taken for public use without just compensation.

Laches
Delay barring the right to special forms of relief.

Legatee
One to whom personal property is given by will.

Lessee
A tenant.

Lessor
A landlord.

Libel
Written defamation; in maritime cases, a suit in court.

Lien
A charge upon property for the payment of a debt.

Local action
A lawsuit, especially one involving rights to land, which can be brought only in the place where the wrong was committed.

Maintenance and cure
The legal duty of a seaman's employer to care for him during his illness.

Mandamus
A judicial command to perform an official duty.

Misdemeanor
Any crime not punishable by death or by imprisonment in a state prison.

Patent
The exclusive right of manufacture, sale, or use secured by statute to one who invents or discovers a new and useful device or process.

Per curiam
By the court as a whole.

Per se
By itself.

Plaintiff
A person who brings a lawsuit.

Plenary
Full or complete.

Police power
The power inherent in the states as sovereigns and not derived under any written constitution.

Prima facie
At first sight; with regard to evidence, that which, if unexplained or uncontradicted, is sufficient to establish a fact.

Privileges and immunities clause
The provision of the United States Constitution that no state shall make or enforce any law which abridges the privileges or immunities of citizens of the United States.

Pro hac vice
For this occasion.

Pro se
For himself; in his own behalf.

Proximate cause
The immediate cause of injury.

Public defender
A lawyer employed by the public to defend persons accused of crime.

Recognizance
A bail bond.

Remand
To order to be sent back.

Res judicata
The doctrine that a final judgment is binding on the parties to the lawsuit and the matter cannot be relitigated.

Respondent
The defendant in an action; with regard to appeals, the party against whom the appeal is taken.

Sanction
The penalty to be incurred by a wrongdoer.

Saving clause
A statutory provision preserving rights which would otherwise be annihilated by the statute.

Seaworthy
The reasonable fitness of a vessel to perform the service which she has undertaken to perform.

Statute of frauds
A statute rendering certain types of contracts unenforceable unless in writing.

Statute of limitations
A statute fixing a period of time within which certain types of lawsuits or criminal prosecutions must be begun.

Subpoena
Legal process to require the attendance of a witness.

Substantial federal question

A question of federal law of sufficient merit to warrant decision of the case by a federal court.

Substantive offense

An offense which is complete in itself and does not depend on the establishment of another offense.

Summary judgment

A judgment without a trial.

Supremacy clause

The provision of the United States Constitution that the Constitution, federal laws enacted pursuant thereto, and federal treaties shall be the supreme law of the land, binding the judges in every state, notwithstanding any state law to the contrary.

Surety

One who binds himself with another, called the principal, for the performance of an obligation with respect to which the principal is already bound and primarily liable.

Surrogate

The judge of a court dealing largely with wills and decedents' estates.

Tort

A wrong independent of contract; a breach of duty which the law, as distinguished from a mere contract, has imposed.

Tortfeasor

One who commits a tort; a wrongdoer.

Transitory action

An action which may be brought wherever the defendant may be served with process.

Trespass
An injury intentionally inflicted on the person or property of another.

Trier of fact
One who decides questions of fact.

United States Code
The official compilation of statutes enacted by Congress.

United States Court of Appeals
The intermediate level of federal courts above the United States District Courts but below the Supreme Court of the United States.

United States District Court
A federal trial court.

Unseaworthy
See Seaworthy.

USC
See United States Code.

USCS
The abbreviation for United States Code Service, Lawyers Edition, which is a publication annotating the federal laws, arranged according to the numbering of the United States Code.

Venue
The place where a case may be tried.

Writ of certiorari
See Certiorari.

Writ of error coram nobis
See Coram nobis.

TABLE OF CASES

PAGE

A

Ada, Gutierrez v .... 145 L Ed 2d 747
Adams USA, Inc., Nelson v .... 146 L Ed 2d 530
Adarand Constructors, Inc. v Slater .... 145 L Ed 2d 650
Agard, Portuondo v .... 146 L Ed 2d 47
American Honda Motor Co., Geier v .... 146 L Ed 2d 914
Angelone, Ramdass v .... 147 L Ed 2d 125
Angelone, Weeks v .... 145 L Ed 2d 727
Antonelli v Caridine .... 145 L Ed 2d 4
Apfel, Sims v .... 147 L Ed 2d 80
Apprendi v New Jersey .... 147 L Ed 2d 435
Arizona v California .... 147 L Ed 2d 374

B

Babbitt, Public Lands Council v .... 146 L Ed 2d 753
Baral v United States .... 145 L Ed 2d 949
Bauer, In re .... 145 L Ed 2d 21
Beck v Prupis .... 146 L Ed 2d 561
Bill Harbert Constr. Co., Cortez Byrd Chips,
    Inc. v .... 146 L Ed 2d 171
Board of Regents v Southworth .... 146 L Ed 2d 193
Bond v United States .... 146 L Ed 2d 365
Bossier Parish Sch. Bd., Reno v .... 145 L Ed 2d 845
Brancato v Gunn .... 145 L Ed 2d 1
Brooks, Prunty v .... 145 L Ed 2d 13
Brown & Williamson Tobacco Corp., FDA v . 146 L Ed 2d 121
BSA v Dale .... 147 L Ed 2d 554

C

California, Arizona v .... 147 L Ed 2d 374
California Democratic Party v Jones .... 147 L Ed 2d 502
Carhart, Stenberg v .... 147 L Ed 2d 743
Caridine, Antonelli v .... 145 L Ed 2d 4
Carmell v Texas .... 146 L Ed 2d 577
Carpenter, Edwards v .... 146 L Ed 2d 518
Carter v United States .... 147 L Ed 2d 203
Castillo v United States .... 147 L Ed 2d 94

281

TABLE OF CASES

PAGE

Cayetano, Rice v .... 145 L Ed 2d 1007

Christensen v Harris County .... 146 L Ed 2d 621

Colorado, Hill v .... 147 L Ed 2d 597

Condon, Reno v .... 145 L Ed 2d 587

Cortez Byrd Chips, Inc. v Bill Harbert Constr.
Co. .... 146 L Ed 2d 171

Court of Appeal, Martinez v .... 145 L Ed 2d 597

Crosby v National Foreign Trade Council ... 147 L Ed 2d 352

D

Dale, BSA v .... 147 L Ed 2d 554

Dempsey v Martin .... 145 L Ed 2d 10

Dickerson v United States .... 147 L Ed 2d 405

Doe, Santa Fe Indep. Sch. Dist. v .... 147 L Ed 2d 295

Drye v United States .... 145 L Ed 2d 466

E

Edwards v Carpenter .... 146 L Ed 2d 518

Erie, City of v Pap's A.M. .... 146 L Ed 2d 265

F

FDA v Brown & Williamson Tobacco Corp. ... 146 L Ed 2d 121

Fiore v White .... 145 L Ed 2d 353

Fischer v United States .... 146 L Ed 2d 707

Flippo v West Virginia .... 145 L Ed 2d 16

Flores-Ortega, Roe v .... 145 L Ed 2d 985

Florida v J.L. .... 146 L Ed 2d 254

Florida Bd. of Regents, Kimel v .... 145 L Ed 2d 522

Franchise Tax Bd., Hunt-Wesson, Inc. v ..... 145 L Ed 2d 974

French, Miller v .... 147 L Ed 2d 326

Friends of the Earth, Inc. v Laidlaw Envtl.
Servs. (TOC) .... 145 L Ed 2d 610

G

Garner v Jones .... 146 L Ed 2d 236

Geier v American Honda Motor Co. .... 146 L Ed 2d 914

Granville, Troxel v .... 147 L Ed 2d 49

Gunn, Brancato v .... 145 L Ed 2d 1

Gutierrez v Ada .... 145 L Ed 2d 747

H

Harris County, Christensen v .... 146 L Ed 2d 621

Harris Trust & Sav. Bank v Salomon Smith
Barney Inc. .... 147 L Ed 2d 187

Hartford Underwriters Ins. Co. v Union Planters Bank, N.A. .... 147 L Ed 2d 1

TABLE OF CASES

	PAGE
Helms, Mitchell v	147 L Ed 2d 660
Herdrich, Pegram v	147 L Ed 2d 164
Hill v Colorado	147 L Ed 2d 597
Hill, New York v	145 L Ed 2d 560
Hubbell, United States v	147 L Ed 2d 24
Hunt-Wesson, Inc. v Franchise Tax Bd.	145 L Ed 2d 974

I

Illinois v Wardlow	145 L Ed 2d 570
Illinois Council on Long Term Care, Inc., Shalala v	146 L Ed 2d 1
Illinois Dep't of Revenue, Raleigh v	147 L Ed 2d 13

J

J.L., Florida v	146 L Ed 2d 254
Johnson, United States v	146 L Ed 2d 39
Johnson v United States	146 L Ed 2d 727
Jones, California Democratic Party v	147 L Ed 2d 502
Jones, Garner v	146 L Ed 2d 236
Jones v United States	146 L Ed 2d 902
Judd v United States Dist. Court	145 L Ed 2d 7

K

Kimel v Florida Bd. of Regents	145 L Ed 2d 522

L

Laidlaw Envtl. Servs. (TOC), Friends of the Earth, Inc. v	145 L Ed 2d 610
Lesage, Texas v	145 L Ed 2d 347
Locke, United States v	146 L Ed 2d 69
Los Angeles Police Dep't v United Reporting Publ'g Corp.	145 L Ed 2d 451

M

Marley Co., Weisgram v	145 L Ed 2d 958
Martin, Dempsey v	145 L Ed 2d 10
Martinez v Court of Appeal	145 L Ed 2d 597
Martinez-Salazar, United States v	145 L Ed 2d 792
McDaniel, Slack v	146 L Ed 2d 542
Miller v French	147 L Ed 2d 326
Mitchell v Helms	147 L Ed 2d 660
Mobil Oil Exploration & Producing Southeast, Inc. v United States	147 L Ed 2d 528
Morrison, United States v	146 L Ed 2d 658

N

National Foreign Trade Council, Crosby v	147 L Ed 2d 352

TABLE OF CASES

PAGE

Nelson v Adams USA, Inc. .... 146 L Ed 2d 530
New Jersey, Apprendi v .... 147 L Ed 2d 435
New York v Hill .... 145 L Ed 2d 560
Nixon v Shrink Mo. Gov't PAC .... 145 L Ed 2d 886
Norfolk Southern Ry. v Shanklin .... 146 L Ed 2d 374

O

Ohler v United States .... 146 L Ed 2d 826
Olech, Village of Willowbrook v .... 145 L Ed 2d 1060

P

Pap's A.M., City of Erie v .... 146 L Ed 2d 265
Pegram v Herdrich .... 147 L Ed 2d 164
Playboy Entertainment Group, United States v
.... 146 L Ed 2d 865
Portuondo v Agard .... 146 L Ed 2d 47
Prunty v Brooks .... 145 L Ed 2d 13
Prupis, Beck v .... 146 L Ed 2d 561
Public Lands Council v Babbitt .... 146 L Ed 2d 753

R

Raleigh v Illinois Dep't of Revenue .... 147 L Ed 2d 13
Ramdass v Angelone .... 147 L Ed 2d 125
Reeves v Sanderson Plumbing Prods. ...... 147 L Ed 2d 105
Reno v Bossier Parish Sch. Bd. .... 145 L Ed 2d 845
Reno v Condon .... 145 L Ed 2d 587
Rice v Cayetano .... 145 L Ed 2d 1007
Robbins, Smith v .... 145 L Ed 2d 756
Roe v Flores-Ortega .... 145 L Ed 2d 985
Rotella v Wood .... 145 L Ed 2d 1047

S

Salomon Smith Barney Inc., Harris Trust &
    Sav. Bank v .... 147 L Ed 2d 187
Samara Bros., Wal-Mart Stores, Inc. v ...... 146 L Ed 2d 182
Sanderson Plumbing Prods., Reeves v ...... 147 L Ed 2d 105
Santa Fe Indep. Sch. Dist. v Doe .... 147 L Ed 2d 295
Shalala v Illinois Council on Long Term Care,
    Inc. .... 146 L Ed 2d 1
Shanklin, Norfolk Southern Ry. v .... 146 L Ed 2d 374
Shrink Mo. Gov't PAC, Nixon v .... 145 L Ed 2d 886
Sims v Apfel .... 147 L Ed 2d 80
Slack v McDaniel .... 146 L Ed 2d 542
Slater, Adarand Constructors, Inc. v .... 145 L Ed 2d 650
Smith v Robbins .... 145 L Ed 2d 756

TABLE OF CASES

	PAGE
Southworth, Board of Regents v	146 L Ed 2d 193
Stenberg v Carhart	147 L Ed 2d 743

T

Taylor, Williams v	146 L Ed 2d 389
Taylor, Williams v	146 L Ed 2d 435
Texas, Carmell v	146 L Ed 2d 577
Texas v Lesage	145 L Ed 2d 347
Troxel v Granville	147 L Ed 2d 49

U

Union Planters Bank, N.A., Hartford Under-writers Ins. Co. v	147 L Ed 2d 1
United Reporting Publ'g Corp., Los Angeles Police Dep't v	145 L Ed 2d 451
United States, Baral v	145 L Ed 2d 949
United States, Bond v	146 L Ed 2d 365
United States, Carter v	147 L Ed 2d 203
United States, Castillo v	147 L Ed 2d 94
United States, Dickerson v	147 L Ed 2d 405
United States, Drye v	145 L Ed 2d 466
United States, Fischer v	146 L Ed 2d 707
United States v Hubbell	147 L Ed 2d 24
United States, Johnson v	146 L Ed 2d 727
United States v Johnson	146 L Ed 2d 39
United States, Jones v	146 L Ed 2d 902
United States v Locke	146 L Ed 2d 69
United States v Martinez-Salazar	145 L Ed 2d 792
United States, Mobil Oil Exploration & Pro-ducing Southeast, Inc. v	147 L Ed 2d 528
United States v Morrison	146 L Ed 2d 658
United States, Ohler v	146 L Ed 2d 826
United States v Playboy Entertainment Group	146 L Ed 2d 865
United States Dist. Court, Judd v	145 L Ed 2d 7
United States ex rel. Stevens, Vermont Agency of Natural Resources v	146 L Ed 2d 836

V

Vermont Agency of Natural Resources v United States ex rel. Stevens	146 L Ed 2d 836

W

Wal-Mart Stores, Inc. v Samara Bros.	146 L Ed 2d 182
Wardlow, Illinois v	145 L Ed 2d 570
Weeks v Angelone	145 L Ed 2d 727

TABLE OF CASES

	PAGE
Weisgram v Marley Co.	145 L Ed 2d 958
West Virginia, Flippo v	145 L Ed 2d 16
White, Fiore v	145 L Ed 2d 353
Williams v Taylor	146 L Ed 2d 389
Williams v Taylor	146 L Ed 2d 435
Willowbrook, Village of v Olech	145 L Ed 2d 1060
Wood, Rotella v	145 L Ed 2d 1047

INDEX

A

ABORTION.
Health care facilities.
  Regulation of speech within 100 feet of facility effect on First
    Amendment, 147 L Ed 2d 597.
Partial birth abortion.
  Criminalization of abortion used not to save mother's life.
    Constitutionality, 147 L Ed 2d 743.

ABSENCE OR PRESENCE.
Comment on presence of defendant.
  Tailoring testimony by accused, 146 L Ed 2d 47.

ADDRESS.
Arrestee's addresses.
  First amendment effect of state's withholding arrestee address
    information from private publishing service, 145 L Ed 2d
    451.

ADMINISTRATIVE LAW.
Social security appeals council.
  Waiver of rights not raised on review request.
    Exhaustion of administrative remedies and judicial review, 147
      L Ed 2d 80.

ADMIRALTY.
Preemption of state regulations by federal law.
  Oil tanker regulations, 146 L Ed 2d 69.

ADULT OR X-RATED BUSINESSES OR MOVIES.
Nude dancing.
  Public indecency ordinance to prohibit nude dancing.
    Effect on free expression guarantee, 146 L Ed 2d 265.

AGE DISCRIMINATION.
Age discrimination in employment act.
  Construction and application of act.
    Congressional intent to abrogate states' eleventh amendment
      immunity in Age Discrimination in Employment Act and
      effect on fourteenth amendment, 145 L Ed 2d 522.
Evidence.
  Prima facie case under ADEA and sufficient evidence to disbelieve
    employer's justification, 147 L Ed 2d 105.

AGGRAVATING CIRCUMSTANCES.
Instructions to jury.
  Constitutional effect judge's failure to provide alternative jury
    instruction regarding mitigating circumstances in capital
    murder case, 145 L Ed 2d 727.

AIRBAGS.
State authority to require.
  Common law tort action preempted by National Traffic and Motor
    Vehicle Safety Act, 146 L Ed 2d 914.

ANDERS BRIEFS.
Adoption of new procedures by California court to determine
    frivolity of indigent defendant's criminal appeal; fourteenth
    amendment effect, 145 L Ed 2d 756.

ANTITERRORISM AND EFFECTIVE DEATH PENALTY ACT
OF 1996.
Evidentiary hearings.
  Diligence of federal habeas corpus petitioner in whether he
    "failed to develop" factual basis for claim in state court, 146 L
    Ed 2d 435.
Habeas corpus petitions.
  Appeal of dismissed petition dismissed without adjudication on
    the merits.
    Determination as to whether it is a second or successive
      petition that constitutes abuse of writ, 146 L Ed 2d 542.

APPEAL AND ERROR.
Ineffective assistance of counsel.
  Failure to file notice of appeal.
    Criminal defense counsel effectiveness determined under
      Strickland test, 145 L Ed 2d 985.
Ripeness for review.
  Medicare enforcement regulations.
    Statutory preclusion of ripeness consideration, 146 L Ed 2d 1.
Social security appeals council.
  Exhaustion of administrative remedies and judicial review.
    Waiver of issues raised in request for review by appeals council,
      147 L Ed 2d 80.

APPOINTED COUNSEL.
Frivolous appeal procedures.
  Adoption of procedures by California court to determine frivolity
    of indigent defendant's criminal appeal; fourteenth
    amendment effect, 145 L Ed 2d 756.

ARBITRATION AND AWARD.
Venue provisions.
  District which to bring motion to confirm, vacate or modify, 146 L
    Ed 2d 171.

ARGUMENTS OF COUNSEL.
Tailoring testimony by accused.
  Summation comments on opportunity to tailor, 146 L Ed 2d 47.

ARSON.
Residences.
  Use for commercial purposes.
    Prosecution under 18 USCS § 844(i), 146 L Ed 2d 902.

ATHLETICS.
High school football.
  Prayer before football games effect on First Amendment's
    establishment of religion clause, 147 L Ed 2d 295.

ATTORNEYS AT LAW.
Habeas corpus.
  Ineffective assistance of counsel during sentencing phase of
    capital crime trial.
    Entitlement to federal habeas corpus relief, 146 L Ed 2d 389.
Ineffective assistance of counsel.
  Criminal defense counsel effectiveness determined under
    Strickland test.
    Failure to file notice of appeal, 145 L Ed 2d 985.
  Sentencing phase of capital crime trial.
    Entitlement to federal habeas corpus relief, 146 L Ed 2d 389.
Pro se representation.
  Constitutional rights of lay appellant when required to accept
    state-appointed attorney 145 L Ed 2d 597.
Trial dates.
  Waiver of defendant's Interstate Agreement on Detainers rights
    when defense counsel sets trial date outside time period set
    by agreement, 145 L Ed 2d 560.

ATTORNEYS' FEES.
Corporate officers personal liability.
  Due process effect when joined with no opportunity to contest
    liability, 146 L Ed 2d 530.

AUTOMATIC STAY.
Prison litigation reform act.
  Mandatory stay regarding prospective relief.
    Courts barred from exercising authority to suspend stay; effect
      on separation of powers, 147 L Ed 2d 326.

AUTOMOBILES AND HIGHWAY TRAFFIC.
Airbags.
  Common law tort actions.
    Preemption by National Traffic and Motor Vehicle Safety act,
      146 L Ed 2d 914.
National Traffic and Motor Vehicle Safety Act.
  Preemption of common law tort actions, 146 L Ed 2d 914.

B

BAGGAGE OR LUGGAGE.
Search and seizure.
  Physical manipulation of bus passenger's carryon luggage.
    Fourth Amendment prohibition against unreasonable searches,
      effect on, 146 L Ed 2d 365.

BANKRUPTCY.
Administrative claimants.
   Power to seek payment of claim from estate property encumbered
      by secured creditors lien, 147 L Ed 2d 1.
Burden of proof.
   Trustee in bankruptcy.
      Burden lies on trustee where substantive state law put burden
         on taxpayer, 147 L Ed 2d 13.
Liens and encumbrances.
   Administrative claimants.
      Power to seek payment of claim from estate property
         encumbered by secured creditors lien, 147 L Ed 2d 1.

BEST INTERESTS OF PERSON.
Grandparent visitation.
   Fourteenth Amendment effect on parents due process right to
      raise children, 147 L Ed 2d 49.

BRIBERY.
Medicare.
   Payments considered benefits within meaning of federal bribery
      statute.
      Prohibition of fraud against organizations receiving federal
         benefits, 146 L Ed 2d 707.

BURMA.
State agencies authority to restrict purchase of goods and services
   from companies doing business with Burma.
   Supremacy clause effect, 147 L Ed 2d 352.

C

CABLE TELEVISION.
Free speech.
   Restricting transmission of channels primarily dedicated to
      sexually oriented programming, 146 L Ed 2d 865.

CAMPAIGNS AND CAMPAIGN CONTRIBUTIONS.
Limitations on campaign contributions in Missouri state statute.
   Federal statute and first amendment effect, 145 L Ed 2d 886.

CAPITAL OFFENSES AND PUNISHMENT.
Attorneys at law.
   Ineffective assistance of counsel during sentencing phase of
      capital crime trial.
      Entitlement to federal habeas corpus relief, 146 L Ed 2d 389.
Evidentiary hearings.
   Diligence of federal habeas corpus petitioner in whether he
      "failed to develop" factual basis for claim in state court, 146 L
      Ed 2d 435.
Habeas corpus.
   Ineffective assistance of counsel during sentencing phase of
      capital crime.
      Entitlement to federal habeas corpus relief, 146 L Ed 2d 389.

CAPITAL OFFENSES AND PUNISHMENT —Cont'd
Habeas corpus —Cont'd
Simmons v South Carolina rule.
Entitlement to relief when not ineligible for parole at time of
capital sentencing, 147 L Ed 2d 125.
Ineffective assistance of counsel.
Sentencing phase of capital crime trial.
Entitlement to federal habeas corpus relief, 146 L Ed 2d 389.
Instructions to jury.
Constitutional effect judge's failure to provide alternative jury
instruction regarding mitigating circumstances in capital
murder case, 145 L Ed 2d 727.

CAUSE OF ACTION.
RICO.
Overt act in furtherance of RICO conspiracy creates cause of
action under RICO when overt act was not racketeering, 146
L Ed 2d 561.

CERTIFICATES AND CERTIFICATION.
Contractors.
Certification of contractors as disadvantaged business enterprise.
Mootness of subcontractors challenge of certification procedures
of United States Department of Transportation, 145 L Ed
2d 650.

CERTIFIED CASE OR QUESTION.
Statutory interpretation at time of conviction for operating
hazardous waste facility without permit.
Certification of question to Pennsylvania supreme court and
reservation of judgment pending response, 145 L Ed 2d 353.

CERTIORARI.
Frivolous petitions, 145 L Ed 2d 1 to 15, 756.

CHILDREN AND MINORS.
Parental rights.
Grandparent visitations.
Parents Fourteenth Amendment due process rights, 147 L Ed
2d 49.
Visitation rights.
Grandparents.
Parents Fourteenth Amendment due process rights, 147 L Ed
2d 49.

CIVIL RIGHTS AND DISCRIMINATION.
Contractors.
Certification of contractors as disadvantaged business enterprise.
Mootness of subcontractors challenge of certification procedures
of United States Department of Transportation, 145 L Ed
2d 650.
Hawaiian electoral qualifications.
Constitutionality of Hawaiian statute permitting only
descendants of aboriginal people to vote for state agency
position, 145 L Ed 2d 1007.

CIVIL RIGHTS AND DISCRIMINATION —Cont'd
Homosexuals.
Boy Scouts of America.
Public accommodations law requiring Scouts to admit
homosexuals effect on freedom of association, 147 L Ed 2d
554.
Race conscious university admissions.
Damages claim and summary judgment issuance where
university had race conscious admissions process, 145 L Ed
2d 347.

CLASS ACTIONS OR PROCEEDINGS.
Equal protection.
Cause of action for "class of one" where property owner's claim
did not allege membership in class, 145 L Ed 2d 1060.

CLEAN WATER ACT.
Hazardous waste facilities.
Illegal discharge of pollutants.
Mootness of civil penalties claim under Clean Water Act after
voluntary cessation of illegal activity, 145 L Ed 2d 610.

COASTAL ZONE MANAGEMENT ACT.
Government contracts.
Oil companies granted restitution for breach of lease contracts to
explore for and develop oil, 147 L Ed 2d 528.

COLLEGES AND UNIVERSITIES.
Activity fees.
Freedom of speech.
Mandatory fee for extracurricular student speech with
viewpoint neutrality, 146 L Ed 2d 193.
Admission procedures or policy.
Civil rights and discrimination.
Race conscious admissions process, damages claim and
summary judgment issuance, 145 L Ed 2d 347.
Freedom of speech.
Mandatory fee for extracurricular student speech with viewpoint
neutrality, 146 L Ed 2d 193.

COMMERCE CLAUSE.
Arson.
Prosecution under 18 USCS § 844(i).
Owner-occupied residence not used for commercial purpose, 146
L Ed 2d 902.
Driver's license applications.
Personal information provided.
Driver's Privacy Protection Act, constitutionality of act, 145 L
Ed 2d 587.
Gender motivated violence.
Congressional authority under commerce clause to provide civil
remedy, 146 L Ed 2d 658.

COMMERCE CLAUSE —Cont'd
Income tax.
California's interest-deduction-offset tax on nondomiciliary
corporations.
Due process and commerce clause effect, 145 L Ed 2d 974.
Taxes.
California's interest-deduction-offset tax on nondomiciliary
corporations.
Due process and commerce clause effect, 145 L Ed 2d 974.

COMMERCIAL SPEECH.
Arrestee's addresses.
First amendment effect of state's withholding arrestee address
information from private publishing service, 145 L Ed 2d
451.

CONFLICT OF LAWS.
Bankruptcy.
State claim in bankruptcy court, 147 L Ed 2d 13.

CONFRONTATION OF WITNESSES.
Comments on presence of defendant.
Tailoring testimony by accused, 146 L Ed 2d 47.

CONSENT OR APPROVAL.
Driver's license applications.
Personal information provided.
Driver's Privacy Protection Act, constitutionality of act, 145 L
Ed 2d 587.

CONSPIRACY.
Cause of action under RICO.
Overt act in furtherance of RICO conspiracy creates cause of
action under RICO when overt act was not racketeering, 146
L Ed 2d 561.

CONSTITUTIONAL LAW.
Driver's Privacy Protection Act.
Constitutionality of act, 145 L Ed 2d 587.
Pro se representation.
Constitutional rights of lay appellant when required to accept
state-appointed attorney, 145 L Ed 2d 597.
Vote dilution.
Preclearance of a redistricting plan with a discriminatory but
nonretrogressive purpose.
Interpretation of §5 of the Voting Rights Act of 1965, 145 L Ed
2d 845.

CONSTRUCTION AND INTERPRETATION.
Abortion.
Partial birth abortion.
Constitutionality of criminalization of abortion used not to save
mother's life, 147 L Ed 2d 743.

CONSTRUCTION AND INTERPRETATION —Cont'd
Age discrimination in employment act.
    Congressional intent to abrogate states' eleventh amendment
        immunity in Age Discrimination in Employment Act and
        effect on fourteenth amendment, 145 L Ed 2d 522.
Driver's Privacy Protection Act.
    Constitutionality of act, 145 L Ed 2d 587.
Guam Organic Act.
    Runoff election provisions under the Guam Organic Act regarding
        gubernatorial elections, 145 L Ed 2d 747.
Interstate Agreement on Detainers.
    Federal law subject to federal construction, 145 L Ed 2d 560.
Medicare.
    Payments considered benefits within meaning of federal bribery
        statute.
        Prohibition of fraud against organizations receiving federal
            benefits, 146 L Ed 2d 707.
Miranda v. Arizona.
    Constitutionality of.
        Governs admissibility of statements made by custodial
            interrogation, 147 L Ed 2d 405.
Voting rights act §5.
    Preclearance of a redistricting plan with a discriminatory but
        nonretrogressive purpose, 145 L Ed 2d 845.

**CORPORATE OFFICERS, DIRECTORS, AGENTS, AND
    EMPLOYEES.**
Personal liability for attorneys' fees.
    Due process effect when joined with no opportunity to contest
        liability, 146 L Ed 2d 530.

CORPORATE TAXES.
Nondomiciliary corporations.
    California's interest-deduction-offset tax on nondomiciliary
        corporations.
        Due process and commerce clause effects, 145 L Ed 2d 974.

CORPORATIONS.
Piercing the corporate veil.
    Attorneys' fees.
        Personal liability for fees when joined with no opportunity to
            contest liability, 146 L Ed 2d 530.

CREDITS.
Income taxes.
    Remittance by tax payer and employer of federal withholding tax
        held paid under § 6511 of the IRC, 145 L Ed 2d 949.

CRIMINAL LAW.
Trial dates.
    Waiver of defendant's Interstate Agreement on Detainers rights
        when defense counsel sets trial date outside time period set
        by agreement, 145 L Ed 2d 560.

CROSSING AND CROSSINGS.
Federal Railroad Safety Act preemption of state tort claims.
Railroad's failure to maintain adequate warning devices at
crossings where federal funds were used in installation of
devices, 146 L Ed 2d 374.

D

DAMAGES.
Treble.
Limitation of actions in RICO actions; effect of "injury and
pattern discovery" rule, 145 L Ed 2d 1047.

DEFERENCE TO ADMINISTRATIVE DETERMINATIONS.
Tobacco and tobacco products.
Food and drug administration, 146 L Ed 2d 121.

DEFERENCE TO DISTRICT COURTS.
Venue jurisdiction.
Arbitration awards, 146 L Ed 2d 171.

DEPRIVATION OF FEDERAL RIGHT.
Pro se representation.
Constitutional rights of lay appellant when required to accept
state-appointed attorney, 145 L Ed 2d 597.

DISMISSAL, DISCONTINUANCE, AND NONSUIT.
Habeas corpus appeals.
Appeal of dismissed petition dismissed without adjudication on
the merits.
Determination as to whether it was a second or successive
petition that constitutes abuse of writ, 146 L Ed 2d 542.
Interstate Agreement on Detainers.
Waiver of defendant's Interstate Agreement on Detainers rights
when defense counsel sets trial date outside time period set
by agreement, 145 L Ed 2d 560.

DISTRICT COURTS AND JUDGES.
Supervised release.
District court authority to impose additional term after
revocation and reimprisonment.
Retroactive application implications, 146 L Ed 2d 727.

DRIVERS' LICENSES.
Personal information.
Driver's Privacy Protection Act, constitutionality of act, 145 L Ed
2d 587.

DRUGS AND NARCOTICS.
Search and seizure.
Pat-down and search of fleeing suspect where fourth amendment
exceptions not invoked, 145 L Ed 2d 570.

DUE PROCESS.
Income tax.
   California's interest-deduction-offset tax on nondomiciliary
      corporations.
   Due process and commerce clause effect, 145 L Ed 2d 974.
Parental rights.
   Grandparent visitation.
      Fourteenth Amendment effect on parents due process right to
         raise children, 147 L Ed 2d 49.

E

ELECTIONS.
Primary election blanket system.
   Violation of freedom of association, 147 L Ed 2d 502.

ELECTIONS AND VOTING.
Campaigns and campaign contributions.
   Limitations on campaign contributions in Missouri state statute.
   Federal statute and first amendment effect, 145 L Ed 2d 886.
Electoral qualifications.
   Constitutionality of Hawaiian statute permitting only
      descendants of aboriginal people to vote for state agency
      position, 145 L Ed 2d 1007.
Guam.
   Runoff election provisions under the Guam Organic Act regarding
      gubernatorial elections, 145 L Ed 2d 747.
Preclearance.
   Louisiana redistricting plan with a discriminatory but
      nonretrogressive purpose.
      Interpretation of §5 of the Voting Rights Act of 1965, 145 L Ed
         2d 845.
Runoff elections.
   Runoff election provisions under the Guam Organic Act regarding
      gubernatorial elections, 145 L Ed 2d 747.

EMPLOYERS' LIABILITY.
Age discrimination in employment act.
   Congressional intent to abrogate states' eleventh amendment
      immunity in Age Discrimination in Employment Act and
      effect on fourteenth amendment, 145 L Ed 2d 522.

EQUAL PROTECTION.
Class of one.
   Cause of action for "class of one" where property owner's claim
      did not allege membership in class, 145 L Ed 2d 1060.
Contractors.
   Certification of contractors as disadvantaged business enterprise.
      Subcontractors challenge of certification procedures of United
         States Department of Transportation, 145 L Ed 2d 650.

EQUITY.
ERISA.
Nonfiduciary party in interest.
    Liability to be sued under 502(a)(3) of ERISA, 147 L Ed 2d 187.

ESCAPE OR FLIGHT.
Fleeing suspect.
    Pat-down and search of fleeing suspect where fourth amendment
        exceptions not invoked, 145 L Ed 2d 587.

ESTABLISHMENT OF RELIGION.
High school football.
    Prayer before football games effect on First Amendment's
        establishment of religion clause, 147 L Ed 2d 295.
Private and parochial schools.
    Educational materials loaned to private schools effect on First
        Amendment, 147 L Ed 2d 660.

ESTATES.
Tax lien on disclaimed inheritance property.
    Federal law to determine existence of a property interest in an
        estate disclaimed under Arkansas state law subject to a
        federal tax lien, 145 L Ed 2d 466.

EVIDENCE.
Indictments.
    Dismissal of indictment.
        Source of evidence in indictment independent of documents
           produced under grant of immunity, 147 L Ed 2d 24.
Judgment as a matter of law.
    Appropriateness of entry of judgment as a matter of law by
        federal court of appeals when evidence was both erroneously
        admitted and insufficient to support a verdict, 145 L Ed 2d
        958.
Prior convictions.
    Preemptive introduction on direct examination.
        Admission challenged on appeal, 146 L Ed 2d 826.

EXCLUSION OR SUPPRESSION OF EVIDENCE.
Fleeing suspect.
    Pat-down and search of fleeing suspect where fourth amendment
        exceptions not invoked, 145 L Ed 2d 587.
Prior convictions.
    Preemptive introduction on direct examination.
        Admission challenged on appeal, 146 L Ed 2d 826.

EXHAUSTION OF REMEDIES.
Medicare enforcement regulations.
    Statutory preclusion of exhaustion consideration, 146 L Ed 2d 1.

EXPERT AND OPINION EVIDENCE.
Judgment as a matter of law.
    Appropriateness of entry of judgment as a matter of law by
        federal court of appeals when evidence was both erroneously
        admitted and insufficient to support a verdict, 145 L Ed 2d
        958.

EXPERT WITNESSES.
Judgment as a matter of law.
Appropriateness of entry of judgment as a matter of law by
federal court of appeals when evidence was both erroneously
admitted and insufficient to support a verdict, 145 L Ed 2d
958.

EX POST FACTO.
Crime victim testimony.
Retrospective application of statutory provision allowing sexual
abuse victim's uncorroborated testimony to support
conviction, 146 L Ed 2d 577.
Parole.
Retroactive application of Georgia provision extending intervals
between parole considerations, 146 L Ed 2d 236.
Supervised release.
District court authority to impose additional term after
revocation and reimprisonment.
Retroactive application implications, 146 L Ed 2d 727.

F

FAIR LABOR STANDARDS ACT.
Compensatory time.
Compelling use of compensatory time by public employer, 146 L
Ed 2d 621.

FALSE CLAIMS ACT.
Sovereign immunity.
State and state agency liability in qui tam action brought under
act, 146 L Ed 2d 836.
Standing.
Qui tam actions, 146 L Ed 2d 836.

FEDERALISM.
Concurrent powers.
Determining concurrence or preemption, 146 L Ed 2d 69.
Driver's Privacy Protection Act.
Constitutionality of act, 145 L Ed 2d 587.

FEDERAL QUESTION.
Preclusion.
Medicare enforcement regulations.
Statutory preclusion, 146 L Ed 2d 1.

FEDERAL RAILROAD SAFETY ACT.
Preemption.
State tort claims.
Railroad's failure to maintain adequate warning devices at
crossings where federal funds were used in installation of
devices, 146 L Ed 2d 374.

FIDUCIARIES.
ERISA.
Treatment-and-eligibility mixed decisions.
Fiduciary act of HMO acting through physician employee, 147 L Ed 2d 164.

FINALITY OR CONCLUSIVENESS.
Conviction.
Statutory interpretation at time of conviction for operating hazardous waste facility without permit.
Certification of question to Pennsylvania supreme court and reservation of judgment pending response, 145 L Ed 2d 353.

FINES, FORFEITURES AND PENALTIES.
Civil money penalties.
Mootness of civil penalties claim under Clean Water Act after voluntary cessation of illegal activity, 145 L Ed 2d 610.
Machine guns.
Imposition of stiffer penalty for using machine gun element of separate offense not sentencing factor, 147 L Ed 2d 94.
Weapons and firearms.
Imposition of stiffer penalty for using machine gun element of separate offense not sentencing factor, 147 L Ed 2d 94.

FIRST AMENDMENT.
Campaign finance.
See CAMPAIGNS AND CAMPAIGN CONTRIBUTIONS.

FOOD AND DRUG ADMINISTRATION.
Tobacco regulation.
Jurisdiction, 146 L Ed 2d 121.

FOOTBALL.
High school football.
Prayer before football games effect on First Amendment's establishment of religion clause, 147 L Ed 2d 295.

FORMA PAUPERIS.
Frivolous petitions, 145 L Ed 2d 1 to 15, 756.

FOURTEENTH AMENDMENT.
Congressional abrogation of states' sovereign immunity from federal court suit
Age discrimination in employment act, abrogation of eleventh amendment immunity and effect on fourteenth amendment, 145 L Ed 2d 522.
Frivolous appeal procedures.
Adoption of procedures by California court to determine frivolity of indigent defendant's criminal appeal; fourteenth amendment effect, 145 L Ed 2d 756.
Parental rights.
Grandparent visitation.
Effect on parents due process right to raise children, 147 L Ed 2d 49.

INDEX

FOURTH AMENDMENT.
Fleeing suspect.
> Pat-down and search of fleeing suspect where fourth amendment exceptions not invoked, 145 L Ed 2d 587.

FRAUD AND DECEIT.
Medicare.
> Payments considered benefits within meaning of federal bribery statute.
>> Prohibition of fraud against organizations receiving federal benefits, 146 L Ed 2d 707.

FREEDOM OF ASSOCIATION.
Boy Scouts of America.
> Public accommodations law requiring Scouts to admit homosexuals.
>> Violation of freedom of association, 147 L Ed 2d 554.

Elections.
> Primary election blanket system.
>> Violation of freedom of association, 147 L Ed 2d 502.

FREEDOM OF SPEECH AND PRESS.
Arrestee's addresses.
> First amendment effect of state's withholding arrestee address information from private publishing service, 145 L Ed 2d 451.

Cable television.
> Restricting transmission of channels primarily dedicated to sexually oriented programming, 146 L Ed 2d 865.

Colleges and universities.
> Mandatory fee for extracurricular student speech with viewpoint neutrality, 146 L Ed 2d 193.

Health care facilities.
> Regulation of speech within 100 feet of facility effect on First Amendment, 147 L Ed 2d 597.

Nude dancing.
> Public indecency ordinance to prohibit nude dancing.
>> Effect on free expression guarantee, 146 L Ed 2d 265.

FRIVOLOUS APPEALS.
Indigents, 145 L Ed 2d 756.
> Adoption of procedures by California court to determine frivolity of indigent defendant's criminal appeal; fourteenth amendment effect, 145 L Ed 2d 756.

FRUIT OF POISONOUS TREE DOCTRINE.
Anonymous tip.
> Stop and frisk based on anonymous tip where informant's knowledge or credibility is unknown, 146 L Ed 254.

Homicide crime scene.
> Warrantless search where Fourth Amendment exceptions not invoked, 145 L Ed 2d 16.

INDEX

G

GAS AND OIL.
Government contracts.
Oil companies granted restitution for breach of lease contracts to explore for and develop oil, 147 L Ed 2d 528.

GENDER MOTIVATED VIOLENCE.
Congressional authority under commerce clause to provide civil remedy, 146 L Ed 2d 658.

GERRYMANDERING.
Preclearance of a Louisiana redistricting plan with a discriminatory but nonretrogressive purpose.
Interpretation of §5 of the Voting Rights Act of 1965, 145 L Ed 2d 845.

GOVERNING LAW.
Tax lien on inheritance property.
Federal law to determine existence of a property interest in an estate disclaimed under Arkansas state law subject to a federal tax lien, 145 L Ed 2d 466.
Venue.
Arbitration award.
Motion to confirm, vacate or modify, 146 L Ed 2d 171.

GOVERNORS.
Guam.
Runoff election provisions under the Guam Organic Act regarding gubernatorial elections, 145 L Ed 2d 747.

GRANDPARENTS.
Visitation rights.
Violation of parents Fourteenth Amendment due process rights, 147 L Ed 2d 49.

GUAM.
Elections.
Runoff election provisions under the Guam Organic Act regarding gubernatorial elections, 145 L Ed 2d 747.

H

HABEAS CORPUS.
Abuse of writ.
Appeal of dismissed petition dismissed without adjudication on the merits.
Determination as to whether it was a second or successive petition that constitutes abuse of writ, 146 L Ed 2d 542.
Appeal and error.
Dismissed petition dismissed without adjudication on the merits.
Determination as to whether it was a second or successive petition that constitutes abuse of writ, 146 L Ed 2d 542.

HABEAS CORPUS —Cont'd
Attorneys at law.
  Ineffective assistance of counsel during sentencing phase of
    capital crime trial.
    Entitlement to federal habeas corpus relief, 146 L Ed 2d 389.
Evidentiary hearings.
  Diligence of federal habeas corpus petitioner in whether he
    "failed to develop" factual basis for claim in state court, 146 L
    Ed 2d 435.
Ineffective assistance of counsel.
  Cause and prejudice standard exception of procedurally defaulted
    ineffective assistance of counsel claim.
    Effect on procedurally defaulted insufficient evidence claim, 146
      L Ed 2d 518.
  Sentencing phase of capital crime trial.
    Entitlement to federal habeas corpus relief, 146 L Ed 2d 389.
Procedural default.
  Cause and prejudice standard exception for procedurally
    defaulted ineffective assistance of counsel claim.
    Effect on procedurally defaulted insufficient evidence claim, 146
      L Ed 2d 518.
Simmons v South Carolina rule.
  Entitlement to relief when not ineligible for parole at time of
    capital sentencing, 147 L Ed 2d 125.

HATE CRIMES.
Sentencing.
  Facts that increase penalties beyond statutory maximums must
    be submitted to jury and proven beyond reasonable doubt,
    147 L Ed 2d 435.

HEALTH MAINTENANCE ORGANIZATIONS.
ERISA.
  Treatment-and-eligibility mixed decisions.
    Fiduciary act of HMO acting through physician employee, 147
      L Ed 2d 164.

HEARINGS.
Evidentiary hearings.
  Diligence of federal habeas corpus petitioner in whether he
    "failed to develop" factual basis for claim in state court, 146 L
    Ed 2d 435.

HOMICIDE.
Search and seizure of crime scene.
  Warrantless search where Fourth Amendment exceptions not
    invoked, 145 L Ed 2d 16.

HOMOSEXUALITY.
Boy Scouts of America.
  Public accommodations law requiring Scouts to admit
    homosexuals.
    Violation of freedom of association, 147 L Ed 2d 554.

I

INCINERATORS AND INCINERATION.
Hazardous waste incinerator facility.
Illegal discharge of pollutants.
Mootness of civil penalties claim under Clean Water Act after voluntary cessation of illegal activity, 145 L Ed 2d 610.

INCOME TAXES.
Corporations.
California's interest-deduction-offset tax on nondomiciliary corporations.
Due process and commerce clause effects, 145 L Ed 2d 974.
Credits and refunds.
Remittance by taxpayer and employer of federal withholding tax held paid under §6511 of the IRC, 145 L Ed 2d 949.

INDECENCY, LEWDNESS, AND OBSCENITY.
Cable TV.
Restricting transmission of channels primarily dedicated to sexually oriented programming, 146 L Ed 2d 865.
Nude dancing.
Public indecency ordinance to prohibit nude dancing.
Effect on free expression guarantee, 146 L Ed 2d 265.

INDEPENDENT CONTRACTORS.
Certification of contractors as disadvantaged business enterprise.
Mootness of subcontractors challenge of certification procedures of United States Department of Transportation, 145 L Ed 2d 650.

INDIANS.
Electoral qualifications.
Constitutionality of Hawaiian statute permitting only descendants of aboriginal people to vote for state agency position, 145 L Ed 2d 1007.
Water rights.
Res judicata effect on claims for additional water rights, 147 L Ed 2d 374.

INDICTMENT, INFORMATION OR COMPLAINT IN CRIMINAL CASE.
Dismissal of indictment.
Source of evidence in indictment independent of documents produced under grant of immunity, 147 L Ed 2d 24.

INEFFECTIVE ASSISTANCE OF COUNSEL.
Habeas corpus, federal relief.
Cause and prejudice standard exception of procedurally defaulted ineffective assistance of counsel claim.
Effect on procedurally defaulted insufficient evidence claim, 146 L Ed 2d 518.

INEFFECTIVE ASSISTANCE OF COUNSEL —Cont'd
Habeas corpus, federal relief —Cont'd
Ineffective assistance of counsel during sentencing phase of
capital crime trial, 146 L Ed 2d 389.
Strickland test.
Criminal defense counsel effectiveness determined under
Strickland test.
Failure to file notice of appeal, 145 L Ed 2d 985.

INFORMATION.
Arrestee's addresses.
First amendment effect of state's withholding arrestee address
information from private publishing service, 145 L Ed 2d
451.

INJURY IN FACT.
Hazardous waste facility illegal discharge of pollutants.
Mootness of civil penalties claim under Clean Water Act after
voluntary cessation of illegal activity, 145 L Ed 2d 610.

INSTRUCTIONS TO JURY.
Alternative instructions.
Constitutional effect judge's failure to provide alternative jury
instruction regarding mitigating circumstances in capital
murder case, 145 L Ed 2d 727.

INTEREST IN PROPERTY OR SUBJECT MATTER.
Tax liens.
Federal law to determine existence of a property interest in an
estate disclaimed under Arkansas state law subject to a
federal tax lien, 145 L Ed 2d 466.

INTERIOR DEPARTMENT OR SECRETARY.
Government contracts.
Oil companies granted restitution for breach of lease contracts to
explore for and develop oil, 147 L Ed 2d 528.
Taylor Grazing Act.
Livestock grazing on federal public rangelands, 146 L Ed 2d 753.

INTERSTATE AGREEMENT ON DETAINERS.
Trial dates.
Waiver of defendant's Interstate Agreement on Detainers rights
when defense counsel sets trial date outside time period set
by agreement, 145 L Ed 2d 560.

J

JOINDER OF PARTIES.
Corporate officers personal liability for attorneys' fees.
Due process effect when joined with no opportunity to contest
liability, 146 L Ed 2d 530.

JUDGMENT AS A MATTER OF LAW.
Federal court of appeals.
Appropriateness of entry of judgment as a matter of law when
evidence was both erroneously admitted and insufficient to
support a verdict, 145 L Ed 2d 958.

JUDGMENT NOTWITHSTANDING THE VERDICT.
Federal court of appeals.
Appropriateness of entry of judgment as a matter of law when evidence was both erroneously admitted and insufficient to support a verdict, 145 L Ed 2d 958.

JURISDICTION.
Food and drug administration.
Tobacco and tobacco products, 146 L Ed 2d 121.

JURY AND JURY TRIAL.
Peremptory challenges.
Curative use.
Impairment or denial of defendant's exercise of peremptory challenge when used for curative purposes 145 L Ed 2d 792.

L

LABOR AND EMPLOYMENT.
Compensatory time.
Fair Labor Standards Act effect on public employer's compelling use of compensatory time off, 146 L Ed 2d 621.

LANHAM ACT.
Trade dress.
Unregistered protectible upon showing secondary meaning, 146 L Ed 2d 182.

LESSER AND INCLUDED OFFENSES.
Instructions to jury.
Robbery, 147 L Ed 2d 203.

LIENS AND ENCUMBRANCES.
Inheritance property.
Federal law to determine existence of a property interest in an estate disclaimed under Arkansas state law subject to a federal tax lien, 145 L Ed 2d 466.

LIMITATION OF ACTIONS.
RICO actions.
"Injury and pattern discovery" rule effect on start of limitations period for treble damages action, 145 L Ed 2d 1047.

LIVESTOCK.
Taylor Grazing Act.
Grazing on federal public rangelands.
Authority of Secretary of Interior, 146 L Ed 2d 753.

M

MACHINE GUNS.
Penalties.
Imposition of stiffer penalty for using machine gun element of separate offense not sentencing factor, 147 L Ed 2d 94.

MEDICARE.
Enforcement regulations challenged.
Federal question jurisdiction not available, 146 L Ed 2d 1.
Fraud.
Payments considered benefits within meaning of federal bribery statute.
Prohibition of fraud against organizations receiving federal benefits, 146 L Ed 2d 707.

MINORITY VOTE DILUTION.
Preclearance of a redistricting plan with a discriminatory but nonretrogressive purpose.
Interpretation of §5 of the Voting Rights Act of 1965. 145 L Ed 2d 845.

MIRANDA V. ARIZONA.
Constitutionality of.
Governs admissibility of statements made by custodial interrogation, 147 L Ed 2d 405.
Reaffirmation of.
Governs admissibility of statements made by custodial interrogation, 147 L Ed 2d 405.

MOOT OR ABSTRACT QUESTIONS OR MATTERS.
Certification of contractors as disadvantaged business enterprise.
Subcontractors challenge of certification procedures of United States Department of Transportation, 145 L Ed 2d 650.
Civil money penalties.
Mootness of civil penalties claim under Clean Water Act after voluntary cessation of illegal activity, 145 L Ed 2d 610.
Nude dancing.
Public indecency ordinance to prohibit nude dancing.
Effect when establishment no longer operates as nude dance club, 146 L Ed 2d 265.
Redistricting plans, 145 L Ed 2d 845.

MOTIONS.
Venue.
Arbitration awards.
Confirm, vacate, or modify, 146 L Ed 2d 171.

N

NATIONAL TRAFFIC AND MOTOR VEHICLE SAFETY ACT OF 1966.
Preemption.
Common law tort action claiming cars to be equipped with airbags preempted, 146 L Ed 2d 914.

NONDOMICILIARY CORPORATIONS.
Income tax.
California's interest-deduction-offset tax on nondomiciliary corporations.
Due process and commerce clause effects, 145 L Ed 2d 974.

NUDE DANCING.
Public indecency law, free expression guarantee of First
Amendment, 146 L Ed 2d 265.

O

OUTER CONTINENTAL SHELF LANDS ACT.
Government contracts.
Oil companies granted restitution for breach of lease contracts to
explore for and develop oil, 147 L Ed 2d 528.

OVERBREADTH.
Arrestee's addresses.
First amendment effect of state's withholding arrestee address
information from private publishing service, 145 L Ed 2d
451.

OVERTIME.
Compensatory time.
Fair Labor Standards Act effect on public employer's compelling
use of compensatory time off, 146 L Ed 2d 621.

P

PAROLE, PROBATION AND PARDON.
Ex post facto.
Retroactive application Georgia provision extending intervals
between parole considerations, 146 L Ed 2d 236.
Habeas corpus relief.
Entitlement to relief when not ineligible for parole at time of
capital sentencing, 147 L Ed 2d 125.
Supervised release.
District court authority to impose additional term after
revocation and reimprisonment.
Retroactive application implications, 146 L Ed 2d 727.

PARTIES.
Primary elections.
Blanket system.
Violation of freedom of association, 147 L Ed 2d 502.
Standing.
Qui tam actions.
False Claims Act, 146 L Ed 2d 836.
Taxpayer actions.
Civil penalties, 145 L Ed 2d 610.

PENSIONS AND RETIREMENT.
Employee Retirement Income Security Act.
Civil action for appropriate equitable relief.
Nonfiduciary parties in interest liability to be sued under
502(a)(3) of ERISA, 147 L Ed 2d 187.

PENSIONS AND RETIREMENT —Cont'd
Employee Retirement Income Security Act —Cont'd
Fiduciary acts.
Treatment-and-eligibility mixed decisions by HMO acting
through physician employee, 147 L Ed 2d 164.

PIERCING OF CORPORATE VEIL.
Attorneys' fees.
Personal liability of president when joined with no opportunity to
contest liability, 146 L Ed 2d 530.

POLICE POWER.
Gender motivated violence and suppression of crime.
Congressional authority under commerce clause to provide civil
remedy, 146 L Ed 2d 658.

POLITICS AND POLITICAL MATTERS.
Primary elections.
Blanket system.
Violation of freedom of association, 147 L Ed 2d 502.

POOR PERSONS.
Frivolous appeal procedures.
Adoption of procedures by California court to determine frivolity
of indigent defendant's criminal appeal; fourteenth
amendment effect, 145 L Ed 2d 756.

PORTS AND HARBORS.
Preemption of state regulations by federal law.
Oil tanker regulations, 146 L Ed 2d 69.

PRAYER.
Schools and education.
High school football.
Prayer before football games effect on First Amendment's
establishment of religion clause, 147 L Ed 2d 295.

PRECEDENTS.
Overturning.
Sub silentio overturning or limiting, 146 L Ed 2d 1.

PRECLUSION OF JURISDICTION.
Federal question jurisdiction.
Medicare enforcement regulations.
Statutory preclusion, 146 L Ed 2d 1.

PREEMPTION AND PREEMPTIVE RIGHTS.
National Traffic and Motor Safety Act.
Common law tort action preempted in case regarding equipping
cars with airbags, 146 L Ed 2d 914.
Oil tanker regulations, 146 L Ed 2d 69.
Railroads.
Federal Railroad Safety Act preemption of state tort claims.
Railroad's failure to maintain adequate warning devices at
crossings where federal funds were used in installation of
devices, 146 L Ed 2d 374.

PREEMPTION AND PREEMPTIVE RIGHTS —Cont'd
State agencies' authority to restrict purchase of goods or services
from companies doing business with Burma.
Supremacy clause effect, 147 L Ed 2d 352.
State law.
National Traffic and Motor Safety Act preempts common law tort
action regarding equipping car with airbags, 146 L Ed 2d
914.
Tort actions.
National Traffic and Motor Safety Act preempts common law tort
action regarding equipping cars with airbags, 146 L Ed 2d
914.

PREJUDICE OR BIAS.
Instructions to jury.
Constitutional effect judge's failure to provide alternative jury
instruction regarding mitigating circumstances in capital
murder case, 145 L Ed 2d 727.
Peremptory challenges.
Impairment or denial of defendant's exercise of peremptory
challenge when used for curative purposes 145 L Ed 2d 792.

PRESUMPTIONS AND BURDEN OF PROOF.
Bankruptcy.
Trustee in bankruptcy.
Burden lies on trustee where state substantive law put burden
on taxpayer, 147 L Ed 2d 13.
Sentence and punishment.
Hate crimes.
Facts that increase penalties beyond statutory maximums must
be submitted to jury to be proven beyond a reasonable
doubt, 147 L Ed 2d 435.

PRIMARY ELECTIONS.
Blanket system.
Violation of freedom of association, 147 L Ed 2d 502.

PRIOR CONVICTIONS.
Preemptive introduction on direct examination.
Admission challenged on appeal, 146 L Ed 2d 826.

PRIORITIES AND PREFERENCES.
Inheritance property.
Federal law to determine existence of a property interest in an
estate disclaimed under Arkansas state law subject to a
federal tax lien, 145 L Ed 2d 466.

PRISONS AND PRISONERS.
Interstate Agreement on Detainers.
Waiver of defendant's Interstate Agreement on Detainers rights
when defense counsel sets trial date outside time period set
by agreement, 145 L Ed 2d 560.

PRISONS AND PRISONERS —Cont'd
Prison litigation reform act.
  Mandatory stay regarding prospective relief.
    Courts barred from exercising authority to suspend stay; effect
      on separation of powers, 147 L Ed 2d 326.

PRIVACY.
Baggage or luggage.
  Bus passenger's opaque carryon luggage.
    Physical manipulation of and effect on Fourth Amendment
      prohibition against unreasonable searches, 146 L Ed 2d
      365.

PRIVATE OR PAROCHIAL SCHOOLS.
Establishment of religion.
  Educational materials loaned to private schools effect on First
    Amendment, 147 L Ed 2d 660.

PRIVILEGES AND IMMUNITIES.
Self-incrimination.
  Indictment dismissed.
    Source of evidence in indictment independent of documents
      produced under grant of immunity, 147 L Ed 2d 24.

PROCEDURAL DEFAULT.
Ineffective assistance of counsel.
  Cause and prejudice standard exception of procedurally defaulted
    ineffective assistance of counsel claim.
    Effect on procedurally defaulted insufficient evidence claim, 146
      L Ed 2d 518.

PRODUCTS LIABILITY.
Judgment as a matter of law.
  Appropriateness of entry of judgment as a matter of law by
    federal court of appeals when evidence was both erroneously
    admitted and insufficient to support a verdict, 145 L Ed 2d
    958.

PROPERTY.
Inheritance property.
  Federal law to determine existence of a property interest in an
    estate disclaimed under Arkansas state law subject to a
    federal tax lien, 145 L Ed 2d 466.

PRO SE REPRESENTATION.
Constitutional rights of lay appellant when required to accept
  state-appointed attorney, 145 L Ed 2d 597.

PROSPECTIVE AND RETROSPECTIVE MATTERS.
Crime victim testimony.
  Ex post facto effect on statutory provision allowing sexual abuse
    victim's uncorroborated testimony to support conviction, 146
    L Ed 2d 577.

PROSPECTIVE OR RETROSPECTIVE MATTERS.
Statutory interpretation at time of conviction for operating
hazardous waste facility without permit.
Certification of question to Pennsylvania supreme court and
reservation of judgment pending response, 145 L Ed 2d 353.

PUBLIC ACCOMMODATIONS.
Boy Scouts of America.
Public accommodations law requiring Scouts to admit
homosexuals.
Violation of freedom of association, 147 L Ed 2d 554.

PUBLICATION.
Arrestee's addresses.
First amendment effect of state's withholding arrestee address
information from private publishing service, 145 L Ed 2d
451.

PUBLIC OFFICERS AND EMPLOYEES.
Compensatory time.
Fair Labor Standards Act effect on public employer's compelling
use of compensatory time off, 146 L Ed 2d 621.

PUBLIC WORKS AND CONTRACTS.
Restitution.
Oil companies granted restitution for government's breach of
lease contracts to explore for and develop oil, 147 L Ed 2d
528.

Q

QUI TAM ACTIONS.
False claims act.
Standing, 146 L Ed 2d 836.

R

RACIAL DISCRIMINATION.
College and university admissions.
Damages claim and summary judgment issuance where
university had race conscious admissions process, 145 L Ed
2d 347.

RACKETEERING.
Causes of action.
Overt act in furtherance of RICO conspiracy creates cause of
action under RICO when overt act was not racketeering, 146
L Ed 2d 561.
Limitation of action in RICO actions.
"Injury and pattern discovery" rule effect on start of limitations
period for treble damages action, 145 L Ed 2d 1047.

RAILROADS.
Preemption.
  Federal Railroad Safety Act preemption of state tort claims.
    Railroad's failure to maintain adequate warning devices at
      crossings where federal funds were used in installation of
      devices, 146 L Ed 2d 374.

RANGELANDS.
Taylor Grazing Act.
  Livestock grazing on federal public rangelands.
    Authority of Secretary of Interior, 146 L Ed 2d 753.

RAPE.
Gender motivated violence.
  Congressional authority under commerce clause to provide civil
    remedy, 146 L Ed 2d 658.

**RATIONAL RELATIONSHIP TO LEGITIMATE
GOVERNMENT INTEREST.**
Nude dancing.
  Public indecency ordinance to prohibit nude dancing.
    Effect on free expression guarantee, 146 L Ed 2d 265.

REASONABLE SUSPICION.
Fleeing suspect.
  Pat-down and search of fleeing suspect where fourth amendment
    exceptions not invoked, 145 L Ed 2d 587.

RECORDS AND RECORDING.
Arrestee's addresses.
  First amendment effect of state's withholding arrestee address
    information from private publishing service, 145 L Ed 2d
    451.
Driver's license applications.
  Driver's Privacy Protection Act, constitutionality of act, 145 L Ed
    2d 587.

REDISTRICTING.
Preclearance of a redistricting plan with a discriminatory but
    nonretrogressive purpose.
  Interpretation of §5 of the Voting Rights Act of 1965, 145 L Ed 2d
    845.

REFUND OR REPAYMENT.
Income taxes.
  Remittance by tax payer and employer of federal withholding tax
    held paid under §6511 of the IRC, 145 L Ed 2d 949.

REGISTRATION.
Driver's license applications.
  Driver's Privacy Protection Act, constitutionality of act, 145 L Ed
    2d 587.

RELEASE OR DISCHARGE.
Supervised release.
  Excess time served in prison.
    Offset against length of supervised release not available, 146 L
      Ed 2d 39.

INDEX

RELIGIOUS FREEDOM.
Schools and education.
  Educational materials loaned to private schools effect on First
    Amendment, 147 L Ed 2d 660.
  High school football.
    Prayer before football games effect on First Amendment's
      establishment of religion clause, 147 L Ed 2d 295.

REMAND.
Warrantless search of homicide crime scene.
  Fourth Amendment exceptions not invoked, issues to be resolved
    on remand, 145 L Ed 2d 16.

RESTITUTION AND IMPLIED CONTRACTS.
Government contracts.
  Oil companies granted restitution for breach of lease contracts to
    explore for and develop oil, 147 L Ed 2d 528.

RETROGRESSION.
Preclearance of a Louisiana redistricting plan with a discriminatory
  but nonretrogressive purpose.
  Interpretation of §5 of the Voting Rights Act of 1965, 145 L Ed 2d
    845.

RIGHT TO COUNSEL.
Frivolous appeal procedures.
  Adoption of procedures by California court to determine frivolity
    of indigent defendant's criminal appeal; fourteenth
    amendment effect 145 L Ed 2d 756.
Pro se representation.
  Constitutional rights of lay appellant when required to accept
    state-appointed attorney, 145 L Ed 2d 597.

ROBBERY.
Jury instructions.
Lesser included offense instruction, 147 L Ed 2d 203.

RULES OF APPELLATE PROCEDURE.
Frivolous appeal procedures.
  Adoption of procedures by California court to determine frivolity
    of indigent defendant's criminal appeal; fourteenth
    amendment effect, 145 L Ed 2d 756.

RULES OF CIVIL PROCEDURE.
Judgment as a matter of law.
  Appropriateness of entry of judgment as a matter of law by
    federal court of appeals when evidence was both erroneously
    admitted and insufficient to support a verdict, 145 L Ed 2d
    958.

RULES OF CRIMINAL PROCEDURE.
Frivolous appeal procedures.
  Adoption of procedures by California court to determine frivolity
    of indigent defendant's criminal appeal; fourteenth
    amendment effect, 145 L Ed 2d 756.

RULES OF CRIMINAL PROCEDURE —Cont'd
Jury instructions.
Robbery of a bank, 147 L Ed 2d 203.
Peremptory challenges.
Impairment or denial of defendant's exercise of peremptory
challenge when used for curative purposes 145 L Ed 2d 792.

S

SCHOOL BOARD.
Preclearance of a Louisiana redistricting plan with a discriminatory
but nonretrogressive purpose.
Interpretation of §5 of the Voting Rights Act of 1965, 145 L Ed 2d
845.

SCHOOLS AND EDUCATION.
Freedom of speech and press.
Mandatory fee for extracurricular student speech with viewpoint
neutrality, 146 L Ed 2d 193.

SEARCH AND SEIZURE.
Anonymous tip.
Stop and frisk based on anonymous tip where informant's
knowledge or credibility is unknown, 146 L Ed 2d 254.
Baggage or luggage.
Physical manipulation of bus passenger's carryon luggage.
Effect on Fourth Amendment prohibition against unreasonable
searches, 146 L Ed 2d 365.
Bus passengers.
Physical manipulation of carryon luggage.
Effect on Fourth Amendment prohibition against unreasonable
searches, 146 L Ed 2d 365.
Fleeing suspect.
Pat-down and search of fleeing suspect where fourth amendment
exceptions not invoked, 145 L Ed 2d 587.
Homicide crime scene.
Warrantless search where Fourth Amendment exceptions not
invoked, 145 L Ed 2d 16.
Plain view doctrine.
Physical manipulation of bus passenger's opaque carryon luggage.
Effect on Fourth Amendment prohibition against unreasonable
searches, 146 L Ed 2d 365.

SECONDARY MEANING.
Trade dress.
Protectibility of unregistered trade dress, 146 L Ed 2d 182.

SECURED TRANSACTIONS.
Bankruptcy estate.
Administrative claimants power to seek claim from encumbered
estate property, 147 L Ed 2d 1.

SELF-INCRIMINATION.
Prior convictions.
  Preemptive introduction on direct examination.
    Admission challenged on appeal, 146 L Ed 2d 826.
Privileges and immunities.
  Indictment dismissed.
    Source of evidence in indictment independent of documents
      produced under grant of immunity, 147 L Ed 2d 24.

SENTENCE OR PUNISHMENT.
Machine guns.
  Imposition of stiffer penalty for using machine gun element as
    separate offense not sentencing factor, 147 L Ed 2d 94.
Maximum sentences.
  Hate crimes.
    Facts that increase penalties beyond statutory maximums must
      be submitted to jury to be proven beyond a reasonable
      doubt, 147 L Ed 2d 435.
Weapons and firearms.
  Imposition of stiffer penalty for using machine gun element as
    separate offense not sentencing factor, 147 L Ed 2d 94.

SENTENCING REFORM ACT.
Supervised release.
  District court authority to impose additional term after
    revocation and reimprisonment.
    Retroactive application implications, 146 L Ed 2d 727.

SEPARATION OF POWERS.
Prison litigation reform act.
  Mandatory stay regarding prospective relief.
    Courts barred from exercising authority to suspend stay; effect
      on separation of powers, 147 L Ed 2d 326.

SEXUAL ABUSE.
Gender motivated violence.
  Congressional authority under commerce clause to provide civil
    remedy, 146 L Ed 2d 658.

SEXUAL ORIENTATION.
Boy Scouts of America.
  Public accommodations law requiring Scouts to admit
    homosexuals.
    Violation of freedom of association, 147 L Ed 2d 554.

SHIPS AND SHIPPING.
Oil tanker regulations.
  Preemption of state regulations by federal law, 146 L Ed 2d 69.

SOCIAL SECURITY.
Appeals council.
  Waiver of issues not raised in request for review after exhaustion
    of administrative remedies and judicial review, 147 L Ed 2d
    80.

SOVEREIGN IMMUNITY.
Age discrimination in employment act.
  Congressional intent to abrogate states' eleventh amendment
      immunity in Age Discrimination in Employment Act and
      effect on fourteenth amendment, 145 L Ed 2d 522.
False Claims Act.
  State and state agency liability in qui tam action brought under
      act, 146 L Ed 2d 836.

SPEEDY TRIAL.
Interstate Agreement on Detainers.
  Waiver of defendant's Interstate Agreement on Detainers rights
      when defense counsel sets trial date outside time period set
      by agreement, 145 L Ed 2d 560.

STANDING.
Qui tam actions.
  False Claims Act, 146 L Ed 2d 836.

STATES, TERRITORIES AND POSSESSIONS.
Age discrimination and employment act.
  Congressional intent to abrogate states' eleventh amendment
      immunity in Age Discrimination in Employment Act and
      effect on fourteenth amendment, 145 L Ed 2d 522.
Burden of proof.
  Trustees in bankruptcy.
    Burden lies on trustee where state substantive law put burden
        on taxpayer, 147 L Ed 2d 13.
Driver's license applications.
  Driver's Privacy Protection Act, constitutionality of act, 145 L Ed
      2d 587.
Electoral qualifications.
  Constitutionality of Hawaiian statute permitting only
      descendants of aboriginal people to vote for state agency
      position, 145 L Ed 2d 1007.
Eleventh amendment.
  Age discrimination in employment act.
    Congressional intent to abrogate states' eleventh amendment
        immunity in Age Discrimination in Employment Act and
        effect on fourteenth amendment, 145 L Ed 2d 522.
Guam.
  Elections.
    Runoff election provisions under the Guam Organic Act
        regarding gubernatorial elections, 145 L Ed 2d 747.
Immunity.
  Age discrimination in employment act.
    Congressional intent to abrogate states' eleventh amendment
        immunity in Age Discrimination in Employment Act and
        effect on fourteenth amendment, 145 L Ed 2d 522.
Income tax.
  California's interest-deduction-offset tax on nondomiciliary
      corporations.
    Due process and commerce clause effects, 145 L Ed 2d 974.

STATES, TERRITORIES AND POSSESSIONS —Cont'd
Inheritance property.
Federal law to determine existence of a property interest in an
estate disclaimed under Arkansas state law subject to a
federal tax lien, 145 L Ed 2d 466.
Railroads.
Federal Railroad Safety Act preemption of state tort claims.
Railroad's failure to maintain adequate warning devices at
crossings where federal funds were used in installation of
devices, 146 L Ed 2d 374.
State agencies' authority to restrict purchase of goods and services
from companies doing business with Burma.
Supremacy clause effect, 147 L Ed 2d 352.

STATUTES.
Facial overbreadth.
First amendment effect of state's withholding arrestee address
information from private publishing service, 145 L Ed 2d
451.

STATUTORY CONSTRUCTION.
Exceptions created by Congress.
Court not to create additional exceptions, 146 L Ed 2d 2.
Lenity, rule of.
Ambiguity necessary to trigger rule of lenity, 146 L Ed 2d 39.

STATUTORY MAXIMUMS.
Hate crimes.
Facts that increase penalties beyond statutory maximums must
be submitted to jury and proven beyond reasonable doubt,
147 L Ed 2d 435.

STOP AND FRISK.
Anonymous tip.
Informant's knowledge or credibility is unknown, 146 L Ed 2d
254.
Fleeing suspect.
Pat-down and search of fleeing suspect where fourth amendment
exceptions not invoked, 145 L Ed 2d 587.

STRICT SCRUTINY.
Cable TV.
Restricting transmission of channels primarily dedicated to
sexually oriented programming, 146 L Ed 2d 865.
Campaigns and campaign contributions.
Limitations on campaign contributions in Missouri state statute.
Federal statute and first amendment effect, 145 L Ed 2d 886.
Race-based measures by United States Department of
Transportation.
Mootness of procedure certifying contractors as disadvantaged
business enterprises 145 L Ed 2d 650.

SUBCONTRACTOR COMPENSATION CLAUSES.
Certification of contractors as disadvantaged business enterprise.
  Mootness of subcontractors challenge of certification procedures of
    United States Department of Transportation, 145 L Ed 2d
    650.

SUMMARY JUDGMENT.
Race conscious university admissions.
  Damages claim and summary judgment issuance where
    university had race conscious admissions process, 145 L Ed
    2d 347.

SUPERVISED RELEASE.
District court authority.
  Imposition of additional term after revocation and
    reimprisonment.
    Retroactive application implications, 146 L Ed 2d 727.
Excess time served in prison.
  Offset against length of supervised release not available, 146 L
    Ed 2d 39.

T

TAXES.
Liens on inheritance property.
  Federal law to determine existence of a property interest in an
    estate disclaimed under Arkansas state law subject to a
    federal tax lien, 145 L Ed 2d 466.

TAX LIENS.
Inheritance property.
  Federal law to determine existence of a property interest in an
    estate disclaimed under Arkansas state law subject to a
    federal tax lien, 145 L Ed 2d 466.

TAXPAYERS' ACTIONS.
Hazardous waste facilities.
  Illegal discharge of pollutants.
    Mootness of civil penalties claim under Clean Water Act after
      voluntary cessation of illegal activity, 145 L Ed 2d 610.

TAYLOR GRAZING ACT.
Secretary of Interior authority.
  Livestock grazing on federal public rangelands, 146 L Ed 2d 753.

TELECOMMUNICATIONS ACT OF 1996.
Cable television.
  Restricting transmission of channels primarily dedicated to
    sexually oriented programming, 146 L Ed 2d 865.

TOBACCO AND TOBACCO PRODUCTS.
Food and drug administration regulation, 146 L Ed 2d 121.

TORTS.
Preemption of common law tort actions.
  National Traffic and Motor Vehicle Safety Act, 146 L Ed 2d 914.

TORTS —Cont'd
Railroads.
    Federal Railroad Safety Act preemption of state tort claims.
        Railroad's failure to maintain adequate warning devices at
            crossings where federal funds were used in installation of
            devices, 146 L Ed 2d 374.

TRADE DRESS.
Unregistered trade dress protectibility.
    Secondary meaning, 146 L Ed 2d 182.

TRADEMARKS AND TRADE NAMES.
Unregistered trade dress protectibility.
    Secondary meaning, 146 L Ed 2d 182.

TRIAL.
Interstate Agreement on Detainers.
    Waiver of defendant's Interstate Agreement on Detainers rights
        when defense counsel sets trial date outside time period set
        by agreement, 145 L Ed 2d 560.
Presence of defendant.
    Comment on presence.
        Tailoring testimony by accused, 146 L Ed 2d 47.

V

VENUE.
Arbitration act provisions.
    District to bring motion to confirm, vacate or modify, 146 L Ed 2d
        171.

VOTING RIGHTS ACT.
Interpretation and construction.
    Voting Rights Act of 1965 §5.
        Preclearance of a Louisiana redistricting plan with a
            discriminatory but nonretrogressive purpose, 145 L Ed 2d
            845.
Preclearance.
    Redistricting plan with a discriminatory but nonretrogressive
        purpose, 145 L Ed 2d 845.

W

WAGES, SALARY, AND OTHER COMPENSATION.
Compensatory time.
    Fair Labor Standards Act effect on public employers compelling
        use of compensatory time off, 146 L Ed 2d 621.

WAIVER.
Interstate Agreement on Detainers.
    Waiver of defendant's Interstate Agreement on Detainers rights
        when defense counsel sets trial date outside time period set
        by agreement, 145 L Ed 2d 560.

WAIVER —Cont'd
Social security appeals council.
Exhaustion of administrative remedies and judicial review.
Effect on issues raised in request for review by appeals council, 147 L Ed 2d 80.

WARNINGS.
Railroads.
Federal Railroad Safety Act preemption of state tort claims.
Railroad's failure to maintain adequate warning devices at crossings where federal funds were used in installation of devices, 146 L Ed 2d 374.

WARRANTLESS SEARCH.
Homicide crime scene.
Where Fourth Amendment exceptions not invoked, 145 L Ed 2d 16.

WATERS AND WATER COURSES.
Indians.
Water rights.
Res judicata effect on claims for additional water rights, 147 L Ed 2d 374.

WEAPONS AND FIREARMS.
Fleeing suspect.
Pat-down and search of fleeing suspect where fourth amendment exceptions not invoked, 145 L Ed 2d 587.
Penalties.
Imposition of stiffer penalty for using machine gun element of separate offense not sentencing factor, 147 L Ed 2d 94.

WITNESSES.
Tailoring testimony by accused.
Comments on opportunity to tailor, 146 L Ed 2d 47.